FIA
FFA

ACCA
PAPER F3

FINANCIAL ACCOUNTING

D1353503

PRACTICE & REVISION KIT

Welcome to BPP Learning Media's Practice and Revision Kit for FFA. In this, **the only FFA/F3 Practice and Revision Kit to be reviewed by the examiner:**

- We include **Do you know?** Checklists to test your knowledge and understanding of topics

- We provide you with **two** mock exams including the Specimen exam

- We provide the **ACCA examiner's answers** as well as our own to the Specimen exam as an additional revision aid

BPP's **i-Pass** product also supports this paper and is a vital tool if you are taking the computer based exam.

Note
FIA *FFA* and ACCA *Paper F3* are examined under the same syllabus and study guide.

FOR EXAMS FROM FEBRUARY 2014 TO AUGUST 2015

First edition May 2011
Third edition November 2013

ISBN 9781 4453 7034 7
Previous ISBN 9781 4453 9977 5
e-ISBN 9781 4453 7069 9

British Library Cataloguing-in-Publication Data
A catalogue record for this book
is available from the British Library

Published by

BPP Learning Media Ltd
BPP House, Aldine Place
London W12 8AA

www.bpp.com/learningmedia

Printed in the United Kingdom by Polestar Wheatons

Hennock Road
Marsh Barton
Exeter
EX2 8RP

Your learning materials, published by BPP Learning
Media Ltd, are printed on paper sourced from
sustainable, managed forests.

We are grateful to the Association of Chartered
Certified Accountants for permission to reproduce past
examination questions. The suggested solutions in the
exam answer bank have been prepared by BPP
Learning Media Ltd, except where otherwise stated.

Contents

Question index

	Marks	Time allocation	Page	
		Mins	Questions	Answers
Part A: The context and purpose of financial reporting				
The context and purpose of financial reporting				
Questions 1.1 to 1.14	28	34	5	175
Part B: The qualitative characteristics of financial information				
The qualitative characteristics of financial information				
Questions 2.1 to 2.11	22	26	11	175
Part C: The use of double entry and accounting systems				
Double entry bookkeeping				
Questions 3.1 to 3.17	34	41	17	176
Questions 4.1 to 4.16	32	38	20	177
Part D: Recording transactions and events				
Sales tax				
Questions 5.1 to 5.8	16	19	27	179
Inventory				
Questions 6.1 to 6.18	36	43	28	180
Tangible non-current assets				
Questions 7.1 to 7.17	34	41	33	181
Questions 8.1 to 8.20	40	48	38	183
Intangible non-current assets				
Questions 9.1 to 9.12	24	29	43	185
Accruals and prepayments				
Questions 10.1 to 10.15	30	36	46	186
Receivables and payables				
Questions 11.1 to 11.19	38	46	50	188
Provisions and contingencies				
Questions 12.1 to 12.10	20	24	54	189

BPP
LEARNING MEDIA

Helping you with your revision

BPP Learning Media – Approved Learning Partner – content

As ACCA's **Approved Learning Partner – content**, BPP Learning Media gives you the **opportunity** to use **examiner-reviewed** revision materials for exams from February 2014 to August 2015. By incorporating the examiner's comments and suggestions regarding syllabus coverage, the BPP Learning Media Practice and Revision Kit provides excellent, **ACCA-approved** support for your revision.

Selecting questions

We provide signposts to help you plan your revision.

- A full **question index** listing questions that cover each part of the syllabus, so that you can locate the questions that provide practice on key topics, and see the different ways in which they might be tested

Attempting mock exams

There are two mock exams that provide practice at coping with the pressures of the exam day. We strongly recommend that you attempt them under exam conditions. **Mock exam 1** is the Specimen exam. **Mock exam 2** reflects the question styles and syllabus coverage of the exam.

Using your BPP Practice and Revision Kit

Aim of this Practice and Revision Kit

To provide the practice to help you succeed in both the paper based and computer based examinations for Paper FFA/F3 *Financial Accounting*.

To pass the examination you need a thorough understanding in all areas covered by the syllabus and teaching guide.

Recommended approach

- Make sure you are able to answer questions on **everything** specified by the syllabus and teaching guide. You cannot make any assumptions about what questions may come up on your paper. The examiners aim to discourage 'question spotting'.

- Learning is an **active** process. Use the **DO YOU KNOW?** Checklists to test your knowledge and understanding of the topics covered in FFA/F3 *Financial Accounting* by filling in the blank spaces. Then check your answers against the **DID YOU KNOW?** Checklists. Do not attempt any questions if you are unable to fill in any of the blanks - go back to your **BPP Interactive Text** and revise first.

- When you are revising a topic, think about the mistakes that you know that you should avoid by writing down **POSSIBLE PITFALLS** at the end of each **DO YOU KNOW?** Checklist.

- Once you have completed the checklists successfully, you should attempt the questions on that topic. Each question is worth 2 marks and carries with it a time allocation of 2.4 minutes.

- Once you have completed all of the questions in the body of this Practice & Revision Kit, you should attempt the **MOCK EXAMS** under examination conditions. Check your answers against our answers to find out how well you did.

BPP
LEARNING MEDIA

Passing the FFA/F3 exam

Paper FFA/F3 aims to develop your knowledge and understanding of the underlying principles, concepts and regulations relating to financial accounting. You will need to demonstrate technical proficiency in the use of double entry techniques, including the preparation of basic financial statements for incorporated and unincorporated entities, as well as simple consolidated financial statements for group incorporated entities. You also need to be able to conduct a basic interpretation of financial statements. If you plan to progress through the ACCA qualification, the skills you learn at FFA/F3 will be built upon in papers F7 and P2.

To access FIA and ACCA syllabuses, visit the ACCA website.

http://www.accaglobal.com/

The exam

You can take this exam as a paper based exam or by computer based exam. All questions in the exam are compulsory. This means you cannot avoid any topic, but also means that you do not need to waste time in the exam deciding which questions to attempt. There are fifty MCQs in the paper-based exam and a mixture of MCQs and other types of objective test question (number entry, multiple response and multiple response matching) in the CBE. This means that the examiner is able to test most of the syllabus at each sitting, so you need to have revised right across the syllabus for this exam.

Revision

This kit has been reviewed by the FFA/F3 examiner and contains the Specimen exam, so if you just worked through it to the end you would be very well prepared for the exam. It is important to tackle questions under exam conditions. Allow yourself just the number of minutes shown next to the questions in the index and don't look at the answers until you have finished. Then correct your answer and go back to the Interactive Text for any topic you are really having trouble with. Try the same question again a week later – you will be surprised how much better you are getting. Doing the questions like this will really show you what you know, and will make the exam experience less worrying.

Doing the exam

If you have honestly done your revision you can pass this exam. There are a couple of points to bear in mind:

- Read the question properly.

- Don't spend more than the allotted time on each question. If you are having trouble with a question leave it and carry on. You can come back to it at the end.

Approach to examining the syllabus

FFA/F3 is a two-hour paper. It can be taken as a paper based or a computer based exam.

The exam is structured as follows:

	No of marks
Section A – 35 compulsory objective test questions of 2 marks each	70
Section B – 2 compulsory multi-part questions of 15 marks each	30
	100

The Computer Based Examination

Computer based examinations (CBEs) are available for the first seven FIA papers (not papers FAU, FTM or FFM), and the first three ACCA exams (F1, F2 and F3), in addition to the conventional paper based examination.

Computer based examinations must be taken at an ACCA CBE Licensed Centre.

How do CBEs work?

- Questions are displayed on a monitor

- Candidates enter their answer directly onto the computer

- Candidates have two hours to complete the examination

- When the candidate has completed their examination, the final percentage score is calculated and displayed on screen

- Candidates are provided with a Provisional Result Notification showing their results before leaving the examination room

- The CBE Licensed Centre uploads the results to the ACCA (as proof of the candidate's performance) within 72 hours

- Candidates can check their exam status on the ACCA website by logging into myACCA.

Benefits

- **Flexibility** as a CBE can be sat at any time.

- **Resits** can also be taken at any time and there is no restriction on the number of times a candidate can sit a CBE.

- **Instant feedback** as the computer displays the results at the end of the CBE.

- Results are notified to ACCA **within 72 hours**.

CBE question types

- Multiple choice – choose one answer from four options

- Number entry – key in a numerical response to a question

- Multiple response – select more than one response by clicking the appropriate tick boxes

- Multiple response matching – select a response to a number of related part questions by choosing one option from a number of drop down menus

For more information on computer-based exams, visit the ACCA website.

http://www.accaglobal.com/en/student/Exams/Computer-based-exams.html

Tackling Multiple Choice Questions

MCQs are part of all FIA exams and the first three ACCA exams (F1, F2 and F3). MCQs may feature in the CBE, along with other types of question, while the paper based exam is made up entirely of MCQs.

The MCQs in your exam contain four possible answers. You have to **choose the option that best answers the question**. The three incorrect options are called distracters. There is a skill in answering MCQs quickly and correctly. By practising MCQs you can develop this skill, giving you a better chance of passing the exam.

You may wish to follow the approach outlined below, or you may prefer to adapt it.

Step 1	Skim read all the MCQs and identify what appear to be the easier questions.
Step 2	Attempt each question – **starting with the easier questions** identified in Step 1. Read the question **thoroughly**. You may prefer to work out the answer before looking at the options, or you may prefer to look at the options at the beginning. Adopt the method that works best for you.
Step 3	Read the four options and see if one matches your own answer. Be careful with numerical questions as the distracters are designed to match answers that incorporate common errors. Check that your calculation is correct. Have you followed the requirement exactly? Have you included every stage of the calculation?
Step 4	You may find that none of the options matches your answer. • Re-read the question to ensure that you understand it and are answering the requirement • Eliminate any obviously wrong answers • Consider which of the remaining answers is the most likely to be correct and select the option
Step 5	If you are still unsure make a note and continue to the next question
Step 6	Revisit unanswered questions. When you come back to a question after a break you often find you are able to answer it correctly straight away. If you are still unsure have a guess. You are not penalised for incorrect answers, so **never leave a question unanswered!**

After extensive practice and revision of MCQs, you may find that you recognise a question when you sit the exam. Be aware that the detail and/or requirement may be different. If the question seems familiar read the requirement and options carefully – do not assume that it is identical.

Using your BPP products

This Kit gives you the question practice and guidance you need in the exam. Our other products can also help you pass:

- **Passcards** provide you with clear topic summaries and exam tips

- **i-Pass CDs** are a vital revision tool for anyone taking FIA/ACCA CBEs and offer tests of knowledge against the clock in an environment similar to that encountered in a computer based exam

You can purchase these products by visiting www.bpp.com/learningmedia

Questions

Do you know? – The context and purpose of financial reporting

Check that you can fill in the blanks in the statements below before you attempt any questions. If in doubt, you should go back to your BPP Interactive Text and revise first.

- **F**............. **r** .... is a way of recording, analysing and summarising financial data.

- Businesses of whatever size or nature exist to make a ....

- **P**............. is the excess of .... over expenditure. When **e**.............. exceeds .... the business is running at a **l**.......

- A **s**........ **t**.............. is a business owned and run by one individual, perhaps employing one or two assistants and controlling their work.

- **L** .... **l**........... status means that the business's debts and the personal debts of the business's owners (shareholders) are legally separate.

- .... are arrangements between individuals to carry on business in common with a view to profit. Partnerships are governed by a ....

- Financial accounting is mainly a method of reporting the .... and .... of a business. Financial accounts provide .... information.

- There are various groups of people who need .... about the activities of a business.

- Those charged with **g**................. of a company are responsible for the preparation of the financial statements.

- The statement of financial position is simply a list of all the a........... owned and all the **l**.............. owed by a business as at a particular date.

- An .... is a resource controlled by an entity as a result of past events and from which future economic benefits are expected to flow to the entity.

- A .... is a present obligation of the entity arising from past events, the settlement of which is expected to result in an outflow from the entity of resources embodying economic benefits.

- **E**............ is the residual interest in the assets of the entity after deducting all its liabilities.

- A statement of profit or loss is a record of .... generated and .... incurred over a given period.

- Accounting standards were developed to try to address **s**..............**y**

- The IASB develops ....

- The main objectives of the IFRS Foundation are to:

    - .... a single set of high quality, understandable, enforceable and globally accepted **l**..... through its standard-setting body, the **l**......

    - promote the .... and rigours application of those standards

    - take account of the financial reporting needs of emerging economies and .... and .... entities

    - bring about **c**................. of national accounting standards and IFRSs to high quality solutions.

Did you know? – The context and purpose of financial reporting

Could you fill in the blanks? The answers are in bold. Use this page for revision purposes as you approach the exam.

- **Financial reporting** is a way of recording, analysing and summarising financial data.

- Businesses of whatever size or nature exist to make a **profit**.

- **Profit** is the excess of **income** over expenditure. When **expenditure** exceeds **revenue**, the business is running at a **loss**.

- A **sole tradership** is a business owned and run by one individual, perhaps employing one or two assistants and controlling their work.

- **Limited liability** status means that the business's debts and the personal debts of the business's owners (shareholders) are legally separate.

- **Partnerships** are arrangements between individuals to carry on business in common with a view to profit. Partnerships are governed by a **partnership agreement**.

- Financial accounting is mainly a method of reporting the **financial performance** and **financial position** of a business. Financial accounts provide **historical** information.

- There are various groups of people who need **information** about the activities of a business.

- Those charged with **governance** of a company are responsible for the preparation of the financial statements.

- The statement of financial position is simply a list of all the **assets** owned and all the **liabilities** owed by a business as at a particular date.

- An **asset** is a resource controlled by an entity as a result of past events and from which future economic benefits are expected to flow to the entity.

- A **liability** is a present obligation of the entity arising from past events, the settlement of which is expected to result in an outflow from the entity of resources embodying economic benefits.

- **Equity** is the residual interest in the assets of the entity after deducting all its liabilities.

- A statement of profit or loss is a record of **income** generated and **expenditure** incurred over a given period.

- Accounting standards were developed to try to address **subjectivity**.

- The IASB develops **International Financial Reporting Standards (IFRSs)**.

- The main objectives of the IFRS Foundation are to:

  - **develop** a single set of high quality, understandable, enforceable and globally accepted **international financial reporting standards (IFRSs)** through its standard-setting body, the **IASB**

  - promote the **use** and rigorous application of those standards

  - take account of the financial reporting needs of emerging economies and **small** and **medium-sized entities (SMEs)**

  - bring about **convergence** of national accounting standards and IFRSs to high quality solutions.

1 The context and purpose of financial reporting

34 mins

1.1 Who issues International Financial Reporting Standards?

    A   The IFRS Advisory Committee

    B   The stock exchange

    C   The International Accounting Standards Board

    D   The government   **(2 marks)**

1.2 Which groups of people are most likely to be interested in the financial statements of a sole trader?

    1   Shareholders of the company

    2   The business's bank manager

    3   The tax authorities

    4   Financial analysts

    A   1 and 2 only

    B   2 and 3 only

    C   2, 3 and 4 only

    D   1, 2 and 3 only   **(2 marks)**

1.3 Which of the following statements is/are true?

    1   The shareholder needs a statement of financial prospects, ie an indication of future progress. However, the supplier of goods on credit needs a statement of financial position, ie an indication of the current state of affairs.

    2   The objective of financial statements is to provide information about the financial position, performance and changes in financial position of an entity that is useful to a wide range of users in making economic decisions.

    A   1 only

    B   2 only

    C   Both 1 and 2

    D   Neither 1 or 2   **(2 marks)**

1.4 Which of the following are advantages of trading as a limited liability company?

    1   Operating as a limited liability company makes raising finance easier because additional shares can be issued to raise additional cash.

    2   Operating as a limited liability company is more risky than operating as a sole trader because the shareholders of a business are liable for all the debts of the business whereas the sole trader is only liable for the debts up to the amount he has invested.

    A   1 only

    B   2 only

    C   Both 1 and 2

    D   Neither 1 or 2   **(2 marks)**

1.5 Which of the following best describes corporate governance?

    A   Corporate governance is the system of rules and regulations surrounding financial reporting.

    B   Corporate governance is the system by which companies and other entities are directed and controlled.

    C   Corporate governance is carried out by the finance department in preparing the financial accounts.

    D   Corporate governance is the system by which an entity monitors its impact on the natural environment.   **(2 marks)**

1.6 Which of the following statements is/are true?

1 The directors of a company are ultimately responsible for the preparation of financial statements, even if the majority of the work on them is performed by the finance department.

2 If financial statements are audited, then the responsibility for those financial statements instead falls on the auditors instead of the directors.

3 There are generally no laws surrounding the duties of directors in managing the affairs of a company.

A 1 only
B 1 and 2 only
C 1, 2 and 3
D 1 and 3 only **(2 marks)**

1.7 According to the IASB *Conceptual framework* which of the following is **not** an objective of financial statements?

A Providing information regarding the financial position of a business
B Providing information regarding the performance of a business
C Enabling users to assess the performance of management to aid decision making
D Helping to assess the going concern status of a business **(2 marks)**

1.8 The IASB *Conceptual framework* identifies user groups. Which of the following is **not** an information need for the 'Investor' group?

A Assessment of repayment ability of an entity
B Measuring performance, risk and return
C Taking decisions regarding holding investments
D Taking buy/sell decisions **(2 marks)**

1.9 Which of the following statements about accounting concepts and policies is/are correct?

1 Companies should never change the presentation or classification of items in their financial statements, even if there is a significant change in the nature of operations.

2 Information in financial statements should be presented so as to be understood by users with a reasonable knowledge of business and accounting.

3 Companies should create large provisions in times of company growth so that they can be utilised in more difficult times to keep profits the same.

A 1 and 2
B 2 and 3
C 1 only
D 2 only **(2 marks)**

1.10 Which of the following are TRUE of partnerships?

1 The partners' individual exposure to debt is limited.
2 Financial statements for the partnership by law must be produced and made public.
3 A partnership is not a separate legal entity from the partners themselves.

A 1 and 2 only
B 2 only
C 3 only
D 1 and 3 only **(2 marks)**

1.11 Which of the following correctly defines 'equity' according to the IASB's *Conceptual Framework for Financial Reporting*?

A Equity is a present obligation of the entity arising from past events, the settlement of which is expected to result in an outflow from the entity of resources embodying economic benefit.

B Equity is a resource controlled by an entity as a result of past events and from which future economic benefits are expected to flow to the entity.

C Equity is the residual interest in the assets of the entity after deducting all its liabilities.

D Equity is increases in economic benefits during the accounting period in the form of inflows or enhancements of assets or decreases of liabilities. **(2 marks)**

1.12 Which of the following statements is/are true?

1 Directors of companies have a duty of care to show reasonable competence in their management of the affairs of a company.

2 Directors of companies must act honestly in what they consider to be the best interest of the company.

3 A Director's main aim should be to create wealth for the shareholders of the company.

A 1 and 2 only
B 2 only
C 1, 2 and 3
D 1 and 3 only **(2 marks)**

1.13 Which of the following statements is/are true?

1 The IFRS Interpretations Committee is a forum for the IASB to consult with the outside world.

2 The IFRS Foundation produces IFRSs. The IFRS Foundation is overseen by the IASB.

3 One of the objectives of the IFRS Foundation is to bring about convergence of national accounting standards and IFRSs.

A 1 and 3 only
B 2 only
C 2 and 3 only
D 3 only **(2 marks)**

1.14 What is the role of the IASB?

A Oversee the standard setting and regulatory process
B Formulate international financial reporting standards
C Review defective accounts
D Control the accountancy profession **(2 marks)**

(Total = 28 marks)

Do you know? – The qualitative characteristics of financial information

Check that you can fill in the blanks in the statements below before you attempt any questions. If in doubt, you should go back to your BPP Interactive Text and revise first.

- In preparing financial statements, accountants follow certain fundamental **a**..................

- The IASB's **C**..........**l f**...............**k** provides the basis for its IFRSs.

- The main underlying assumption is ....

- The *Conceptual framework* states that .... characteristics are the attributes that make the information provided in financial statements useful to users.

- The four enhancing qualitative characteristics are ...., ..., ... and ....

- Other important qualitative characteristics and concepts include fair ...., **c**.................. and the business .... concept.

- A .... between qualitative characteristics is often necessary, the aim being to achieve an appropriate balance to meet the objective of financial statements.

Did you know? – The qualitative characteristics of financial information

Could you fill in the blanks? The answers are in bold. Use this page for revision purposes as you approach the exam.

- In preparing financial statements, accountants follow certain fundamental **assumptions**.

- The IASB's *Conceptual framework* provides the basis for its IFRSs. .

- The main underlying assumption is **going concern**.

- The *Conceptual framework* states that **qualitative** characteristics are the attributes that make the information provided in financial statements useful to users.

- The four enhancing qualitative characteristics are **understandability, verifiability**, **timeliness** and **comparability**.

- Other important qualitative characteristics and concepts include fair **presentation**, **consistency** and the business **entity** concept.

- A **trade off** between qualitative characteristics is often necessary, the aim being to achieve an appropriate balance to meet the objective of financial statements.

2 The qualitative characteristics of financial information   26 mins

2.1   Which accounting concept should be considered if the owner of a business takes goods from inventory for his own personal use?

A   The substance over form concept
B   The accruals concept
C   The going concern concept
D   The business entity concept   **(2 marks)**

2.2   Sales revenue should be recognised when goods and services have been supplied; costs are incurred when goods and services have been received.

Which accounting concept governs the above?

A   The substance over form concept
B   The materiality concept
C   The accruals concept
D   The duality concept   **(2 marks)**

2.3   Which accounting concept states that omitting or misstating this information could influence users of the financial statements?

A   The consistency concept
B   The accruals concept
C   The materiality concept
D   The going concern concept   **(2 marks)**

2.4   According to the IASB's *Conceptual Framework for Financial Reporting*, which TWO of the following are part of faithful representation?

1   It is neutral
2   It is relevant
3   It is presented fairly
4   It is free from material error

A   1 and 2
B   2 and 3
C   1 and 4
D   3 and 4   **(2 marks)**

2.5   Which of the following accounting concepts means that similar items should receive a similar accounting treatment?

A   Going concern
B   Accruals
C   Substance over form
D   Consistency   **(2 marks)**

2.6 Listed below are some characteristics of financial information.

1   Relevance
2   Comparability
3   Faithful representation
4   Timeliness

Which of these are fundamental characteristics, according to the IASB's *Conceptual Framework for Financial Reporting*?

A   1 and 2 only
B   2 and 4 only
C   3 and 4 only
D   1 and 3 only   **(2 marks)**

2.7 Which of the following statements about accounting concepts are correct?

1   The accruals concept requires that revenue earned must be matched against the expenditure incurred in earning it.

2   The prudence concept means that understating of assets and overstating of liabilities is desirable in preparing financial statements.

3   The reliability concept means that even if information is relevant, if it is very unreliable, it may be misleading to recognise it in the financial statements.

4   The substance over form convention is that, whenever legally possible, the economic substance of a transaction should be reflected in financial statements rather than simply its legal form.

A   1, 2 and 3
B   1, 2 and 4
C   1, 3 and 4
D   2, 3 and 4   **(2 marks)**

2.8 Listed below are some comments on accounting concepts.

1   In achieving a balance between concepts, the most important consideration is satisfying as far as possible the economic decision-making needs of users.

2   Materiality means that only items having a physical existence may be recognised as assets.

3   The substance over form convention means that the legal form of a transaction must always be shown in financial statements, even if this differs from the commercial effect.

Which, if any, of these comments is correct, according to the IASB's *Conceptual Framework for Financial Reporting*?

A   1 only
B   2 only
C   3 only
D   None of them   **(2 marks)**

2.9 Which, if any, of the following statements about accounting concepts and the characteristics of financial information are correct?

1   The concept of substance over form means that the legal form of a transaction must be reflected in financial statements, regardless of the economic substance.

2   Information is not material if its omission or misstatement could influence the economic decisions of users taken on the basis of the financial statements.

3   It may sometimes be necessary to exclude information that is relevant and reliable from financial statements because it is too difficult for some users to understand.

A   1 and 2 only
B   2 and 3 only
C   1 and 3 only
D   None of these statements are correct   **(2 marks)**

2.10 The IASB's *Conceptual Framework for Financial Reporting* gives four enhancing qualitative characteristics. What are these four characteristics?

    A   Consistency, understandability, faithful representation, substance over form
    B   Accruals basis, going concern concept, consistency, true and fair view
    C   Faithful representation, comparability, understandability, relevance
    D   Comparability, timeliness, understandability, verifiability

(2 marks)

2.11 Which one of the following is *not* a qualitative characteristic of financial information according to the *Conceptual framework for Financial Reporting*?

    A   Going concern
    B   Relevance
    C   Timeliness
    D   Accruals

(2 marks)

(Total = 22 marks)

Do you know? – The use of double entry and accounting systems

Check that you can fill in the blanks in the statements below before you attempt any questions. If in doubt, you should go back to your BPP Interactive Text and revise first.

- Business transactions are recorded on **s**.......... **d**................ Examples include sales and purchase orders, ... and ....

- Books of .... are books in which we first record transactions.

- The main books of prime entry are:

  (a) .... day book
  (b) .... day book
  (c) .... day book
  (d) .... day book
  (e) **J**.........**l**
  (f) .... book
  (g) .... book

- Entries in the .... are totalled and analysed before posting to the **n**......... ledger.

- The .... and .... ledgers contain the personal accounts of individual customers and suppliers. They do not normally form part of the double-entry system.

- The **b**........... **e**........ concept means that a business is always treated separately from its owner(s).

- The accounting equation is: .... = ... + LIABILITIES – .... + PROFIT

- Trade accounts payable are **l**......... Trade accounts receivable are **a**.........

- In double entry bookkeeping every transaction is recorded .... so that every .... is balanced by a ....

- A debit entry will:

  – .... an asset
  – .... a liability
  – .... an expense

- A credit entry will:

  – .... an asset
  – .... a liability
  – .... income

- A trial balance can be used to test the .... of the double entry accounting records.

- A .... and .... ledger account is opened up to gather all items relating to income and expenses. When rearranged, the items make up the ....

Did you know? – The use of double entry and accounting systems

Could you fill in the blanks? The answers are in bold. Use this page for revision purposes as you approach the exam.

- Business transactions are recorded on **source documents**. Examples include sales and purchase orders, **invoices** and **credit notes**.

- Books of **prime entry** are books in which we first record transactions.

- The main books of prime entry are:

  (a) **Sales** day book
  (b) **Purchase** day book
  (c) **Sales returns** day book
  (d) **Purchase returns** day book
  (e) **Journal**
  (f) **Cash** book
  (g) **Petty cash** book

- Entries in the **day books** are totalled and analysed before posting to the **nominal** ledger.

- The **receivables** and **payables** ledgers contain the personal accounts of individual customers and suppliers. They do not normally form part of the double-entry system.

- The **business entity** concept means that a business is always treated separately from its owner(s).

- The accounting equation is: **ASSETS** = **CAPITAL** + LIABILITIES – **DRAWINGS** + PROFIT

- Trade accounts payable are **liabilities**. Trade accounts receivable are **assets**.

- In double entry bookkeeping every transaction is recorded **twice** so that every **debit** is balanced by a **credit**.

- A debit entry will:

  - **increase** an asset
  - **decrease** a liability
  - **increase** an expense

- A credit entry will:

  - **decrease** an asset
  - **increase** a liability
  - **increase** income

- A trial balance can be used to test the **accuracy** of the double entry accounting records.

- A **profit** and **loss** ledger account is opened up to gather all items relating to income and expenses. When rearranged, the items make up the **statement of profit or loss**

3 Double entry bookkeeping I 41 mins

3.1 Which one of the following can the accounting equation can be rewritten as?

A   Assets + profit – drawings - liabilities = closing capital
B   Assets – liabilities – drawings = opening capital + profit
C   Assets – liabilities – opening capital + drawings = profit
D   Assets – profit – drawings = closing capital – liabilities   **(2 marks)**

3.2 A trader's net profit for the year may be computed by using which of the following formulae?

A   Opening capital + drawings – capital introduced – closing capital
B   Closing capital + drawings – capital introduced – opening capital
C   Opening capital – drawings + capital introduced – closing capital
D   Opening capital – drawings – capital introduced – closing capital   **(2 marks)**

3.3 The profit earned by a business in 20X7 was $72,500. The proprietor injected new capital of $8,000 during the year and withdrew goods for his private use which had cost $2,200.

If net assets at the beginning of 20X7 were $101,700, what were the closing net assets?

A $35,000
B $39,400
C $168,400
D $180,000   **(2 marks)**

3.4 The profit made by a business in 20X7 was $35,400. The proprietor injected new capital of $10,200 during the year and withdrew a monthly salary of $500.

If net assets at the end of 20X7 were $95,100, what was the proprietor's capital at the beginning of the year?

A $50,000
B $55,500
C $63,900
D $134,700   **(2 marks)**

3.5 A sole trader took some goods costing $800 from inventory for his own use. The normal selling price of the goods is $1,600.

Which of the following journal entries would correctly record this?

		Dr $	Cr $
A	Inventory account	800	
	Purchases account		800
B	Drawings account	800	
	Purchases account		800
C	Sales account	1,600	
	Drawings account		1,600
D	Drawings account	800	
	Sales account		800

(2 marks)

3.6 A business can make a profit and yet have a reduction in its bank balance. Which ONE of the following might cause this to happen?

A   The sale of non-current assets at a loss
B   The charging of depreciation in the statement of profit or loss
C   The lengthening of the period of credit given to customers
D   The lengthening of the period of credit taken from suppliers   **(2 marks)**

3.7 The net assets of Altese, a trader, at 1 January 20X2 amounted to $128,000. During the year to 31 December 20X2 Altese introduced a further $50,000 of capital and made drawings of $48,000. At 31 December 20X2 Altese's net assets totalled $184,000.

What is Altese's total profit or loss for the year ended 31 December 20X2?

A $54,000 profit
B $54,000 loss
C $42,000 loss
D $58,000 profit (2 marks)

3.8 Jones Co has the following transactions:

1 Payment of $400 to J Bloggs for a cash purchase
2 Payment of $250 to J Doe in respect of an invoice for goods purchased last month

What are the correct ledger entries to record these transactions?

A Dr Cash $650
   Cr Purchases $650
B Dr Purchases $650
   Cr Cash $650
C Dr Purchases $400
   Dr Trade Payables $250
   Cr Cash $650
D Dr Cash $650
   Cr Trade Payables $250
   Cr Purchases $400 (2 marks)

3.9 T Tallon had the following transactions:

1 Sale of goods on credit for $150 to F Rogit
2 Return of goods from B Blendigg originally sold for $300 in cash to B Blendigg

What are the correct ledger entries to record these transactions?

A Dr Receivables $150
   Dr Sales Returns $300
   Cr Sales $150
   Cr Cash $300
B Dr Sales $150
   Dr Cash $300
   Cr Receivables $150
   Cr Sales Returns $300
C Dr Receivables $450
   Cr Sales $150
   Cr Sales Returns $300
D Dr Sales Returns $300
   Dr Sales $150
   Cr Cash $450 (2 marks)

3.10 Which of the following documents should accompany a return of goods to a supplier?

A Debit note
B Remittance advice
C Purchase invoice
D Credit note (2 marks)

3.11 Which of the following are books of prime entry?

    1   Sales day book
    2   Cash book
    3   Journal
    4   Purchase ledger

    A   1 and 2 only
    B   1, 2 and 3 only
    C   1 only
    D   All of them   **(2 marks)**

3.12 In which book of prime entry will a business record debit notes in respect of goods which have been sent back to suppliers?

    A   The sales returns day book
    B   The cash book
    C   The purchase returns day book
    D   The purchase day book   **(2 marks)**

3.13 A company's motor vehicles at cost account at 30 June 20X6 is as follows:

MOTOR VEHICLES – COST

	$		$
Balance b/d	150,500	Disposal	85,000
Additions	120,950	Balance c/d	186,450
	271,450		271,450

What opening balance should be included in the following period's trial balance for motor vehicles – cost at 1 July 20X6?

    A $271,450 DR
    B $271,450 DR
    C $186,450 CR
    D $186,450 DR   **(2 marks)**

3.14 A company's trade payables account at 30 September 20X1 is as follows:

TRADE PAYABLES ACCOUNT

	$		$
Cash at bank	21,600	Balance b/d	14,000
Balance c/d	11,900	Purchases	19,500
	33,500		33,500

What was the balance for trade payables in the trial balance at 1 October 20X0?

    A $14,000 DR
    B $14,000 CR
    C $11,900 DR
    D $11,900 CR   **(2 marks)**

3.15 Which of the following would be recorded in the sales day book?

    A   Discounts allowed
    B   Sales invoices
    C   Credit notes received
    D   Trade discounts   **(2 marks)**

3.16 Which of the following statements is true?

A A debit records an increase in liabilities.
B A debit records a decrease in assets.
C A credit records an increase in liabilities.
D A credit records an decrease in capital.   **(2 marks)**

3.17 How is the total of the purchases day book posted to the nominal ledger?

A Debit purchases, Credit cash
B Debit payables control, Credit purchases
C Debit cash, Credit purchases
D Debit purchases, Credit payables control   **(2 marks)**

(Total = 34 marks)

4 Double entry bookkeeping II   38 mins

The following information is relevant for questions 4.1 and 4.2.

On 1 May 20X9 Marshall's cash book showed a cash balance of $224 and an overdraft of $336. During the week ended 6 May the following transactions took place.

May 1   Sold $160 of goods to P Dixon on credit.

May 1   Withdrew $50 of cash from the bank for business use.

May 2   Purchased goods from A Clarke on credit for $380 less 15% trade discount.

May 2   Repaid a debt of $120 owing to R Hill, taking advantage of a 10% cash discount. The payment was by cheque.

May 3   Sold $45 of goods for cash.

May 4   Sold $80 of goods to M Maguire on credit, offering a $12^{1}/_{2}$% discount if payment made within 7 days.

May 4   Paid a telephone bill of $210 by cheque.

May 4   Purchased $400 of goods on credit from D Daley.

May 5   Received a cheque from H Larkin for $180. Larkin has taken advantage of a $20 cash discount offered to him.

May 5   Sold $304 of goods to M Donald on credit.

May 5   Purchased $135 of goods from Honour Co by cheque.

May 6   Received a cheque from D Randle for $482.

May 6   Purchased $100 of goods on credit from G Perkins.

4.1 What is the total of the sales day book?

A $544
B $589
C $534
D $579   **(2 marks)**

4.2 What is the total of the purchases day book?

A $880
B $823
C $1,033
D $958   **(2 marks)**

4.3 Smith Co has the following transactions:

1   Purchase of goods on credit from T Rader: $450
2   Return of goods purchased on credit last month to T Rouble: $700

What are the correct ledger entries to record these transactions?

A	Dr Purchases	$450	
	Dr Purchase Returns	$700	
	Cr Cash		$450
	Cr Trade Payables		$700
B	Dr Purchases	$450	
	Dr Trade Payables	$700	
	Cr Purchase Returns		$1,150
C	Dr Purchases	$450	
	Dr Trade Payables	$250	
	Cr Purchase Returns		$700
D	Dr Purchase Returns	$700	
	Dr Purchases	$450	
	Cr Trade Payables		$1,150

(2 marks)

4.4 Mew Ling has the following transactions:

1   Receipt of cash from R Singh in respect of an invoice for goods sold three weeks ago
2   Receipt of cash from S Kalu for cash sales

What are the ledger entries required to record the above transactions?

A   Dr Cash
        Cr Sales
B   Dr Cash
        Cr Sales
        Cr Trade Receivables
C   Dr Sales
        Cr Cash
D   Dr Trade Receivables
    Dr Sales
        Cr Cash

(2 marks)

4.5 How is the total of the sales day book recorded in the nominal ledger?

	Debit	Credit
A	Receivables Ledger	Receivables Control Account
B	Receivables Control Account	Receivables Ledger
C	Sales	Receivables Control Account
D	Receivables Control Account	Sales

(2 marks)

4.6 Are the following statements about debit entries true or false?

1   A debit entry in the cash book will increase an overdraft in the accounts.
2   A debit entry in the cash book will increase a bank balance in the accounts.

A   Both true
B   Both false
C   1 true and 2 false
D   1 false and 2 true

(2 marks)

4.7 An accountant has inserted all the relevant figures into the trade payables account, but has not yet balanced off the account.

TRADE PAYABLES ACCOUNT

	$		$
Cash at bank	100,750	Balance b/d	250,225
		Purchases	325,010

Assuming there are no other entries to be made, other than to balance off the account, what is the closing balance on the trade payables account?

A $474,485 DR
B $575,235 DR
C $474,485 CR
D $575,235 CR   **(2 marks)**

4.8 You are given the following information:

Receivables at 1 January 20X3	$10,000
Receivables at 31 December 20X3	$9,000
Total receipts during 20X3 (including cash sales of $5,000)	$85,000

What are sales on credit during 20X3?

A $81,000
B $86,000
C $79,000
D $84,000   **(2 marks)**

4.9 A business sells $100 worth of goods to a customer, the customer pays $50 in cash immediately and will pay the remaining $50 in 30 days' time.

What is the double entry to record the purchase in the customer's accounting records?

A   Debit cash $50, credit payables $50, credit purchases $50
B   Debit payables $50, debit cash $50, credit purchases $100
C   Debit purchases $100, credit payables $50, credit cash $50
D   Debit purchases $100, credit cash $100   **(2 marks)**

4.10 Tin Co purchases $250 worth of metal from Steel Co. Tin Co agrees to pay Steel Co in 60 days time.

What is the double entry to record the purchase in Steel Co's books?

A   Debit sales $250, credit receivables $250
B   Debit purchases $250, credit payables $250
C   Debit receivables $250, credit sales $250
D   Debit payables $250, credit purchases $250   **(2 marks)**

4.11 The following totals appear in the day books for March 20X8.

	$
Sales day book	40,000
Purchases day book	20,000
Returns inwards day book	2,000
Returns outward day book	4,000

Opening and closing inventories are both $3,000. What is the gross profit for March 20X8?

A $22,000
B $24,000
C $20,000
D $18,000   **(2 marks)**

4.12 William's trial balance at 30 September 20X5 includes the following balances:

Trade receivables $75,943
Receivables allowance $4,751

How should these balances be reported in William's statement of financial position as at 30 September 20X5?

A   An asset of $71,192
B   An asset of $75,943 and a liability of $4,751
C   A liability of $71,192
D   A liability of $75,943 and an asset of $4,751   **(2 marks)**

4.13 A trial balance is made up of a list of debit balances and credit balances.

Which of the following statements is correct?

A   Every debit balance represents an expense.
B   Assets are represented by debit balances.
C   Liabilities are represented by debit balances.
D   Income is included in the list of debit balances.   **(2 marks)**

4.14 At 30 November 20X5 Jenny had a bank loan of $8,500 and a balance of $678 in hand in her bank account.

How should these amounts be recorded on Jenny's opening trial balance at 1 December 20X5?

A   Debit $7,822
B   Credit $7,822
C   Credit $8,500 and Debit $678
D   Debit $8,500 and Credit $678   **(2 marks)**

4.15 Bert has extracted the following list of balances from his general ledger at 31 October 20X5:

	$
Sales	258,542
Opening inventory	9,649
Purchases	142,958
Expenses	34,835
Non-current assets (carrying amount)	63,960
Receivables	31,746
Payables	13,864
Cash at bank	1,783
Capital	12,525

What is the total of the debit balances in Bert's trial balance at 31 October 20X5?

A $267,049
B $275,282
C $283,148
D $284,931   **(2 marks)**

4.16 At 31 October 20X6 Roger's trial balance included the following balances:

	$
Machinery at cost	12,890
Accumulated depreciation	8,950
Inventory	5,754
Trade receivables	11,745
Trade payables	7,830
Bank overdraft	1,675
Cash at bank	150

What is the value of Roger's current assets at 31 October 20X6?

A $17,649
B $17,499
C $15,974
D $13,734   **(2 marks)**

(Total = 32 marks)

Do you know? – Recording transactions and events

Check that you can fill in the blanks in the statements below before you attempt any questions. If in doubt, you should go back to your BPP Interactive Text and revise first.

- S......... t...... is an indirect tax levied on the sale of goods and services.

- R.................. businesses charge .... sales tax on sales and suffer .... sales tax on purchases.

- The c...... of g...... s.......is calculated as: Opening inventory + purchases – closing inventory.

- Carriage .... is included in the cost of purchases. Carriage .... is a selling expense.

- The value of inventories is calculated at the l......... of c......... and n...... r............ v........

- The cost of inventories can be arrived at by using .... or ....

- C........... expenditure is expenditure which forms part of the cost of non-current assets. R..................
expenditure is expenditure incurred for the purpose of the trade or to maintain non current assets.

- The ...... of a non-current asset, less its estimated residual value, is allocated fairly between accounting periods by means of d....................

- D.................. costs must be capitalised as an i.................. asset if the criteria in IAS 38 are satisfied.

- A.................. are expenses which relate to an accounting period but have not yet been paid for. They are shown in the statement of financial position as a l..................

- P..................are expenses which have already been paid but relate to a future accounting period. They are shown in the statement of financial position as an ....

- I.................. debts are specific debts owed to a business which it decides are never going to be paid. They are written off as an .... in the statement of profit or loss.

- An .... in the allowance for receivables is shown as an expense in the statement of profit or loss.

- A provision should be recognised:
  - When an entity has a p......... o.............
  - It is p........... that a transfer of economic benefits will be required to settle it
  - A r......... e......... can be made of its amount

- A c.................. liability must not be recognised as a liability in the financial statements. Instead it should be d.............. in the notes to the accounts.

Did you know? – Recording transactions and events

Could you fill in the blanks? The answers are in bold. Use this page for revision purposes as you approach the exam.

- **Sales tax** is an indirect tax levied on the sale of goods and services.

- **Registered** businesses charge **output sales tax** on sales and suffer **input sales tax** on purchases.

- The **cost of goods sold** is calculated as: Opening inventory + purchases – closing inventory.

- Carriage **inwards** is included in the cost of purchases. Carriage **outwards** is a selling expense.

- The value of inventories is calculated at the **lower** of **cost** and **net realisable value**.

- The cost of inventories can be arrived at by using **FIFO (first in-first out)** or **AVCO (weighted average costing)**.

- **Capital** expenditure is expenditure which forms part of the cost of non-current assets. **Revenue** expenditure is expenditure incurred for the purpose of the trade or to maintain non current assets.

- The **cost** of a non-current asset, less its estimated residual value, is allocated fairly between accounting periods by means of **depreciation**.

- **Development** costs must be capitalised as an **intangible** asset if the criteria in IAS 38 are satisfied.

- **Accruals** are expenses which relate to an accounting period but have not yet been paid for. They are shown in the statement of financial position as a **liability**.

- **Prepayments** are expenses which have already been paid but relate to a future accounting period. They are shown in the statement of financial position as an **asset**.

- **Irrecoverable** debts are specific debts owed to a business which it decides are never going to be paid. They are written off as an **expense** in the statement of profit or loss.

- An **increase** in the allowance for receivables is shown as an expense in the statement of profit or loss.

- A **provision** should be recognised:

    - When an entity has a **present obligation**
    - It is **probable** that a transfer of economic benefits will be required to settle it
    - A **reliable estimate** can be made of its amount

- A **contingent** liability must not be recognised as a liability in the financial statements. Instead it should be **disclosed** in the notes to the accounts.

5 Sales tax
19 mins

5.1 W is registered for sales tax. The managing director has asked four staff in the accounts department why the output tax for the last quarter does not equal 20% of sales (20% is the rate of tax). Which one of the following four replies she received was *not* correct?

    A   The company had some exports that were not liable to sales tax.
    B   The company made some sales of zero-rated products.
    C   The company made some sales of exempt products.
    D   The company sold some products to businesses not registered for sales tax.   **(2 marks)**

5.2 The following information relates to Eva Co's sales tax for the month of March 20X3:

	$
Sales (including sales tax)	109,250
Purchases (net of sales tax)	64,000

Sales tax is charged at a flat rate of 15%. Eva Co's sales tax account showed an opening credit balance of $4,540 at the beginning of the month and a closing debit balance of $2,720 at the end of the month.

What was the total sales tax paid to regulatory authorities during the month of March 20X3?

    A $6,470.00
    B $11,910.00
    C $14,047.50
    D $13,162.17   **(2 marks)**

5.3 Alana is not registered for sales tax purposes. She has recently received an invoice for goods for resale which cost $500 before sales tax, which is levied at 15%. The total value was therefore $575.

What is the correct entry to be made in Alana's general ledger in respect of the invoice?

    A   Dr Purchases $500, Dr Sales tax $75, Cr Payables $575
    B   Dr Purchases $575, Cr Sales tax $75, Cr Payables $500
    C   Dr Purchases $500, Cr Payables $500
    D   Dr Purchases $575, Cr Payables $575   **(2 marks)**

5.4 A sales tax registered business sells goods costing $200 plus sales tax at 17.5% on credit. Which of the following entries correctly records this transaction?

A	Dr	Receivables	$235	
		Cr Sales		$235
B	Dr	Receivables	$200	
		Cr Sales		$165
		Cr Sales tax a/c		$35
C	Dr	Receivables	$235	
		Cr Sales		$200
		Cr Sales tax a/c		$35
D	Dr	Sales	$200	
	Dr	Sales tax	$35	
		Cr Payables		$235

(2 marks)

5.5 A business commenced with capital in cash of $1,000. Inventory costing $800 plus sales tax is purchased on credit, and half is sold for $1,000 plus sales tax, the customer paying in cash at once. The sales tax rate is 20%.

What would the accounting equation after these transactions show?

A   Assets $1,800 less Liabilities $200 equals Capital $1,600
B   Assets $2,200 less Liabilities $1,000 equals Capital $1,200
C   Assets $2,600 less Liabilities $800 equals Capital $1,800
D   Assets $2,600 less Liabilities $1,000 equals Capital $1,600   **(2 marks)**

5.6 Trade receivables and payables in the final accounts of a sales tax registered trader will appear as described by which of the following?

A   Inclusive of sales tax in the statement of financial position

B   Exclusive of sales tax in the statement of financial position

C   The sales tax is deducted and added to the sales tax account in the statement of financial position

D   Sales tax does not appear in the statement of financial position because the business simply acts as a collector on behalf of the tax authorities   **(2 marks)**

5.7 Which of the following correctly describe the entry in the sales account for a sale for a sales tax registered trader?

A   Credited with the total of sales made, including sales tax
B   Credited with the total of sales made, excluding sales tax
C   Debited with the total of sales made, including sales tax
D   Debited with the total of sales made, excluding sales tax   **(2 marks)**

5.8 Sales (including sales tax) amounted to $27,612.50, and purchases (excluding sales tax) amounted to $18,000. What is the balance on the sales tax account, assuming all items are subject to sales tax at 17.5%?

A $962.50 debit
B $962.50 credit
C $1,682.10 debit
D $1,682.10 credit   **(2 marks)**

(Total = 16 marks)

6 Inventory   43 mins

6.1 The inventory value for the financial statements of Global Inc for the year ended 30 June 20X3 was based on a inventory count on 7 July 20X3, which gave a total inventory value of $950,000.

Between 30 June and 7 July 20X6, the following transactions took place.

	$
Purchase of goods	11,750
Sale of goods (mark up on cost at 15%)	14,950
Goods returned by Global Inc to supplier	1,500

What figure should be included in the financial statements for inventories at 30 June 20X3?

A $952,750
B $949,750
C $926,750
D $958,950   **(2 marks)**

6.2 Which of the following costs may be included when arriving at the cost of finished goods inventory for inclusion in the financial statements of a manufacturing company?

1   Carriage inwards
2   Carriage outwards
3   Depreciation of factory plant
4   Finished goods storage costs
5   Factory supervisors' wages

A   1 and 5 only
B   2, 4 and 5 only
C   1, 3 and 5 only
D   1, 2, 3 and 4 only   (2 marks)

6.3 The closing inventory at cost of a company at 31 January 20X3 amounted to $284,700.

The following items were included at cost in the total:

1   400 coats, which had cost $80 each and normally sold for $150 each. Owing to a defect in manufacture, they were all sold after the reporting date at 50% of their normal price. Selling expenses amounted to 5% of the proceeds.

2   800 skirts, which had cost $20 each. These too were found to be defective. Remedial work in February 20X3 cost $5 per skirt, and selling expenses for the batch totalled $800. They were sold for $28 each.

What should the inventory value be according to IAS 2 *Inventories* after considering the above items?

A $281,200
B $282,800
C $329,200
D   None of these   (2 marks)

6.4 A company values its inventory using the first in, first out (FIFO) method. At 1 May 20X2 the company had 700 engines in inventory, valued at $190 each.

During the year ended 30 April 20X3 the following transactions took place:

20X2
1 July   Purchased 500 engines at $220 each
1 November   Sold 400 engines for $160,000

20X3
1 February   Purchased 300 engines at $230 each
15 April   Sold 250 engines for $125,000

What is the value of the company's closing inventory of engines at 30 April 20X3?

A $188,500
B $195,500
C $166,000
D   None of these figures   (2 marks)

6.5 Which of the following statements about the valuation of inventory are correct, according to IAS 2 *Inventories*?

1 Inventory items are normally to be valued at the higher of cost and net realisable value.

2 The cost of goods manufactured by an entity will include materials and labour only. Overhead costs cannot be included.

3 LIFO (last in, first out) cannot be used to value inventory.

4 Selling price less estimated profit margin may be used to arrive at cost if this gives a reasonable approximation to actual cost.

A 1, 3 and 4 only
B 1 and 2 only
C 3 and 4 only
D None of the statements are correct (2 marks)

6.6 A company with an accounting date of 31 October carried out a physical check of inventory on 4 November 20X3, leading to an inventory value at cost at this date of $483,700.

Between 1 November 20X3 and 4 November 20X3 the following transactions took place:

1 Goods costing $38,400 were received from suppliers.

2 Goods that had cost $14,800 were sold for $20,000.

3 A customer returned, in good condition, some goods which had been sold to him in October for $600 and which had cost $400.

4 The company returned goods that had cost $1,800 in October to the supplier, and received a credit note for them.

What figure should appear in the company's financial statements at 31 October 20X3 for closing inventory, based on this information?

A $458,700
B $505,900
C $508,700
D $461,500 (2 marks)

6.7 In preparing its financial statements for the current year, a company's closing inventory was understated by $300,000.

What will be the effect of this error if it remains uncorrected?

A The current year's profit will be overstated and next year's profit will be understated.
B The current year's profit will be understated but there will be no effect on next year's profit.
C The current year's profit will be understated and next year's profit will be overstated.
D The current year's profit will be overstated but there will be no effect on next year's profit.
(2 marks)

6.8 At 30 September 20X3 the closing inventory of a company amounted to $386,400.

The following items were included in this total at cost:

1   1,000 items which had cost $18 each. These items were all sold in October 20X3 for $15 each, with selling expenses of $800.

2   Five items which had been in inventory since 19W3, when they were purchased for $100 each, sold in October 20X3 for $1,000 each, net of selling expenses.

What figure should appear in the company's statement of financial position at 30 September 20X3 for inventory?

A $382,600
B $384,200
C $387,100
D $400,600   **(2 marks)**

6.9 The financial year of Mitex Co ended on 31 December 20X1. An inventory count on January 4 20X2 gave a total inventory value of $527,300.

The following transactions occurred between January 1 and January 4.

	$
Purchases of goods	7,900
Sales of goods (gross profit margin 40% on sales)	15,000
Goods returned to a supplier	800

What inventory value should be included in Mitex Co's financial statements at 31 December 20X1?

A $525,400
B $527,600
C $529,200
D $535,200   **(2 marks)**

6.10 Which of the following statements about IAS 2 *Inventories* is correct?

A   Production overheads should be included in cost on the basis of a company's normal level of activity in the period.

B   In arriving at the net realisable value of inventories, trade discounts and settlement discounts must be deducted.

C   In arriving at the cost of inventories, FIFO, LIFO and weighted average cost formulas are acceptable.

D   It is permitted to value finished goods inventories at materials plus labour cost only, without adding production overheads.

                                                                                              (2 marks)

6.11 You are preparing the final accounts for a business. The cost of the items in closing inventory is $41,875. This includes some items which cost $1,960 and which were damaged in transit. You have estimated that it will cost $360 to repair the items, and they can then be sold for $1,200.

What is the correct inventory valuation for inclusion in the final accounts?

A $39,915
B $40,755
C $41,515
D $42,995   **(2 marks)**

6.12 S sells three products – Basic, Super and Luxury. The following information was available at the year end.

	Basic	Super	Luxury
	$ per unit	$ per unit	$ per unit
Original cost	6	9	18
Estimated selling price	9	12	15
Selling and distribution costs	1	4	5
	units	units	units
Units of inventory	200	250	150

What is the value of inventory at the year end?

A $4,200
B $4,700
C $5,700
D $6,150 **(2 marks)**

6.13 An inventory record card shows the following details.

February	1	50 units in stock at a cost of $40 per unit
	7	100 units purchased at a cost of $45 per unit
	14	80 units sold
	21	50 units purchased at a cost of $50 per unit
	28	60 units sold

What is the value of inventory at 28 February using the FIFO method?

A $2,450
B $2,700
C $2,950
D $3,000 **(2 marks)**

6.14 IAS 2 *Inventories* defines the items that may be included in computing the value of an inventory of finished goods manufactured by a business.

Which one of the following lists consists only of items which may be included in the statement of financial position value of such inventories, according to IAS 2?

A Supervisor's wages, carriage inwards, carriage outwards, raw materials
B Raw materials, carriage inwards, costs of storage of finished goods, plant depreciation
C Plant depreciation, carriage inwards, raw materials, Supervisor's wages
D Carriage outwards, raw materials, Supervisor's wages, plant depreciation **(2 marks)**

6.15 The closing inventory of X amounted to $116,400 *excluding* the following two inventory lines:

1 400 items which had cost $4 each. All were sold after the reporting period for $3 each, with selling expenses of $200 for the batch.

2 200 different items which had cost $30 each. These items were found to be defective at the end of the reporting period. Rectification work after the statement of financial position amounted to $1,200, after which they were sold for $35 each, with selling expenses totalling $300.

Which of the following total figures should appear in the statement of financial position of X for inventory?

A $122,300
B $121,900
C $122,900
D $123,300 **(2 marks)**

6.16 The inventory value for the financial statements of Q for the year ended 31 December 20X4 was based on an inventory count on 4 January 20X5, which gave a total inventory value of $836,200.

Between 31 December and 4 January 20X5, the following transactions took place:

	$
Purchases of goods	8,600
Sales of goods (profit margin 30% on sales)	14,000
Goods returned by Q to supplier	700

What adjusted figure should be included in the financial statements for inventories at 31 December 20X4?

A $838,100
B $853,900
C $818,500
D $834,300   **(2 marks)**

6.17 A company has decided to switch from using the FIFO method of inventory valuation to using the average cost method (AVCO).

In the first accounting period where the change is made, opening inventory valued by the FIFO method was $53,200. Closing inventory valued by the AVCO method was $59,800.

Total purchases and during the period were $136,500. Using the AVCO method, opening inventory would have been valued at $56,200.

What is the cost of materials that should be included in the statement of profit or loss for the period?

A $129,900
B $132,900
C $135,900
D $140,100   **(2 marks)**

6.18 Which one of the following statements about the use of a continuous inventory system is INCORRECT?

A   In a retail organisation, a continuous inventory system can be used to keep track of the quantity of each stock item available in its distribution centres.

B   Under continuous inventory, the cost of each receipt of inventory and the cost of each issue from inventory is recorded individually.

C   A continuous inventory system removes the need for periodic physical inventory counts.

D   Both the FIFO and average cost (AVCO) methods of pricing inventory may be used within a continuous inventory system.   **(2 marks)**

(Total = 36 marks)

7   Tangible non-current assets I   41 mins

7.1 What is the purpose of charging depreciation in accounts?

A   To allocate the cost of a non-current asset over the accounting periods expected to benefit from its use

B   To ensure that funds are available for the eventual replacement of the asset

C   To reduce the cost of the asset in the statement of financial position to its estimated market value

D   To account for the 'wearing-out' of the asset over its life   **(2 marks)**

7.2 Your firm bought a machine for $5,000 on 1 January 20X1, which had an expected useful life of four years and an expected residual value of $1,000; the asset was to be depreciated on the straight-line basis. The firm's policy is to charge depreciation in the year of disposal. On 31 December 20X3, the machine was sold for $1,600.

What amount should be entered in the 20X3 statement of profit or loss and other comprehensive income for profit or loss on disposal?

A   Profit of $600
B   Loss of $600
C   Profit of $350
D   Loss of $400   **(2 marks)**

7.3 An asset register showed a carrying value of $67,460. A non-current asset costing $15,000 had been sold for $4,000, making a loss on disposal of $1,250. No entries had been made in the asset register for this disposal.

What is the correct balance on the asset register?

A $42,710
B $51,210
C $53,710
D $62,210   **(2 marks)**

7.4 An organisation's asset register shows a carrying value of $145,600. The non-current asset account in the nominal ledger shows a carrying value of $135,600. The difference could be due to a disposed asset not having been deducted from the asset register. Which one of the following could represent that asset?

A   Asset with disposal proceeds of $15,000 and a profit on disposal of $5,000
B   Asset with disposal proceeds of $15,000 and a carrying value of $5,000
C   Asset with disposal proceeds of $15,000 and a loss on disposal of $5,000
D   Asset with disposal proceeds of $5,000 and a carrying value of $5,000   **(2 marks)**

7.5 Which one of the following would occur if the purchase of computer stationary was debited to the computer equipment at cost account?

A   An overstatement of profit and an overstatement of non-current assets
B   An understatement of profit and an overstatement of non-current assets
C   An overstatement of profit and an understatement of non-current assets
D   An understatement of profit and an understatement of non-current assets   **(2 marks)**

7.6 A company's plant and machinery ledger account for the year ended 30 September 20X2 was as follows:

PLANT AND MACHINERY – COST

		$			$
20X1			*20X2*		
1 Oct	Balance	381,200	1 Jun	Disposal account – cost of asset sold	36,000
1 Dec	Cash – addition	18,000	30 Sep	Balance	363,200
		399,200			399,200

The company's policy is to charge depreciation at 20% per year on the straight line basis, with proportionate depreciation in years of purchase and disposal.

What is the depreciation charge for the year ended 30 September 20X2?

A $74,440
B $84,040
C $72,640
D $76,840   **(2 marks)**

7.7 A company bought a property four years ago on 1 January for $ 170,000. Since then property prices have risen substantially and the property has been revalued at $210,000.

The property was estimated as having a useful life of 20 years when it was purchased. What is the balance on the revaluation surplus reported in the statement of financial position?

A $210,000
B $136,000
C $74,000
D $34,000   **(2 marks)**

7.8 A business purchased a motor car on 1 July 20X3 for $20,000. It is to be depreciated at 20 per cent per year on the straight line basis, assuming a residual value at the end of five years of $4,000, with a proportionate depreciation charge in the years of purchase and disposal.

The $20,000 cost was correctly entered in the cash book but posted to the debit of the motor vehicles repairs account.

How will the business profit for the year ended 31 December 20X3 be affected by the error?

A Understated by $18,400
B Understated by $16,800
C Overstated by $18,400
D Overstated by $16,800   **(2 marks)**

7.9 A company's policy is to charge depreciation on plant and machinery at 20% per year on cost, with proportional depreciation for items purchased or sold during a year.

The company's plant and machinery at cost account for the year ended 30 September 20X3 is shown below.

PLANT AND MACHINERY – COST

		$			$
20X2			20X3		
1 Oct	Balance	200,000	30 Jun Transfer disposal account		40,000
			30 Sep Balance		210,000
20X3					
1 Apr	Cash-purchase of plant	50,000			
		250,000			250,000

What should be the depreciation charge for plant and machinery (excluding any profit or loss on the disposal) for the year ended 30 September 20X3?

A $43,000
B $51,000
C $42,000
D $45,000   **(2 marks)**

7.10   The plant and machinery at cost account of a business for the year ended 30 June 20X4 was as follows:

PLANT AND MACHINERY – COST

		$			$
20X3			*20X3*		
1 Jul	Balance	240,000	30 Sep Transfer disposal account		60,000
20X4			*20X4*		
1 Jan	Cash – purchase of plant	160,000	30 Jun Balance		340,000
		400,000			400,000

The company's policy is to charge depreciation at 20% per year on the straight line basis, with proportionate depreciation in the years of purchase and disposal.

What should be the depreciation charge for the year ended 30 June 20X4?

A $68,000
B $64,000
C $61,000
D $55,000   **(2 marks)**

7.11   A manufacturing company receives an invoice on 29 February 20X2 for work done on one of its machines. $25,500 of the cost is actually for a machine upgrade, which will improve efficiency. The accounts department do not notice and charge the whole amount to maintenance costs. Machinery is depreciated at 25% per annum on a straight-line basis, with a proportional charge in the years of acquisition and disposal. By what amount will the profit for the year to 30 June 20X2 be understated?

A $19,125
B $25,500
C $23,375
D $21,250   **(2 marks)**

7.12   W bought a new printing machine. The cost of the machine was $80,000. The installation costs were $5,000 and the employees received training on how to use the machine, at a cost of $2,000. Before using the machine to print customers' orders, a test was undertaken and the paper and ink cost $1,000.

What should be the cost of the machine in the company's statement of financial position?

A $80,000
B $85,000
C $86,000
D $88,000   **(2 marks)**

7.13   What are the correct ledger entries to record an acquisition of a non-current asset on credit?

	Debit	*Credit*
A	Non-current assets – cost	Receivables
B	Payables	Non-current assets – cost
C	Non-current assets – cost	Payables
D	Non-current assets – cost	Revaluation surplus

                                                                              (2 marks)

7.14 Alpha sells machine B for $50,000 cash on 30 April 20X4. Machine B cost $100,000 when it was purchased and has a carrying value of $65,000 at the date of disposal. What are the journal entries to record the disposal of machine B?

A	Dr Accumulated depreciation	$35,000	
	Dr Loss on disposal (SPL)	$15,000	
	Dr Cash	$50,000	
	Cr Non-current assets – cost		$100,000

B	Dr Accumulated depreciation	$65,000	
	Dr Loss on disposal (SPL)	$35,000	
	Cr Non-current assets – cost		$100,000

C	Dr Accumulated depreciation	$35,000	
	Dr Cash	$50,000	
	Cr Non-current assets		$65,000
	Cr Profit on disposal (SPL)		$20,000

D	Dr Non-current assets	$65,000	
	Dr Accumulated depreciation	$35,000	
	Cr Cash		$50,000
	Cr Profit on disposal (SPL)		$50,000

(2 marks)

7.15 Which of the following statements are correct?

1 IAS 16 *Property, plant and equipment* requires entities to disclose the purchase date of each asset.

2 The carrying amount of a non-current asset is the cost or valuation of that asset less accumulated depreciation.

3 IAS 16 *Property, plan and equipment* permits entities to make a transfer from the revaluation surplus to retained earnings for excess depreciation on revalued assets.

4 Once decided, the useful life of a non-current asset should not be changed.

A 1, 2 and 3
B 2 and 3 only
C 2 and 4 only
D 1, 2 and 4 only **(2 marks)**

The following information is relevant for questions 7.16 and 7.17.

Gusna Co purchased a building on 31 December 20X1 for $750,000. At the date of acquisition, the useful life of the building was estimated to be 25 years and depreciation is calculated using the straight-line method. At 31 December 20X6, an independent valuer valued the building at $1,000,000 and the revaluation was recognised in the financial statements. Gusna's accounting policies state that excess depreciation arising on revaluation of non-current assets can be transferred from the revaluation surplus to retained earnings.

7.16 What is the depreciation charge on the building for the year ended 31 December 20X7?

A $40,000
B $50,000
C $30,000
D $42,500 **(2 marks)**

7.17 What is the journal entry to record the transfer of excess depreciation from the revaluation surplus to retained earnings?

A Dr Revaluation surplus $20,000
     Cr Retained earnings $20,000

B Dr Revaluation surplus $12,500
     Cr Retained earnings $12,500

C Dr Retained earnings $20,000
     Cr Revaluation surplus $20,000

D Dr Revaluation surplus $12,500
     Cr Retained earnings $12,500

(2 marks)

(Total = 34 marks)

8 Tangible non-current assets II   48 mins

8.1 A car was purchased by a newsagent business in May 20X0 for:

	$
Cost	10,000
Road tax	150
Total	10,150

The business adopts a date of 31 December as its year end.

The car was traded in for a replacement vehicle in August 20X3 at an agreed value of $5,000.

It has been depreciated at 25% per annum on the reducing balance method, charging a full year's depreciation in the year of purchase and none in the year of sale.

What was the profit or loss on disposal of the vehicle during the year ended December 20X3?

A Profit: $718
B Profit: $781
C Profit: $1,788
D Profit: $1,836   **(2 marks)**

8.2 The carrying value of a company's non-current assets was $200,000 at 1 August 20X0. During the year ended 31 July 20X1, the company sold non-current assets for $25,000 on which it made a loss of $5,000. The depreciation charge for the year was $20,000. What was the carrying value of non-current assets at 31 July 20X1?

A $150,000
B $155,000
C $160,000
D $180,000   **(2 marks)**

8.3 Y purchased some plant on 1 January 20X0 for $38,000. The payment for the plant was correctly entered in the cash book but was entered on the debit side of the plant repairs account.

Y charges depreciation on the straight line basis at 20% per year, with a proportionate charge in the years of acquisition and disposal, and assuming no scrap value at the end of the life of the asset.

How will Y's profit for the year ended 31 March 20X0 be affected by the error?

A Understated by $30,400
B Understated by $36,100
C Understated by $38,000
D Overstated by $1,900   **(2 marks)**

8.4 B acquired a lorry on 1 May 20X0 at a cost of $30,000. The lorry has an estimated useful life of four years, and an estimated resale value at the end of that time of $6,000. B charges depreciation on the straight line basis, with a proportionate charge in the period of acquisition.

What will the depreciation charge for the lorry be in B's accounting period to 30 September 20X0?

A $3,000
B $2,500
C $2,000
D $5,000 **(2 marks)**

8.5 At 31 December 20X3 Q, a limited liability company, owned a building that had cost $800,000 on 1 January 20W4.

It was being depreciated at 2% per year.

On 31 December 20X3 a revaluation to $1,000,000 was recognised. At this date the building had a remaining useful life of 40 years.

What is the balance on the revaluation surplus at 31 December 20X3 and the depreciation charge in the statement of profit or loss for the year ended 31 December 20X4?

	Depreciation charge for year ended 31 December 20X4 (statement of profit or loss) $	Revaluation surplus as at 31 December 20X3 (statement of financial position) $
A	25,000	200,000
B	25,000	360,000
C	20,000	200,000
D	20,000	360,000

(2 marks)

8.6 Which of the following best explains what is meant by 'capital expenditure'?

A Expenditure on non-current assets, including repairs and maintenance
B Expenditure on expensive assets
C Expenditure relating to the issue of share capital
D Expenditure relating to the acquisition or improvement of non-current assets **(2 marks)**

8.7 Which of the following costs would be classified as capital expenditure for a restaurant business?

A A replacement for a broken window
B Repainting the restaurant
C An illuminated sign advertising the business name
D Cleaning of the kitchen floors **(2 marks)**

8.8 Which one of the following costs would be classified as revenue expenditure on the invoice for a new company car?

A Road tax
B Number plates
C Fitted stereo radio
D Delivery costs **(2 marks)**

8.9 Lance is entering an invoice for a new item of equipment in the accounts. The invoice shows the following costs:

Water treatment equipment	$39,800
Delivery	$1,100
Maintenance charge	$3,980
Sales tax	$7,854
Invoice total	$52,734

Lance is registered for sales tax. What is the total value of capital expenditure on the invoice?

A $39,800
B $40,900
C $44,880
D $52,734   **(2 marks)**

8.10 Which one of the following assets may be classified as a non-current asset in the accounts of a business?

A A tax refund due next year
B A motor vehicle held for resale
C A computer used in the office
D Cleaning products used to clean the office floors   **(2 marks)**

8.11 Which of the following items should be included in current assets?

(i) Assets which are not intended to be converted into cash
(ii) Assets which will be converted into cash in the long term
(iii) Assets which will be converted into cash in the near future

A (i) only
B (i) only
C (iii) only
D (ii) and (iii)   **(2 marks)**

8.12 Which of the following statements describes current assets?

A Assets which are currently located on the business premises
B Assets which are used to conduct the organisation's current business
C Assets which are expected to be converted into cash in the short-term
D Assets which are not expected to be converted into cash in the short-term   **(2 marks)**

8.13 Gamma purchases a motor vehicle on 30 September 20X1 for $15,000 on credit. Gamma has a policy of depreciating motor vehicles using the reducing balance method at 15% per annum, pro rata in the years of purchase and sale.

What are the correct ledger entries to record the purchase of the vehicle at 30 September 20X1 and what is the depreciation charge for the year ended 30 November 20X1?

		Purchase of motor vehicle on 30.9.X1		Depreciation charge for year ended 30.11.X1
A	Dr Non-current assets – cost	$15,000		$2,250
	Cr Payables		$15,000	
B	Dr Payables	$15,000		$2,250
	Cr Non-current assets – cost		$15,000	
C	Dr Non-current assets – cost	$15,000		$375
	Cr Payables		$15,000	
D	Dr Payables	$15,000		$375
	Cr Non-current assets – cost		$15,000	**(2 marks)**

8.14 Banjo Co purchased a building on 30 June 20X8 for $1,250,000. At acquisition, the useful life of the building was 50 years. Depreciation is calculated on the straight-line basis. 10 years later, on 30 June 20Y8 when the carrying amount of the building was $1,000,000, the building was revalued to $1,600,000. Banjo Co has a policy of transferring the excess depreciation on revaluation from the revaluation surplus to retained earnings.

Assuming no further revaluations take place, what is the balance on the revaluation surplus at 30 June 20Y9?

A $335,000
B $310,000
C $560,000
D $585,000   **(2 marks)**

8.15 Baker Co purchased an asset for $100,000 on 1.1.X1. It had an estimated useful life of 5 years and it was depreciated using the reducing balance method at a rate of 40%. On 1.1.X3 it was decided to change the method to straight line.

What is the carrying amount of the asset at 31.12.X3?

A $24,000
B $76,000
C $16,000
D $40,000   **(2 marks)**

8.16 Baxter Co purchased an asset for $100,000 on 1.1.X1. It had an estimated useful life of 5 years and it was depreciated using the straight line method. On 1.1.X3 Baxter Co revised the remaining estimated useful life to 8 years.

What is the carrying amount of the asset at 31.12.X3?

A $40,000
B $52,500
C $40,000
D $62,500   **(2 marks)**

8.17 Senakuta Co purchased a machine with an estimated useful life of 5 years for $34,000 on 30 September 20X5. Senakuta Co planned to scrap the machine at the end of its useful life and estimated that the scrap value at the purchase date was $4,000. On 1 October 20X8, Senakuta revised the scrap value to $2,000 due to the decreased value of scrap metal.

What is the depreciation charge for the year ended 30 September 20X9?

A $7,000
B $6,800
C $2,800
D $6,400   **(2 marks)**

8.18 Evans Co purchased a machine with an estimated useful life of 10 years for $76,000 on 30 September 20X5. The machine had a residual value of $16,000.

What are the ledger entries to record the depreciation charge for the machine in the year ended 30 September 20X8?

A   Dr Depreciation charge $6,000
        Cr Accumulated depreciation $6,000

B   Dr Depreciation charge $6,000
     Dr Non-current assets $12,000
        Cr Accumulated depreciation $18,000

C   Dr Accumulated depreciation $6,000
        Cr Depreciation charge $6,000

D   Dr Accumulated depreciation $18,000
        Cr Non-current assets $18,000

(2 marks)

8.19 Banter Co purchased an office building on 1 January 20X1. The building cost was $1,600,000 and this was depreciated by the straight line method at 2% per year, assuming a 50-year life and nil residual value. The building was re-valued to $2,250,000 on 1 January 20X6. The useful life was not revised. The company's financial year ends on 31 December.

What is the balance on the revaluation reserve at 31 December 20X6?

A $650,000
B $792,000
C $797,000
D $810,000

(2 marks)

8.20 A company purchased an asset on 1 January 20X3 at a cost of $1,000,000. It is depreciated over 50 years by the straight line method (nil residual value), with a proportionate charge for depreciation in the year of acquisition and the year of disposal. At 31 December 20X4 the asset was re-valued to $1,200,000. There was no change in the expected useful life of the asset.

The asset was sold on 30 June 20X5 for $1,195,000.

What profit or loss on disposal of the asset will be reported in the statement of profit or loss of the company for the year ended 31 December 20X5?

A   Profit of $7,500
B   Profit of $235,000
C   Profit of $247,500
D   Loss of $5,000

(2 marks)

(Total = 40 marks)

9 Intangible non-current assets · 29 mins

9.1 According to IAS 38 *Intangible assets*, which of the following statements about research and development expenditure are correct?

1 Research expenditure, other than capital expenditure on research facilities, should be recognised as an expense as incurred.

2 In deciding whether development expenditure qualifies to be recognised as an asset, it is necessary to consider whether there will be adequate finance available to complete the project.

3 Development expenditure recognised as an asset must be amortised over a period not exceeding five years.

A 1, 2 and 3
B 1 and 2 only
C 1 and 3 only
D 2 and 3 only **(2 marks)**

9.2 According to IAS 38 *Intangible assets,* which of the following statements about research and development expenditure are correct?

1 If certain conditions are met, an entity may decide to capitalise development expenditure.

2 Research expenditure, other than capital expenditure on research facilities, must be written off as incurred.

3 Capitalised development expenditure must be amortised over a period not exceeding 5 years.

4 Capitalised development expenditure must be disclosed in the statement of financial position under intangible non-current assets.

A 1, 2 and 4 only
B 1 and 3 only
C 2 and 4 only
D 3 and 4 only **(2 marks)**

9.3 According to IAS 38 *Intangible assets,* which of the following statements concerning the accounting treatment of research and development expenditure are **true**?

1 Development costs recognised as an asset must be amortised over a period not exceeding five years.

2 Research expenditure, other than capital expenditure on research facilities, should be recognised as an expense as incurred.

3 In deciding whether development expenditure qualifies to be recognised as an asset, it is necessary to consider whether there will be adequate finance available to complete the project.

4 Development projects must be reviewed at each reporting date, and expenditure on any project no longer qualifying for capitalisation must be amortised through the statement of profit or loss and other comprehensive income over a period not exceeding five years.

A 1 and 4
B 2 and 4
C 2 and 3
D 1 and 3 **(2 marks)**

9.4 According to IAS 38 *Intangible assets,* which of the following statements is/are correct?

1   Capitalised development expenditure must be amortised over a period not exceeding five years.

2   If all the conditions specified in IAS 38 are met, development expenditure may be capitalised if the directors decide to do so.

3   Capitalised development costs are shown in the statement of financial position under the heading of non-current assets.

4   Amortisation of capitalised development expenditure will appear as an item in a company's statement of changes in equity.

A   3 only
B   2 and 3
C   1 and 4
D   1 and 3   **(2 marks)**

9.5 According to IAS 38 *Intangible assets*, which of the following are intangible non-current assets in the accounts of Iota Co?

1   A patent for a new glue purchased for $20,000 by Iota Co

2   Development costs capitalised in accordance with IAS 38

3   A licence to broadcast a television series, purchased by Iota Co for $150,000

4   A state of the art factory purchased by Iota Co for $1.5million

A   1 and 3 only
B   1, 2 and 3 only
C   2 and 4 only
D   2, 3 and 4 only   **(2 marks)**

9.6 According to IAS 38 *Intangible assets,* which of the following statements about intangible assets are correct?

1   If certain criteria are met, research expenditure must be recognised as an intangible asset.
2   If certain criteria are met, development expenditure must be capitalised
3   Intangible assets must be amortised if they have a definite useful life

A   2 and 3 only
B   1 and 3 only
C   1 and 2 only
D   All three statements are correct   **(2 marks)**

9.7 According to IAS 38 *Intangible assets,* which of the following statements concerning the accounting treatment of research and development expenditure are true?

1   If certain criteria are met, research expenditure may be recognised as an asset.

2   Research expenditure, other than capital expenditure on research facilities, should be recognised as an expense as incurred.

3   In deciding whether development expenditure qualifies to be recognised as an asset, it is necessary to consider whether there will be adequate finance available to complete the project.

4   Development expenditure recognised as an asset must be amortised over a period not exceeding five years.

5   The financial statements should disclose the total amount of research and development expenditure recognised as an expense during the period.

A   1, 4 and 5
B   2, 4 and 5
C   2, 3 and 4
D   2, 3 and 5   **(2 marks)**

9.8 According to IAS 38 *Intangible assets,* which of the following statements are correct?

1   Research expenditure should not be capitalised.
2   Intangible assets are never amortised.
3   Development expenditure must be capitalised if certain conditions are met.

A   1 and 3 only
B   1 and 2 only
C   2 and 3 only
D   All three statements are correct   **(2 marks)**

The following information is relevant for questions 9.9 and 9.10.

The following balances existed in the accounting records of Koppa Co, at 31 December 20X7.

	$'000
Development costs capitalised, 1 January 20X7	180
Research and development expenditure for the year	162

In preparing the company's statement of profit or loss and other comprehensive income and statement of financial position at 31 December 20X7 the following further information is relevant.

(a)   The $180,000 total for development costs as at 1 January 20X7 relates to two projects:

	$'000
Project 836: completed project	82
(balance being amortised over the period expected to benefit from it.	
Amount to be amortised in 20X7: $20,000)	
Project 910: in progress	98
	180

(b)   The research and development expenditure for the year is made up of:

	$'000
Research expenditure	103
Development costs on Project 910 which continues to satisfy the	
requirements in IAS 38 for capitalisation	59
	162

9.9 According to IAS 38 *Intangible assets*, what amount should be charged in the statement of profit or loss and other comprehensive income for research and development costs for the year ended 31 December 20X7?

A $123,000
B $182,000
C $162,000
D $103,000   **(2 marks)**

9.10 According to IAS 38 *Intangible assets,* what amount should be disclosed as an intangible asset in the statement of financial position for the year ended 31 December 20X7?

A $219,000
B $180,000
C $160,000
D $59,000   **(2 marks)**

9.11 Theta Co purchased a patent on 30 November 20X3 for $25,000. Theta Co expects to use the patent for the next ten years, after which it will be valueless. According to IAS 38 *Intangible assets,* what is the value of the patent in Theta Co's statement of financial position as at 30 November 20X5?

A $25,000
B $20,000
C $5,000
D $15,000   **(2 marks)**

9.12 PF purchased a quota for carbon dioxide emissions for $15,000 on 30 April 20X6 and capitalised it as an intangible asset in its statement of financial position. PF estimates that the quota will have a useful life of 3 years. What is the journal entry required to record the amortisation of the quota in the accounts for the year ended 30 April 20X9?

A   Dr Expenses $15,000
        Cr Accumulated amortisation $15,000

B   Dr Expenses $5,000
        Cr Accumulated amortisation $5,000

C   Dr Intangible assets $5,000
        Cr Accumulated amortisation $5,000

D   Dr Accumulated amortisation $15,000
        Cr Intangible assets $15,000   **(2 marks)**

(Total = 24 marks)

10 Accruals and prepayments   36 mins

10.1 A company receives rent for subletting part of its office block.

Rent, receivable quarterly in advance, is received as follows:

Date of receipt	Period covered			$
1 October 20X1	3 months to	31 December 20X1		7,500
30 December 20X1	3 months to	31 March 20X2		7,500
4 April 20X2	3 months to	30 June 20X2		9,000
1 July 20X2	3 months to	30 September 20X2		9,000
1 October 20X2	3 months to	31 December 20X2		9,000

What figures, based on these receipts, should appear in the company's financial statements for the year ended 30 November 20X2?

	Statement of profit or loss	Statement of financial position
A	$34,000 Debit	Rent in arrears (Dr) $3,000
B	$34,500 Credit	Rent received in advance (Cr) $6,000
C	$34,000 Credit	Rent received in advance (Cr) $3,000
D	$34,000 Credit	Rent in arrears (Dr) $3,000

(2 marks)

10.2 A company pays rent quarterly in arrears on 1 January, 1 April, 1 July and 1 October each year. The rent was increased from $90,000 per year to $120,000 per year as from 1 October 20X2.

What rent expense and accrual should be included in the company's financial statements for the year ended 31 January 20X3?

	Rent expense $	Accrual $
A	100,000	20,000
B	100,000	10,000
C	97,500	10,000
D	97,500	20,000

(2 marks)

10.3 At 31 March 20X2 a company had oil in hand to be used for heating costing $8,200 and an unpaid heating oil bill for $3,600.

At 31 March 20X3 the heating oil in hand was $9,300 and there was an outstanding heating oil bill of $3,200.

Payments made for heating oil during the year ended 31 March 20X3 totalled $34,600.

Based on these figures, what amount should appear in the company's statement of profit or loss and other comprehensive income for heating oil for the year?

A $23,900
B $36,100
C $45,300
D $33,100   (2 marks)

10.4 A company has sublet part of its offices and in the year ended 30 November 20X3 the rent receivable was:

Until 30 June 20X3 $8,400 per year
From 1 July 20X3 $12,000 per year

Rent was paid quarterly in advance on 1 January, April, July, and October each year.

What amounts should appear in the company's financial statements for the year ended 30 November 20X3?

	Rent receivable	Statement of financial position	
A	$9,900	$2,000 in sundry payables	
B	$9,900	$1,000 in sundry payables	
C	$10,200	$1,000 in sundry payables	
D	$9,900	$2,000 in sundry receivables	(2 marks)

10.5 A business compiling its financial statements for the year to 31 July each year pays rent quarterly in advance on 1 January, 1 April, 1 July and 1 October each year. The annual rent was increased from $60,000 per year to $72,000 per year as from 1 October 20X3.

What figure should appear for rent expense in the business's statement of profit or loss and other comprehensive income for the year ended 31 July 20X4?

A $69,000
B $62,000
C $70,000
D $63,000   (2 marks)

10.6 Diesel fuel in inventory at 1 November 20X7 was $12,500, and there were invoices awaited for $1,700. During the year to 31 October 20X8, diesel fuel bills of $85,400 were paid, and a delivery worth $1,300 had yet to be invoiced. At 31 October 20X8, the inventory of diesel fuel was valued at $9,800. What is the value of diesel fuel to be charged to the statement of profit or loss and other comprehensive income for the year to 31 October 20X8?

A $87,700
B $89,400
C $88,500
D $91,100   (2 marks)

10.7 The electricity account for the year ended 30 June 20X1 was as follows.

	$
Opening balance for electricity accrued at 1 July 20X0	300
Payments made during the year	
1 August 20X0 for three months to 31 July 20X0	600
1 November 20X0 for three months to 31 October 20X0	720
1 February 20X1 for three months to 31 January 20X1	900
30 June 20X1 for three months to 30 April 20X1	840
1 August 20X1 for three months to 31 July 20X1	840

Which of the following is the appropriate entry for electricity?

	Accrued at 30 June 20X1	*Charge to SPL year ended 30 June 20X1*
A	$Nil	$3,060
B	$460	$3,320
C	$560	$3,320
D	$560	$3,420

(2 marks)

10.8 The year end of M Inc is 30 November 20X0. The company pays for its gas by a standing order of $600 per month. On 1 December 20W9, the statement from the gas supplier showed that M Inc had overpaid by $200. M Inc received gas bills for the four quarters commencing on 1 December 20W9 and ending on 30 November 20X0 for $1,300, $1,400, $2,100 and $2,000 respectively.

Which of the following is the correct charge for gas in M Inc's statement of profit or loss for the year ended 30 November 20X0?

A $6,800
B $7,000
C $7,200
D $7,400

(2 marks)

10.9 A business compiling its accounts for the year to 31 January each year pays rent quarterly in advance on 1 January, 1 April, 1 July and 1 October each year. After remaining unchanged for some years, the rent was increased from $24,000 per year to $30,000 per year as from 1 July 20X0.

Which of the following figures is the rent expense which should appear in the statement of profit or loss for year ended 31 January 20X1?

A $27,500
B $29,500
C $28,000
D $29,000

(2 marks)

10.10 B, a limited liability company, receives rent for subletting part of its office premises to a number of tenants.

In the year ended 31 December 20X4 B received cash of $318,600 from its tenants.

Details of rent in advance and in arrears at the beginning and end of 20X4 are as follows:

	31 December	
	20X4	20X3
	$	$
Rent received in advance	28,400	24,600
Rent owing by tenants	18,300	16,900

All rent owing was subsequently received

What figure for rental income should be included in the statement of profit or loss of B for 20X4?

A $341,000
B $336,400
C $300,800
D $316,200   **(2 marks)**

10.11 During 20X4, B, a limited liability company, paid a total of $60,000 for rent, covering the period from 1 October 20X3 to 31 March 20X5.

What figures should appear in the company's financial statements for the year ended 31 December 20X4?

	Statement of profit or loss and other comprehensive income	Statement of financial position
	$	$
A	40,000	10,000 Prepayment
B	40,000	15,000 Prepayment
C	50,000	10,000 Accrual
D	50,000	15,000 Accrual **(2 marks)**

10.12 What are the correct ledger entries to record an accrual in the accounts?

A   Dr Asset
    Cr Expenses

B   Dr Expenses
    Cr Liability

C   Dr Liability
    Cr Expenses

D   Dr Expenses
    Cr Asset   **(2 marks)**

The following information is relevant for questions 10.13 and 10.14.

10.13 The trainee accountant at Judd Co has forgotten to make an accrual for rent for December in the financial statements for the year ended 31 December 20X2. Rent is charged in arrears at the end of February, May, August and November each year. The bill payable in February is expected to be $30,000. Judd Co's draft statement of profit or loss shows a profit of $25,000 and draft statement of financial position shows net assets of $275,000.

What is the profit or loss for the year and what is the net asset position after the accrual has been included in the financial statements?

	Profit for the year	Net asset position
A	$15,000	$265,000
B	$15,000	$285,000
C	$35,000	$265,000
D	$35,000	$285,000	**(2 marks)**

10.14 What are the correct ledger entries to record a prepayment in the accounts?

A	Dr Asset
	Cr Expenses
B	Dr Expenses
	Cr Liability
C	Dr Liability
	Cr Expenses
D	Dr Expenses
	Cr Asset **(2 marks)**

10.15 Buster's draft accounts for the year to 31 October 20X5 report a loss of $1,486. When he prepared the accounts, Buster did not include an accrual of $1,625 and a prepayment of $834.

What is Buster's profit or loss for the year to 31 October 20X5 following the inclusion of the accrual and prepayment?

A	A loss of $695
B	A loss of $2,277
C	A loss of $3,945
D	A profit of $1,807 **(2 marks)**

(Total = 30 marks)

---

11 Receivables and payables   46 mins

11.1 At 31 December 20X2 a company's receivables totalled $400,000 and an allowance for receivables of $50,000 had been brought forward from the year ended 31 December 20X1.

It was decided to write off debts totalling $38,000 and to adjust the allowance for receivables to 10% of the receivables.

What charge for receivables expense should appear in the company's statement of profit or loss for the year ended 31 December 20X2?

A	$74,200
B	$51,800
C	$28,000
D	$24,200 **(2 marks)**

11.2 At 1 July 20X2 the receivables allowance of Q was $18,000.

During the year ended 30 June 20X3 debts totalling $14,600 were written off. It was decided that the receivables allowance should be $16,000 as at 30 June 20X3.

What amount should appear in Q's statement of profit or loss for receivables expense for the year ended 30 June 20X3?

A $12,600
B $16,600
C $48,600
D $30,600 (2 marks)

11.3 At 30 September 20X2 a company's allowance for receivables amounted to $38,000, which was five per cent of the receivables at that date.

At 30 September 20X3 receivables totalled $868,500. It was decided to write off $28,500 of debts as irrecoverable and to keep the allowance for receivables at five per cent of receivables.

What should be the charge in the statement of profit or loss for the year ended 30 September 20X3 for receivables expense?

A $42,000
B $33,925
C $70,500
D $32,500 (2 marks)

11.4 At 1 July 20X3 a limited liability company had an allowance for receivables of $83,000.
During the year ended 30 June 20X4 debts totalling $146,000 were written off. At 30 June 20X4 it was decided that a receivables allowance of $218,000 was required.

What figure should appear in the company's statement of profit or loss for the year ended 30 June 20X4 for receivables expense?

A $155,000
B $364,000
C $281,000
D $11,000 (2 marks)

11.5 A company has received cash for a debt that was previously written off. Which of the following is the correct double entry to record the cash received?

	Debit	Credit
A	Irrecoverable debts expense	Accounts receivable
B	Cash	Irrecoverable debts expense
C	Allowance for receivables	Accounts receivable
D	Cash	Allowance for receivables

(2 marks)

11.6 At 31 December 20X4 a company's trade receivables totalled $864,000 and the allowance for receivables was $48,000.

It was decided that debts totalling $13,000 were to be written off, and the allowance for receivables adjusted to five per cent of the receivables.

What figures should appear in the statement of financial position for trade receivables (after deducting the allowance) and in the statement of profit or loss for receivables expense?

	Statement of profit or loss $	Statement of financial position $
A	8,200	807,800
B	7,550	808,450
C	18,450	808,450
D	55,550	808,450

(2 marks)

11.7 Which of the following would a decrease in the allowance for receivables result in?

    A   An increase in liabilities
    B   A decrease in working capital
    C   A decrease in net profit
    D   An increase in net profit   **(2 marks)**

11.8 A company has been notified that a customer has been declared bankrupt. The company had previously made an allowance for this debt. Which of the following is the correct double entry to account for this new information?

	Debit	*Credit*
A	Irrecoverable debts	Receivables
B	Receivables	Irrecoverable debts
C	Allowance for receivables	Receivables
D	Receivables	Allowance for receivables

    (2 marks)

11.9 An increase in an allowance for receivables of $8,000 has been treated as a reduction in the allowance in the financial statements. Which of the following explains the resulting effects?

    A   Net profit is overstated by $16,000, receivables overstated by $8,000
    B   Net profit understated by $16,000, receivables understated by $16,000
    C   Net profit overstated by $16,000, receivables overstated by $16,000
    D   Gross profit overstated by $16,000, receivables overstated by $16,000   **(2 marks)**

11.10 At 1 January 20X1, there was an allowance for receivables of $3,000. During the year, $1,000 of debts were written off as irrecoverable, and $800 of debts previously written off were recovered. At 31 December 20X1, it was decided to adjust the allowance for receivables to 5% of receivables which are $20,000.

What is the total receivables expense for the year?

    A $200 debit
    B $1,800 debit
    C $2,200 debit
    D $1,800 credit   **(2 marks)**

11.11 Allowances for receivables are an example of which accounting concept?

    A   Accruals
    B   Consistency
    C   Matching
    D   Prudence   **(2 marks)**

11.12 At the beginning of the year, the allowance for receivables was $850. At the year-end, the allowance required was $1,000. During the year $500 of debts were written off, which includes $100 previously included in the allowance for receivables.

What is the charge to statement of profit or loss for receivables expense for the year?

    A $1,500
    B $1,000
    C $650
    D $550   **(2 marks)**

11.13 Which of the following statements are correct?

    1   An aged receivables analysis shows how long invoices for each customer have been outstanding.

    2   A credit limit is a tool applied by the credit control department to make suppliers provide goods on time.

    3   Receivables are included in the statement of financial position net of the receivables allowance.

    4   Credit limits are applied to customers who purchase goods using cash only.

    A   1 and 2
    B   2 and 3
    C   1 and 3
    D   3 and 4   **(2 marks)**

11.14 At 31 May 20X7 Roberta's trial balance included the following items.

	$
Inventory at 1 June 20X6	23,856
Trade receivables	55,742
Trade payables	32,165
Bank overdraft	5,855
Loan due for repayment in 20X9	15,000

What is the value of Roberta's current liabilities at 31 May 20X7?

    A $38,020
    B $53,020
    C $61,597
    D $76,597   **(2 marks)**

11.15 At 1 November 20X5, Sanjay Motors is owed $20,000 by Jackson for servicing and repair work carried out on Jackson's fleet of motor vehicles.

Of the $20,000 outstanding, $3,500 relates to work that Jackson feels was sub-standard. Despite discussions and negotiation, and although Jackson is generally a 'good customer', Sanjay is doubtful that Jackson will ever pay this $3,500.

What allowance for receivables should Sanjay Motors make to account for this doubtful debt?

    A   None, Jackson is a good customer so Sanjay Motors should assume they will eventually pay
    B   A specific allowance of $20,000 as Jackson may decide not to pay any of their debt
    C   A general allowance of $3,500
    D   A specific allowance of $3,500   **(2 marks)**

11.16 At the end of its first trading period after commencing business, Khan & Co has a receivables balance of $500,000. It wishes to provide a specific allowance on a debt of $10,000. (The customer that owes this $10,000 is in severe financial difficulty, it is unlikely any of this $10,000 will be recovered).

Khan & Co also wishes to set up a general allowance of 2%.

What is the charge to the statement of profit or loss?

    A $19,800
    B $20,000
    C $10,000
    D $9,800   **(2 marks)**

11.17 At 1 January 20X4, Tartar Co had total receivables of $380,000. A specific allowance of $20,000 had been made for a business customer, Drab. The general allowance for receivables was 2.5%. During the year, Drab went out of business owing Tartar Co $28,000, none of which is expected to be recovered. At 31 December 20X4, Tatar had total receivables of $420,000. There were no specific allowances but the general allowance for receivables was increased to 3%.

What is the charge in the statement of profit or loss for the year to 31 December for the allowance for receivables and irrecoverable debts?

A $16,400
B $31,600
C $44,400
D $11,600   (2 marks)

11.18 Which one of the following statements about an imprest system of petty cash is correct?

A An imprest system for petty cash controls small cash expenditures because a fixed amount is paid into petty cash at the beginning of each period.

B The imprest system provides a control over petty cash spending because the amount of cash held in petty cash at any time must be equal to the value of the petty cash vouchers for the period.

C An imprest system for petty cash can operate without the need for petty cash vouchers or receipts for spending.

D An imprest system for petty cash helps with management of small cash expenditures are reduces the risk of fraud.

                                                                                      (2 marks)

11.19 Which one of the following provides evidence that an item of expenditure on petty cash has been approved or authorised?

A Petty cash voucher

B Record of the transaction in the petty cash book

C Receipt for the expense

D Transfer of cash from the bank account into petty cash   (2 marks)

                                                                              (Total = 38 marks)

12 Provisions and contingencies   24 mins

12.1 Which of the following statements about provisions and contingencies is/are correct?

1 A company should disclose details of the change in carrying value of a provision from the beginning to the end of the year.

2 Contingent assets must be recognised in the financial statements in accordance with the prudence concept.

3 Contingent liabilities must be treated as actual liabilities and provided for if it is probable that they will arise.

A 3 only
B 2 and 3 only
C 1 and 3 only
D All three statements are correct   (2 marks)

12.2 Which of the following statements about contingent assets and contingent liabilities are correct?

1   A contingent asset should be disclosed by note if an inflow of economic benefits is probable.

2   A contingent liability should be disclosed by note if it is probable that a transfer of economic benefits to settle it will be required, with no provision being made.

3   No disclosure is required for a contingent liability if it is not probable that a transfer of economic benefits to settle it will be required.

4   No disclosure is required for either a contingent liability or a contingent asset if the likelihood of a payment or receipt is remote.

A   1 and 4 only
B   2 and 3 only
C   2, 3 and 4
D   1, 2 and 4   **(2 marks)**

12.3 An ex-director of X company has commenced an action against the company claiming substantial damages for wrongful dismissal. The company's solicitors have advised that the ex-director is unlikely to succeed with his claim, although the chance of X paying any monies to the ex-director is not remote. The solicitors' estimates of the company's potential liabilities are:

	$
Legal costs (to be incurred whether the claim is successful or not)	50,000
Settlement of claim if successful	500,000
	550,000

According to IAS 37 *Provisions, contingent liabilities and continent assets*, how should this claim be treated in the financial statements?

A   Provision of $550,000
B   Disclose a contingent liability of $550,000
C   Disclose a provision of $50,000 and a contingent liability of $500,000
D   Provision for $500,000 and a contingent liability of $50,000   **(2 marks)**

12.4 The following items have to be considered in finalising the financial statements of Q, a limited liability company:

1   The company gives warranties on its products. The company's statistics show that about 5% of sales give rise to a warranty claim.

2   The company has guaranteed the overdraft of another company. The likelihood of a liability arising under the guarantee is assessed as possible.

According to IAS 37 *Provisions, contingent liabilities and continent assets*, what is the correct action to be taken in the financial statements for these items?

	Create a provision	Disclose by note only	No action
A	1	2	
B		1	2
C	1, 2		
D	2	1	

(2 marks)

12.5 Which of the following statements about the requirements of IAS 37 *Provisions, contingent liabilities and contingent assets* are correct?

1   A contingent asset should be disclosed by note if an inflow of economic benefits is probable.

2   No disclosure of a contingent liability is required if the possibility of a transfer of economic benefits arising is remote.

3   Contingent assets must not be recognised in financial statements unless an inflow of economic benefits is virtually certain to arise.

A   All three statements are correct
B   1 and 2 only
C   1 and 3 only
D   2 and 3 only   **(2 marks)**

12.6 Wanda Co allows customers to return faulty goods within 14 days of purchase. At 30 November 20X5 a provision of $6,548 was made for sales returns. At 30 November 20X6, the provision was re-calculated and should now be $7,634.

What should be reported in Wanda Co's statement of profit or loss for the year to 31 October 20X6 in respect of the provision?

A   A charge of $7,634
B   A credit of $7,634
C   A charge of $1,086
D   A credit of $1,086   **(2 marks)**

12.7 Doggard Co is a business that sells second hand cars. If a car develops a fault within 30 days of the sale, Doggard Co will repair it free of charge.

At 30 April 20X4 Doggard Co had made a provision for repairs of $2,500. At 30 April 20X5 Doggard Co calculated that the provision should be $2,000.

What entry should be made for the provision in Doggard Co's statement of profit or loss for the year to 30 April 20X5?

A   A charge of $500
B   A credit of $500
C   A charge of $2,000
D   A credit of $2,000   **(2 marks)**

12.8 Which of the following best describes a provision according to IAS 37 *Provisions, contingent liabilities and contingent assets*?

A   A provision is a liability of uncertain timing or amount.

B   A provision is a possible obligation of uncertain timing or amount.

C   A provision is a credit balance set up to offset a contingent asset so that the effect on the statement of financial position is nil.

D   A provision is a possible asset that arises from past events.   **(2 marks)**

12.9 Which of the following items does the statement below describe?

"A possible obligation that arises from past events and whose existence will be confirmed only by the occurrence or non-occurrence of one or more uncertain future events not wholly within the entity's control"

A   A provision
B   A current liability
C   A contingent liability
D   A contingent asset   **(2 marks)**

12.10 Montague's paint shop has suffered some bad publicity as a result of a customer claiming to be suffering from skin rashes as a result of using a new brand of paint sold by Montague's shop. The customer launched a court action against Montague in November 20X3, claiming damages of $5,000. Montague's lawyer has advised him that the most probable outcome is that he will have to pay the customer $3,000.

What amount should Montague include as a provision in his accounts for the year ended 31 December 20X3?

    A $nil
    B $5,000
    C $3,000
    D $8,000   **(2 marks)**

(Total = 20 marks)

Do you know? – Preparing a trial balance

Check that you can fill in the blanks in the statements below before you attempt any questions. If in doubt, you should go back to your BPP Interactive Text and revise first.

- A ...... reconciliation is a comparison of a **b**...... **s**............. (sent monthly, weekly or even daily by the bank) with the cash book. Differences between the balance on the bank statement and the balance in the cash book will be errors or .... differences, and they should be identified and satisfactorily explained.

- Differences between the cash book and the bank statement arise for three reasons:

    - .... – usually in the cash book
    - Omissions – such as **b**...... **c**............not posted in the cash book
    - **T**............ differences – such as unpresented cheques

- There are five main types of error: errors of **t**..............., **o**............, **pr**............, **c**............, and **comp**............ errors.

- A suspense account is an account showing a balance equal to the difference in a **t** ...... **b**...........

- Suspense accounts are only .... None should exist when it comes to drawing up the financial statements at the end of the accounting period.

- The two most important control accounts are those for .... and .... They are part of the double entry system.

- Cash books and day books are totalled periodically and the totals posted to the **c**............ accounts. The balance totals on the **p**............ accounts should agree to the balance on the **c**............... account.

- Discounts can be defined as follows:

    - A......... discount is a reduction in the list price of an article, given by a wholesaler or manufacturer to a retailer.

    - A..................... discount is a reduction in the amount payable for the purchase of goods or services in return for payment in cash, or within an agreed period.

- .... discounts received are **d**............ from the cost of purchases. **C**...... discounts received are included as **o**......... **i**.......... of the period in the statement of profit or loss.

- .... discounts allowed are **d**............ from sales and **c**...... discounts allowed are shown as .... of the period.

Did you know? – Preparing a trial balance

Could you fill in the blanks? The answers are in bold. Use this page for revision purposes as you approach the exam.

- A **bank** reconciliation is a comparison of a **bank statement** (sent monthly, weekly or even daily by the bank) with the cash book. Differences between the balance on the bank statement and the balance in the cash book will be errors or **timing** differences, and they should be identified and satisfactorily explained.

- Differences between the cash book and the bank statement arise for three reasons:

    - **Errors** – usually in the cash book
    - Omissions – such as **bank charges** not posted in the cash book
    - **Timing** differences – such as unpresented cheques

- There are five main types of error: errors of **transposition**, **omission**, **principle**, **commission** and **compensating** errors.

- A suspense account is an account showing a balance equal to the difference in a **trial balance**.

- Suspense accounts are only **temporary**. None should exist when it comes to drawing up the financial statements at the end of the accounting period.

- The two most important control accounts are those for **receivables** and **payables**. They are part of the double entry system.

- Cash books and day books are totalled periodically and the totals posted to the **control** accounts. The balance totals on the **personal** accounts should agree to the balance on the **control** account.

- Discounts can be defined as follows:

    - A **trade** discount is a reduction in the list price of an article, given by a wholesaler or manufacturer to a retailer.

    - A **cash (settlement)** discount is a reduction in the amount payable for the purchase of goods or services in return for payment in cash, or within an agreed period.

- **Trade** discounts received are **deducted** from the cost of purchases. **Cash** discounts received are included as **other income** of the period in the statement of profit or loss.

- **Trade** discounts allowed are **deducted** from sales and **cash** discounts allowed are shown as **expenses** of the period.

13 Control accounts

48 mins

13.1 You are given the following information:

Receivables at 1 January 20X3	$10,000
Receivables at 31 December 20X3	$9,000
Total receipts during 20X3 (including cash sales of $5,000)	$85,000

What is the figure for sales on credit during 20X3?

A $81,000
B $86,000
C $79,000
D $84,000 **(2 marks)**

13.2 A supplier sends you a statement showing a balance outstanding of $14,350. Your own records show a balance outstanding of $14,500.

Which one of the following could be the reason for this difference?

A The supplier sent an invoice for $150 which you have not yet received.
B The supplier has allowed you $150 cash discount which you had omitted to enter in your ledgers.
C You have paid the supplier $150 which he has not yet accounted for.
D You have returned goods worth $150 which the supplier has not yet accounted for.

(2 marks)

13.3 Your payables control account has a balance at 1 October 20X8 of $34,500 credit. During October, credit purchases were $78,400, cash purchases were $2,400 and payments made to suppliers, excluding cash purchases, and after deducting settlement discounts of $1,200, were $68,900. Purchase returns were $4,700.

What was the closing balance?

A $38,100
B $40,500
C $47,500
D $49,900 **(2 marks)**

13.4 A receivables ledger control account had a closing balance of $8,500. It contained a contra to the payables ledger of $400, but this had been entered on the wrong side of the control account.

What should be the correct balance on the control account?

A $7,700 debit
B $8,100 debit
C $8,400 debit
D $8,900 debit **(2 marks)**

13.5 Which of the following items could appear on the credit side of a receivables ledger control account?

1 Cash received from customers
2 Irrecoverable debts written off
3 Increase in allowance for receivables
4 Discounts allowed
5 Sales
6 Credits for goods returned by customers
7 Cash refunds to customers

A 1, 2, 4 and 6
B 1, 2, 4 and 7
C 3, 4, 5 and 6
D 5 and 7 **(2 marks)**

13.6 An inexperienced bookkeeper has drawn up the following receivables ledger control account:

RECEIVABLES LEDGER CONTROL ACCOUNT

	$		$
Opening balance	180,000	Credit sales	190,000
Cash from credit customers	228,000	Irrecoverable debts written off	1,500
Sales returns	8,000	Contras against payables	2,400
Cash refunds to credit customers	3,300	Closing balance (balancing figure)	229,600
Discount allowed	4,200		
	423,500		423,500

What should the closing balance be after correcting the errors made in preparing the account?

A $130,600
B $129,200
C $142,400
D $214,600 (2 marks)

13.7 The following receivables ledger control account has been prepared by a trainee accountant:

		$			$
20X3			20X3		
1 Jan	Balance	284,680	31 Dec	Cash received from credit	
31 Dec	Credit sales	189,120		customers	179,790
	Discounts allowed	3,660		Contras against amounts	
	Irrecoverable debts			owing by company in	
	written off	1,800		payables ledger	800
	Sales returns	4,920		Balance	303,590
		484,180			484,180

What should the closing balance on the account be when the errors in it are corrected?

A $290,150
B $286,430
C $282,830
D $284,430 (2 marks)

13.8 The following control account has been prepared by a trainee accountant:

RECEIVABLES LEDGER CONTROL ACCOUNT

	$		$
Opening balance	308,600	Cash received from credit customers	147,200
Credit sales	154,200	Discounts allowed to credit	
Cash sales	88,100	customers	1,400
Contras against credit balances in		Interest charged on overdue	
payables ledger	4,600	accounts	2,400
		Irrecoverable debts written off	4,900
		Allowance for receivables	2,800
		Closing balance	396,800
	555,500		555,500

What should the closing balance be when all the errors made in preparing the receivables ledger control account have been corrected?

A $395,200
B $304,300
C $307,100
D $309,500 (2 marks)

13.9 The following receivables ledger control account prepared by a trainee accountant contains a number of errors:

RECEIVABLES LEDGER CONTROL ACCOUNT

		$			$
20X4			*20X4*		
1 Jan	Balance	614,000	31 Dec	Credit sales	301,000
31 Jan	Cash from credit customers	311,000		Discounts allowed	3,400
	Contras against amounts			Irrecoverable debts	
	due to suppliers in			written off	32,000
	payables ledger	8,650		Interest charged on overdue	
				accounts	1,600
				Balance	595,650
		933,650			933,650

What should the closing balance on the control account be after the errors in it have been corrected?

A $561,550
B $578,850
C $581,550
D $568,350   **(2 marks)**

13.10 Your organisation sold goods to PQ Co for $800 less trade discount of 20% and cash discount of 5% for payment within 14 days. The invoice was settled by cheque five days later. Which one of the following gives the entries required to record BOTH of these transactions?

		DEBIT	CREDIT
		$	$
A	PQ Co	640	
	Sales		640
	Bank	608	
	Discount allowed	32	
	PQ Co		640
B	PQ Co	640	
	Sales		640
	Bank	600	
	Discount allowed	40	
	PQ Co		640
C	PQ Co	640	
	Sales		640
	Bank	608	
	Discount received	32	
	PQ Co		640
D	PQ Co	800	
	Sales		800
	Bank	608	
	Discount allowed	182	
	PQ Co		800

(2 marks)

13.11 Which one of the following is **not** the purpose of a receivables ledger control account?

A   A receivables ledger control account provides a check on the arithmetical accuracy of the personal ledger.

B   A receivables ledger control account helps to locate errors in the trial balance.

C   A receivables ledger control account ensures that there are no errors in the personal ledger.

D   Control accounts deter fraud.   **(2 marks)**

13.12 Which of the following lists is composed only of items which would appear on the credit side of the receivables control account?

A   Cash received from customers, sales returns, irrecoverable debts written off, contras against amounts due to suppliers in the accounts payable ledger

B   Sales, cash refunds to customers, irrecoverable debts written off, discounts allowed

C   Cash received from customers, discounts allowed, interest charged on overdue accounts, irrecoverable debts written off

D   Sales, cash refunds to customers, interest charged on overdue accounts, contras against amounts due to suppliers in the accounts payable ledger   **(2 marks)**

13.13 The following receivables ledger control account has been prepared by a trainee accountant:

RECEIVABLES LEDGER CONTROL ACCOUNT

20X5		$	20X5		$
1 Jan	Balance	318,650	31 Jan	Cash from credit customers	181,140
	Credit sales	161,770		Interest charged on overdue accounts	280
	Cash sales	84,260		Irrecoverable debts written off	1,390
	Discounts allowed to			Sales returns from credit	
	credit customers	1,240		customers	3,990
				Balance	379,120
		565,920			565,920

What should the closing balance at 31 January 20X5 be after correcting the errors in the account?

A $292,380
B $295,420
C $292,940
D $377,200   **(2 marks)**

13.14 At 1 April 20X9, the payables ledger control account showed a balance of $142,320.

At the end of April the following totals are extracted from the subsidiary books for April:

	$
Purchases day book	183,800
Returns outwards day book	27,490
Returns inwards day book	13,240
Payments to payables, after deducting $1,430 cash discount	196,360

It is also discovered that:

(a)   the purchase day book figure is net of sales tax at 17.5%; the other figures all include sales tax.

(b)   a customer's balance of $2,420 has been offset against his balance of $3,650 in the payables ledger.

(c)   a supplier's account in the payables ledger, with a debit balance of $800, has been included on the list of payables as a credit balance.

What is the corrected balance on the payables ledger control account?

A $130,585
B $144,835
C $98,429
D $128,985   **(2 marks)**

The following scenario relates to questions 13.15 to 13.17.

P & Co maintain a receivables ledger control account within the nominal ledger. At 30 November 20X0, the total of the list of individual balances extracted from the receivables ledger was $15,800, which did not agree with the balance on the receivables ledger control account. An examination of the books revealed the following information, which can be used to reconcile the receivables ledger and the receivables ledger control account.

1   The credit balance of $420 in Ahmed's payables ledger account had been set off against his account in the receivables ledger, but no entries had been made in the receivables and payables ledger control accounts.

2   The personal account of Mahmood was undercast by $90.

3   Yasmin's balance of (debit) $780 had been omitted from the list of balances.

4   Thomas' personal account balance of $240 had been removed from the receivables ledger as a bad debt, but no entry had been made in the receivables ledger control account.

5   The January total of $8,900 in the sales daybook had been posted as $9,800.

6   A credit note to Charles for $1,000, plus sales tax of $300, had been posted to the receivables ledger control account as $1,300 and to Charles' personal account as $1,000.

7   The total on the credit side of Edward's personal account had been overcast by $125.

13.15 Which of these items need to be corrected by journal entries in the nominal ledger?

    A   1, 3, 4 and 5 only
    B   1, 4 and 5 only
    C   1, 2, 5 and 6 only
    D   2, 3, 6 and 7 only   **(2 marks)**

13.16 What is the revised total of the balances in the receivables ledger after the errors have been corrected?

    A $15,105
    B $16,195
    C $16,495
    D $16,915   **(2 marks)**

13.17 Assuming that the closing balance on the receivables ledger control account should be $16,000, what is the opening balance on the receivables ledger control account before the errors were corrected?

    A $14,440
    B $15,760
    C $17,560
    D $17,860   **(2 marks)**

13.18 The balance on Jude Co's payables ledger control account is $31,554. The accountant at Jude Co has discovered that she has not recorded:

A settlement discount of $53 received from a supplier; and
A supplier's invoice for $622.

What amount should be reported for payables on Jude Co's statement of financial position?

    A $30,879
    B $30,985
    C $32,123
    D $32,229   **(2 marks)**

13.19 The accountant at Borris Co has prepared the following reconciliation between the balance on the trade payables ledger control account in the general ledger and the list of balances from the suppliers ledger:

	$
Balance on general ledger control account	68,566
Credit balance omitted from list of balances from payables ledger	(127)
	68,439
Undercasting of purchases day book	99
Total of list of balances	68,538

What balance should be reported on Borris Co's statement of financial position for trade payables?

A $68,439
B $68,538
C $68,566
D $68,665   (2 marks)

13.20 How should the balance on the payables ledger control account be reported in the final accounts?

A   As an expense account
B   As a non-current liability
C   As a current asset
D   As a current liability   (2 marks)

(Total = 40 marks)

14 Bank reconciliations   36 mins

14.1 Your cash book at 31 December 20X3 shows a bank balance of $565 overdrawn. On comparing this with your bank statement at the same date, you discover the following.

1   A cheque for $57 drawn by you on 29 December 20X3 has not yet been presented for payment.

2   A cheque for $92 from a customer, which was paid into the bank on 24 December 20X3, has been dishonoured on 31 December 20X3.

What is the correct bank balance to be shown in the statement of financial position at 31 December 20X3?

A $714 overdrawn
B $657 overdrawn
C $473 overdrawn
D $53 overdrawn   (2 marks)

14.2 The cash book shows a bank balance of $5,675 overdrawn at 31 August 20X5. It is subsequently discovered that a standing order for $125 has been entered twice, and that a dishonoured cheque for $450 has been debited in the cash book instead of credited.

What is the correct bank balance?

A $5,100 overdrawn
B $6,000 overdrawn
C $6,250 overdrawn
D $6,450 overdrawn   (2 marks)

14.3 A business had a balance at the bank of $2,500 at the start of the month. During the following month, it paid for materials invoiced at $1,000 less trade discount of 20% and cash discount of 10%. It received a cheque from a customer in respect of an invoice for $200, subject to cash discount of 5%.

What was the balance at the bank at the end of the month?

 A $1,970
 B $1,980
 C $1,990
 D $2,000   **(2 marks)**

14.4 The bank statement on 31 October 20X7 showed an overdraft of $800. On reconciling the bank statement, it was discovered that a cheque drawn by your company for $80 had not been presented for payment, and that a cheque for $130 from a customer had been dishonoured on 30 October 20X7, but that this had not yet been notified to you by the bank.

What is the correct bank balance to be shown in the statement of financial position at 31 October 20X7?

 A $1,010 overdrawn
 B $880 overdrawn
 C $750 overdrawn
 D $720 overdrawn   **(2 marks)**

14.5 Your firm's cash book at 30 April 20X8 shows a balance at the bank of $2,490. Comparison with the bank statement at the same date reveals the following differences:

	$
Unpresented cheques	840
Bank charges not in cash book	50
Receipts not yet credited by the bank	470
Dishonoured cheque not in cash book	140

What is the adjusted bank balance per the cash book at 30 April 20X8?

 A $1,460
 B $2,300
 C $2,580
 D $3,140   **(2 marks)**

14.6 The following bank reconciliation statement has been prepared by a trainee accountant:

BANK RECONCILIATION 30 SEPTEMBER 20X2

	$
Balance per bank statement (overdrawn)	36,840
Add: lodgements credited after date	51,240
	88,080
Less: outstanding cheques	43,620
Balance per cash book (credit)	44,460

Assuming the amounts stated for items other than the cash book balance are correct, what should the cash book balance be?

 A $44,460 credit as stated
 B $60,020 credit
 C $29,220 debit
 D $29,220 credit   **(2 marks)**

14.7 Listed below are some possible causes of difference between the cash book balance and the bank statement balance when preparing a bank reconciliation:

1   Cheque paid in, subsequently dishonoured
2   Error by bank
3   Bank charges
4   Lodgements credited after date
5   Outstanding cheques not yet presented

Which of these items require an entry in the cash book?

A   1 and 3 only
B   1, 2, 3, 4 and 5
C   2, 4, and 5 only
D   4 and 5 only   (2 marks)

14.8 In preparing a company's bank reconciliation statement at March 20X3, the following items are causing the difference between the cash book balance and the bank statement balance:

1   Bank charges $380
2   Error by bank $1,000 (cheque incorrectly debited to the account)
3   Lodgements not credited $4,580
4   Outstanding cheques $1,475
5   Direct debit $350
6   Cheque paid in by the company and dishonoured $400

Which of these items will require an entry in the cash book?

A   2, 4 and 6
B   1, 5 and 6
C   3 and 4
D   3 and 5   (2 marks)

14.9 The following bank reconciliation statement has been prepared by a trainee accountant:

	$
Overdraft per bank statement	3,860
Less: outstanding cheques	9,160
	5,300
Add: deposits credited after date	16,690
Cash at bank as calculated above	21,990

What should be the correct balance per the cash book?

A $21,990 balance at bank as stated
B $3,670 balance at bank
C $11,390 balance at bank
D $3,670 overdrawn   (2 marks)

14.10 Which of the following statements about bank reconciliations are correct?

1   A difference between the cash book and the bank statement must be corrected by means of a journal entry.
2   In preparing a bank reconciliation, lodgements recorded before date in the cash book but credited by the bank after date should reduce an overdrawn balance in the bank statement.
3   Bank charges not yet entered in the cash book should be dealt with by an adjustment in the bank reconciliation statement.
4   If a cheque received from a customer is dishonoured after date, a credit entry in the cash book is required.

A   2 and 4
B   1 and 4
C   2 and 3
D   1 and 3   (2 marks)

14.11 The following information relates to a bank reconciliation.

(i)   The bank balance in the cashbook before taking the items below into account was $8,970 overdrawn.

(ii)   Bank charges of $550 on the bank statement have not been entered in the cashbook.

(iii)   The bank has credited the account in error with $425 which belongs to another customer.

(iv)   Cheque payments totalling $3,275 have been entered in the cashbook but have not been presented for payment.

(v)   Cheques totalling $5,380 have been correctly entered on the debit side of the cashbook but have not been paid in at the bank.

What was the balance as shown by the bank statement *before* taking the items above into account?

A $8,970 overdrawn
B $11,200 overdrawn
C $12,050 overdrawn
D $17,750 overdrawn   **(2 marks)**

14.12 The following attempt at a bank reconciliation statement has been prepared by Q Co:

	$
Overdraft per bank statement	38,600
Add: deposits not credited	41,200
	79,800
Less: outstanding cheques	3,300
Overdraft per cash book	76,500

Assuming the bank statement balance of $38,600 to be correct, what *should* the cash book balance be?

A $76,500 overdrawn, as stated
B $5,900 overdrawn
C $700 overdrawn
D $5,900 cash at bank   **(2 marks)**

14.13 After checking a business cash book against the bank statement, which of the following items could require an entry in the cash book?

1   Bank charges
2   A cheque from a customer which was dishonoured
3   Cheque not presented
4   Deposits not credited
5   Credit transfer entered in bank statement
6   Standing order entered in bank statement.

A   1, 2, 5 and 6
B   3 and 4
C   1, 3, 4 and 6
D   3, 4, 5 and 6   **(2 marks)**

14.14 The following bank reconciliation statement has been prepared for a company:

	$
Overdraft per bank statement	39,800
Add: Deposits credited after date	64,100
	103,900
Less: Outstanding cheques presented after date	44,200
Overdraft per cash book	59,700

Assuming the amount of the overdraft per the bank statement of $39,800 is correct, what should be the balance in the cash book?

A $158,100 overdrawn
B $19,900 overdrawn
C $68,500 overdrawn
D $59,700 overdrawn as stated   **(2 marks)**

14.15 Listed below are five potential causes of difference between a company's cash book balance and its bank statement balance as at 30 November 20X3:

1   Cheques recorded and sent to suppliers before 30 November 20X3 but not yet presented for payment

2   An error by the bank in crediting to another customer's account a lodgement made by the company

3   Bank charges

4   Cheques paid in before 30 November 20X3 but not credited by the bank until 3 December 20X3

5   A cheque recorded and paid in before 30 November 20X3 but dishonoured by the bank

Which one of the following alternatives correctly analyses these items into those requiring an entry in the cash book and those that would feature in the bank reconciliation?

	Cash book entry	Bank reconciliation
A	1, 2, 4	3, 5
B	3, 5	1, 2, 4
C	3, 4	1, 2, 5
D	2, 3, 5	1, 4

(2 marks)

(Total = 30 marks)

15 Correction of errors   36 mins

15.1   The debit side of a trial balance totals $800 more than the credit side.

Which one of the following errors would fully account for the difference?

A $400 paid for plant maintenance has been correctly entered in the cash book and credited to the plant asset account.

B   Discount received $400 has been debited to discount allowed account.

C   A receipt of $800 for commission receivable has been omitted from the records.

D   The petty cash balance of $800 has been omitted from the trial balance.

(2 marks)

15.2 The bookkeeper of Peri made the following mistakes:

Discount allowed $3,840 was credited to discounts received account.

Discount received $2,960 was debited to discounts allowed account.

Discounts were otherwise correctly recorded.

Which one of the following journal entries will correct the errors?

		Dr $	Cr $
A	Discount allowed	7,680	
	Discount received		5,920
	Suspense account		1,760
B	Discount allowed	880	
	Discount received	880	
	Suspense account		1,760
C	Discount allowed	6,800	
	Discount received		6,800
D	Suspense account	1,760	
	Discount allowed		880
	Discount received		880

(2 marks)

15.3 A company's trial balance failed to agree, the totals being:

Debit	$815,602
Credit	$808,420

Which one of the following errors could fully account for the difference?

A   The omission from the trial balance of the balance on the insurance expense account $7,182 debit

B   Discount allowed $3,591 debited in error to the discount received account

C   No entries made in the records for cash sales totalling $7,182

D   The returns outwards total of $3,591 was included in the trial balance as a debit balance

(2 marks)

15.4 The debit side of a trial balance totals $50 more than the credit side. Which one of the following could this be due to?

A   A purchase of goods for $50 being omitted from the payables control account
B   A sale of goods for $50 being omitted from the receivables control account
C   An invoice of $25 for electricity being credited to the electricity account
D   A receipt for $50 from a customer being omitted from the cash book   **(2 marks)**

15.5 Which one of the following would be an error of principle?

A   Plant and machinery purchased was credited to a non-current assets account.
B   Plant and machinery purchased was debited to the purchases account.
C   Plant and machinery purchased was debited to the equipment account.
D   Plant and machinery purchased was credited to the equipment account.   **(2 marks)**

15.6 What is an error of commission?

    A   An error where a transaction has not been recorded

    B   An error where one side of a transaction has been recorded in the wrong account, and that account is of a different class to the correct account

    C   An error where one side of a transaction has been recorded in the wrong account, and that account is of the same class as the correct account

    D   An error where the numbers in the posting have been transposed   **(2 marks)**

15.7 Where a transaction is entered into the correct ledger accounts, but the wrong amount is used, what is the error known as?

    A   An error of omission
    B   An error of original entry
    C   An error of commission
    D   An error of principle   **(2 marks)**

15.8 A business statement of profit or loss and other comprehensive income for the year ended 31 December 20X4 showed a net profit of $83,600. It was later found that $18,000 paid for the purchase of a motor van had been debited to motor expenses account. It is the company's policy to depreciate motor vans at 25 per cent per year, with a full year's charge in the year of acquisition.

What would the net profit be after adjusting for this error?

    A $106,100
    B $70,100
    C $97,100
    D $101,600   **(2 marks)**

15.9 An organisation restores its petty cash balance to $250 at the end of each month. During October, the total expenditure column in the petty cash book was calculated as being $210, and the imprest was restored by this amount. The analysis columns posted to the nominal ledger totalled only $200.

Which one of the following would this error cause?

    A   The trial balance being $10 higher on the debit side
    B   The trial balance being $10 higher on the credit side
    C   No imbalance in the trial balance
    D   The petty cash balance being $10 lower than it should be   **(2 marks)**

15.10 Net profit was calculated as being $10,200. It was later discovered that capital expenditure of $3,000 had been treated as revenue expenditure, and revenue receipts of $1,400 had been treated as capital receipts.

What is the net profit after correcting this error?

    A $5,800
    B $8,600
    C $11,800
    D $14,600   **(2 marks)**

15.11 The accountant at Investotech discovered the following errors after calculating the company's profit for 20X3:

(a) A non-current asset costing $50,000 has been included in the purchases account

(b) Stationery costing $10,000 has been included as closing inventory of raw materials, instead of stationery expenses

What is the effect of these errors on gross profit and net profit?

A Understatement of gross profit by $40,000 and understatement of net profit by $30,000
B Understatement of both gross profit and net profit by $40,000
C Understatement of gross profit by $60,000 and understatement of net profit by $50,000
D Overstatement of both gross profit and net profit by $60,000 **(2 marks)**

15.12 A purchase return of $48 has been wrongly posted to the debit of the sales returns account, but has been correctly entered in the supplier's account.

Which of the following statements about the trial balance would be correct?

A The credit side to be $48 more than the debit side
B The debit side to be $48 more than the credit side
C The credit side to be $96 more than the debit side
D The debit side to be $96 more than the credit side **(2 marks)**

15.13 Two types of common errors in bookkeeping are errors of *principle* and errors of *transposition*.

Which of the following correctly states whether or not these errors will be revealed by extracting a trial balance?

	Errors of Principle	*Errors of Transposition*
A	Will be revealed	Will not be revealed
B	Will be revealed	Will be revealed
C	Will not be revealed	Will not be revealed
D	Will not be revealed	Will be revealed

(2 marks)

15.14 The following are balances on the accounts of Luigi, a sole trader, as at the end of the current financial year and after all entries have been processed and the profit for the year has been calculated.

	$
Non-current assets	85,000
Receivables	7,000
Trade payables	3,000
Bank loan	15,000
Allowance for depreciation, non-current assets	15,000
Inventory	4,000
Accruals	1,000
Prepayments	2,000
Bank overdraft	2,000

What is the balance on Luigi's capital account?

A $59,000
B $66,000
C $62,000
D $64,000 **(2 marks)**

15.15 The following balances have been extracted from the nominal ledger accounts of Tanya, but the figure for bank loan is unknown. There are no other accounts in the main ledger.

	$
Payables	27,000
Capital	66,000
Purchases	160,000
Sales	300,000
Other expenses	110,000
Receivables	33,000
Purchase returns	2,000
Non-current assets	120,000
Cash in bank	18,000
Bank loan	Unknown

What is the credit balance on the bank loan account?

A $46,000
B $102,000
C $78,000
D $34,000

(2 marks)

(Total = 30 marks)

16 Suspense accounts   24 mins

The following information is relevant for question 16.1 and 16.2

When Q's trial balance failed to agree, a suspense account was opened for the difference. The trial balance totals were:

Debit	$864,390
Credit	$860,930

The company does not have control accounts for its receivables and payables ledgers.

The following errors were found:

1   In recording an issue of shares at par, cash received of $333,000 was credited to the ordinary share capital account as $330,000.

2   Cash $2,800 paid for plant repairs was correctly accounted for in the cash book but was credited to the plant asset account.

3   The petty cash book balance $500 had been omitted from the trial balance.

4   A cheque for $78,400 paid for the purchase of a motor car was debited to the motor vehicles account as $87,400.

5   A contra between the receivables ledger and the payables ledger for $1,200 which should have been credited in the receivables ledger and debited in the payables ledger was actually debited in the receivables ledger and credited in the payables ledger.

16.1   Which of these errors will require an entry to the suspense account to correct them?

A   All five items
B   3 and 5 only
C   2, 4 and 5 only
D   1, 2, 3 and 4 only

(2 marks)

16.2 What will the balance on the suspense account be after making the necessary entries to correct the errors affecting the suspense account?

A $2,440 Debit
B $15,560 Credit
C $13,640 Debit
D $3,440 Debit   **(2 marks)**

16.3 A company's trial balance totals were:

Debit $387,642
Credit $379,511

A suspense account was opened for the difference.

Which one of the following errors would have the effect of reducing the difference when corrected?

A   The petty cash balance of $500 has been omitted from the trial balance.

B $4,000 received for rent of part of the office has been correctly recorded in the cash book and debited to rent account.

C $3,000 paid for repairs to plant has been debited to the plant asset account.

D   An invoice for Mr A Smith for $400 has been posted to the account of Mrs B Smith in error.
                                                                                                      (2 marks)

16.4 A trial balance extracted from a sole trader's records failed to agree, and a suspense account was opened for the difference.

Which of the following errors would require an entry in the suspense account in correcting them?

1   Discount allowed was mistakenly debited to discount received account.

2   Cash received from the sale of a non-current asset was correctly entered in the cash book but was debited to the disposal account.

3   The balance on the rent account was omitted from the trial balance.

4   Goods taken from inventory by the proprietor had been recorded by crediting drawings account and debiting purchases account.

A   All four items
B   2 and 3 only
C   2 and 4 only
D   1 and 3 only   **(2 marks)**

16.5 A suspense account was opened when a trial balance failed to agree. The following errors were later discovered.

• A gas bill of $420 had been recorded in the gas account as $240.
• A discount of $50 given to a customer had been credited to discounts received.
• Interest received of $70 had been entered in the bank account only.

What was the original balance on the suspense account?

A   Debit $210
B   Credit $210
C   Debit $160
D   Credit $160   **(2 marks)**

16.6 The trial balance of Delta, a limited liability company, did not agree and a suspense account was opened for the difference. The following errors were subsequently found:

1 A cash refund due to customer A was correctly treated in the cash book and then credited to the accounts receivable ledger account of customer B.

2 The sale of goods to a director for $300 was recorded by debiting sales revenue account and crediting the director's current account.

3 The total of the discount received column in the cash book had been credited in error to the discount allowed account.

4 Some of the cash received from customers had been used to pay sundry expenses before banking the money.

5 $5,800 paid for plant repairs was correctly treated in the cash book and then credited to plant and equipment asset account.

Which of the above errors would require an entry to the suspense account as part of the process of correcting them?

A   1, 3 and 5
B   1, 2 and 5
C   1 and 5
D   3 and 4   (2 marks)

16.7 The trial balance of Z failed to agree, the totals being: debit $836,200
                                                                   credit $819,700

A suspense account was opened for the amount of the difference and the following errors were found and corrected:

1 The totals of the cash discount columns in the cash book had not been posted to the discount accounts. The figures were discount allowed $3,900 and discount received $5,100.

2 A cheque for $19,000 received from a customer was correctly entered in the cash book but was posted to the control account as $9,100.

What will be the remaining balance on the suspense be **after** the correction of these errors?

A $25,300 credit
B $7,700 credit
C $27,700 debit
D $5,400 credit   (2 marks)

16.8 The trial balance of C, a limited liability company, did not agree, and a suspense account was opened for the difference. Checking in the bookkeeping system revealed a number of errors.

1 $4,600 paid for motor van repairs was correctly treated in the cash book but was credited to motor vehicles asset account.

2 $360 received from B, a customer, was credited in error to the account of BB.

3 $9,500 paid for rent was debited to the rent account as $5,900.

4 The total of the discount allowed column in the cash book had been debited in error to the discounts received account.

5 No entries have been made to record a cash sale of $100.

Which of the errors above would require an entry to the suspense account as part of the process of correcting them?

A   3 and 4
B   1 and 3
C   2 and 5
D   2 and 3   (2 marks)

16.9 The suspense account shows a debit balance of $100. What could this balance be due to?

    A   Entering $50 received from A Turner on the debit side of A Turner's account

    B   Entering $50 received from A Turner on the credit side of A Turner's account

    C   Undercasting the sales day book by $100

    D   Undercasting the purchases account by $100   **(2 marks)**

16.10 A suspense account shows a credit balance of $130. Which of the following could be due to?

    A   Omitting a sale of $130 from the sales ledger

    B   Recording a purchase of $130 twice in the purchases account

    C   Failing to write off a bad debt of $130

    D   Recording an electricity bill paid of $65 by debiting the bank account and crediting the electricity account   **(2 marks)**

(Total = 20 marks)

Do you know? – Preparing basic financial statements

Check that you can fill in the blanks in the statements below before you attempt any questions. If in doubt, you should go back to your BPP Interactive Text and revise first.

- There are some important differences between the accounts of a l............ l............ c........... and those of sole traders or partnerships.

- .... liability means that the maximum amount that an owner stands to lose, in the event that the company becomes insolvent and cannot pay off its debts, is his share of the capital in the business.

- .... capital and .... are 'owned' by the shareholders. They are known collectively as 'shareholders' equity'.

- A company can increase its share capital by means of a .... issue or a .... issue.

- .... are included in a set of financial statements to give users extra information.

- IAS 18 is concerned with the recognition of ....

- Events after the reporting date but before the date the financial statements are approved that provide further **e**............ of conditions that existed at the reporting date should be .... for in the financial statements.

- Events which do not affect the situation at the reporting date should not be .... for but should be .... in the financial statements.

- The approach to incomplete records questions is to build up the information given so as to complete the necessary .... entry.

- ....- .... is the profit as a percentage of cost.

- **G**......... **p**.......... .... is the profit as a percentage of sales.

- Where no trading records have been kept, profit can be derived from opening and closing net assets by use of the **b**............ **e**.............

- The business equation is Profit = increase in .... – capital introduced + ...

- Statements of **c**...... **f**........ are a useful addition to the financial statements of companies because it is recognised that accounting profit is not the only indicator of a company's performance.

- .... activities are the principal revenue-producing activities of the enterprise and other activities that are not investing or financing activities.

- .... activities are the acquisition and disposal of non-current assets and other investments not included in cash equivalents.

- .... activities are activities that result in changes in the size and composition of the equity capital and borrowings of the entity.

Did you know? – Preparing basic financial statements

Could you fill in the blanks? The answers are in bold. Use this page for revision purposes as you approach the exam.

- There are some important differences between the accounts of a **limited liability company** and those of sole traders or partnerships.

- **Limited** liability means that the maximum amount that an owner stands to lose, in the event that the company becomes insolvent and cannot pay off its debts, is his share of the capital in the business.

- **Share** capital and **reserves** are 'owned' by the shareholders. They are known collectively as 'shareholders' equity'.

- A company can increase its share capital by means of a **bonus** issue or a **rights** issue.

- **Notes** are included in a set of financial statements to give users extra information.

- IAS 18 is concerned with the recognition of **revenue**.

- Events after the reporting date but before the date the financial statements are approved that provide further **evidence** of conditions that existed at the reporting date should be **adjusted** for in the financial statements.

- Events which do not affect the situation at the reporting date should not be **adjusted** for, but should be **disclosed** in the financial statements.

- The approach to incomplete records questions is to build up the information given so as to complete the necessary **double** entry.

- **Mark-up** is the profit as a percentage of cost.

- **Gross profit margin** is the profit as a percentage of sales.

- Where no trading records have been kept, profit can be derived from opening and closing net assets by use of the **business equation**.

- The business equation is Profit = increase in **net assets** – capital introduced + **drawings**

- Statements of **cash flows** are a useful addition to the financial statements of companies because it is recognised that accounting profit is not the only indicator of a company's performance.

- **Operating** activities are the principal revenue-producing activities of the enterprise and other activities that are not investing or financing activities.

- **Investing** activities are the acquisition and disposal of non-current assets and other investments not included in cash equivalents.

- **Financing** activities are activities that result in changes in the size and composition of the equity capital and borrowings of the entity.

17 15 mark questions: preparing basic financial statements   162 mins

17.1 Mr Yousef

The following trial balance has been extracted from the ledger of Mr Yousef, a sole trader.

TRIAL BALANCE AS AT 31 MAY 20X6

	Dr $	Cr $
Sales		138,078
Purchases	82,350	
Carriage	5,144	
Drawings	7,800	
Rent and insurance	6,622	
Postage and stationery	3,001	
Advertising	1,330	
Salaries and wages	26,420	
Irrecoverable debts	877	
Allowance for receivables		130
Receivables	12,120	
Payables		6,471
Cash on hand	177	
Cash at bank	1,002	
Inventory as at 1 June 20X5	11,927	
Equipment at cost	58,000	
Accumulated depreciation		19,000
Capital		53,091
	216,770	216,770

The following additional information as at 31 May 20X6 is available.

1   Rent is accrued by $210.
2   Insurance has been prepaid by $880.
3    $2,211 of carriage represents carriage inwards on purchases.
4   Equipment is to be depreciated at 15% per annum using the straight-line method.
5   The allowance for receivables is to be increased by $40.
6   Inventory at the close of business has been valued at $13,551.

Required

(a)   Prepare a statement of profit or loss for the year ended 31 May 20X6.   (8 marks)

(b)   Prepare a statement of financial position as at that date.   (7 marks)

          (15 marks)

17.2 Shuswap

The draft statement of financial position shown below has been prepared for Shuswap, a limited liability company, as at 31 December 20X4:

	Cost $'000	Accumulated depreciation $'000	Carrying value $'000
Assets			
Non-current assets			
Land and buildings	9,000	1,000	8,000
Plant and equipment	21,000	9,000	12,000
	30,000	10,000	20,000
Current assets			
Inventories			3,000
Receivables			2,600
Cash at bank			1,900
Total assets			27,500
Equity and liabilities			
Equity			
Issued share capital (ordinary shares of 50c each)			6,000
Retained earnings			12,400
Non-current liabilities			
Loan notes (redeemable 20Y0)			2,000
Current liabilities			
Trade payables			2,100
			22,500
Suspense account			5,000
			27,500

The following further information is available:

1 It has been decided to revalue the land and buildings to $12,000,000 at 31 December 20X4.

2 Trade receivables totalling $200,000 are to be written off.

3 During the year there was a contra settlement of $106,000 in which an amount due to a supplier was set off against the amount due from the same company for goods sold to it. No entry has yet been made to record the set-off.

4 Some inventory items included in the draft statement of financial position at cost $500,000 were sold after the reporting date for $400,000, with selling expenses of $40,000.

5 The suspense account is made up of two items:

   (a) The proceeds of issue of 4,000,000 50c shares at $1.10 per share, credited to the suspense account from the cash book.

   (b) The balance of the account is the proceeds of sale of some plant on 1 January 20X4 with a carrying value at the date of sale of $700,000 and which had originally cost $1,400,000. No other accounting entries have yet been made for the disposal apart from the cash book entry for the receipt of the proceeds. Depreciation on plant has been charged at 25% (straight line basis) in preparing the draft statement of financial position without allowing for the sale. The depreciation for the year relating to the plant sold should be adjusted for in full.

Required

(a) Prepare the journal entries to clear the suspense account. (4 marks)

(b) Prepare the company's statement of financial position as at 31 December 20X4, complying as far as possible with IAS 1 *Presentation of financial statements*. Details of non-current assets, adjusted appropriately, should appear as they are presented in the question. (11 marks)

(15 marks)

17.3 Malright

You are presented with the following trial balance of Malright, a limited liability company, at 31 October 20X7.

	Dr $'000	Cr $'000
Buildings at cost	740	
Buildings, accumulated depreciation, 1 November 20X6		60
Plant at cost	220	
Plant, accumulated depreciation, 1 November 20X6		110
Land at cost	235	
Bank balance		50
Revenue		1,800
Purchases	1,105	
Discounts received		90
Returns inwards	35	
Wages	180	
Energy expenses	105	
Inventory at 1 November 20X6	160	
Trade payables		250
Trade receivables	320	
Administrative expenses	80	
Allowance for receivables, at 1 November 20X6		10
Directors' remuneration	70	
Retained earnings at 1 November 20X6		130
10% loan notes		50
Dividend paid	30	
$1 ordinary shares		650
Share premium account		80
	3,280	3,280

Additional information as at 31 October 20X7:

(a) Closing inventory has been counted and is valued at $75,000.

(b) The items listed below should be apportioned as indicated.

	Cost of sales %	Distribution costs %	Administrative expenses %
Discounts received	–	–	100
Energy expenses	40	20	40
Wages	40	25	35
Directors' remuneration	–	–	100

(c) An invoice of $15,000 for energy expenses for October 20X7 has not been received.

(d) Loan note interest has not been paid for the year.

(e) The allowance for receivables is to be increased to 5% of trade receivables. Any expenses connected with receivables should be charged to administrative expenses.

(f) Plant is depreciated at 20% per annum using the reducing balance method. The entire charge is to be allocated to cost of sales.

(g) Buildings are depreciated at 5% per annum on their original cost, allocated 30% to cost of sales, 30% to distribution costs and 40% to administrative expenses.

(h) Income tax has been calculated as $45,000 for the year.

Required

Prepare the following financial statements for Malright in accordance with IAS 1 *Presentation of financial statements:*

(a)	The statement of profit or loss for the year ended 31 October 20X7	(6 marks)
(b)	The statement of changes in equity for the year ended 31 October 20X7	(3 marks)
(c)	The statement of financial position as at 31 October 20X7	(6 marks)

(15 marks)

17.4 Sondaw

You have been provided with the following trial balance as at 31 May 20X4 for a limited liability company called Sondaw.

	Debit	Credit
	$'000	$'000
Bank	50	
Inventory at 1 June 20X3	1,200	
General expenses	600	
Heating and lighting	90	
Marketing and advertising expenses	248	
Wages	490	
Buildings at cost	5,000	
Motor vehicles at cost	160	
Plant and equipment at cost	700	
Retained earnings at 1 June 20X3		280
Trade receivables	438	
Purchases	2,200	
Loan note interest paid	30	
5% Loan note		600
Revenue		5,876
Discounts received		150
Trade payables		500
$1 ordinary shares		1,500
Accumulated depreciation at 1 June 20X3		
Buildings		2,000
Motor vehicles		60
Plant and equipment		240
	11,206	11,206

The following notes are relevant.

(a) Inventory at 31 May 20X4 was valued at $800,000.

(b) Marketing and advertising expenses include $6,000 paid in advance for a marketing campaign which will begin in June 20X4. Marketing and advertising expenses should be allocated to administrative expenses.

(c) There are wages outstanding of $10,000 for the year ended 31 May 20X4.

(d) A customer ceased trading owing the company $38,000; the debt is not expected to be recovered.

(e) An allowance for receivables is to be established amounting to 5% of trade receivables.

(f) Depreciation is to be provided for as follows.

    (i) Buildings at 5% per annum on their original cost, allocated 50% to cost of sales, 20% to distribution costs and 30% to administrative expenses.

    (ii) Motor vehicles at 25% per annum of their written down value, allocated to distribution costs.

    (iii) Plant and equipment at 20% per annum of their written down value, allocated to cost of sales.

(g) No dividends have been paid or declared.

(h) Income tax of $250,000 is to be provided for the year.

(i) The audit fee accrual is estimated to be $20,000.

(j) The expenses listed below should be apportioned as follows.

	Cost of sales %	Distribution costs %	Administrative expenses %
General expenses	10	40	50
Heating and lighting	50	30	20
Wages and salaries	60	30	10

Required

Prepare the following financial statements for the year ended 31 May 30X4 for Sondaw, showing workings where appropriate in accordance with IAS 1 *Presentation of financial statements*.

(a) A statement of profit or loss (7 marks)
(b) A statement of financial position (8 marks)

(15 marks)

17.5 Tonson

The following information has been extracted from the books of Tonson, a limited liability company, as at 31 October 20X6.

	Dr $'000	Cr $'000
Cash	15	
Insurance	75	
Inventory at 1 November 20X5	350	
General expenses	60	
Energy expenses	66	
Marketing expenses	50	
Wages and salaries	675	
Discounts received		50
Share premium account		200
Retained earnings at 1 November 20X5		315
Allowance for receivables at 1 November 20X5		40
Sales revenue		5,780
Telephone expenses	80	
Property expenses	100	
Bank		94
Returns inward	95	
Trade payables		290
Loan note interest	33	
Trade receivables	900	
Purchases	3,570	
7% loan notes		470
Irrecoverable debts	150	
$1 ordinary shares		1,800
Accumulated depreciation at 1 November 20X5		
Buildings		360
Motor Vehicles		80
Furniture and equipment		420
Land at cost	740	
Buildings at cost	1,500	
Motor vehicles at cost	240	
Furniture and equipment at cost	1,200	
	9,899	9,899

You have also been provided with the following information:

(a)   Inventory at 31 October 20X6 was valued at $275,000 based on its original cost. However, $45,000 of this inventory has been in the warehouse for over two years and the directors have agreed to sell it in November 20X6 for a cash price of $20,000.

(b)   The marketing expenses include $5,000 which relates to November 20X6.

(c)   Based on past experience the allowance for receivables is to be increased to 5% of trade receivables.

(d)   There are wages and salaries outstanding of $40,000 for the year ended 31 October 20X6.

(e)   Buildings are depreciated at 5% of cost. At 31 October 20X6 the buildings were professionally valued at $1,800,000 and the directors wish this valuation to be incorporated into the accounts.

(f)   Depreciation is to be charged as follows:

    (i)   Motor vehicles at 20% of written down value
    (ii)   Furniture and equipment at 20% of cost

(g)   No dividends have been paid or declared.

(h)   Tax of $150,000 is to be provided for the year.

(i)   During October 20X6 a bonus issue of one for ten shares was made to ordinary shareholders. This has not been entered into the books. The share premium account was used for this purpose.

Required

Prepare the following statements, *for internal use*:

(a)	The statement of profit or loss for the year ended 31 October 20X6	(8 marks)
(b)	The statement of financial position as at 31 October 20X6	(7 marks)

(15 marks)

17.6 Emma

Set out below are the financial statements of Emma, a limited liability company. You have been asked to prepare the company's statement of cash flows, implementing IAS 7 *Statement of cash flows*.

EMMA
STATEMENT OF PROFIT OR LOSS FOR THE YEAR ENDED 31 DECEMBER 20X2

	$'000
Sales revenue	2,553
Cost of sales	1,814
Gross profit	739
Distribution costs	125
Administrative expenses	264
Operating profit	350
Interest received	25
Interest paid	75
Profit before tax	300
Income tax expense	240
Profit for the year	60

EMMA
STATEMENTS OF FINANCIAL POSITION AS AT 31 DECEMBER

	20X2 $'000	20X1 $'000
Non-current assets		
Tangible assets	380	305
Intangible assets	250	200
Investments	–	25
	630	530

	20X2 $'000	20X1 $'000
Current assets		
Inventories	150	102
Receivables	390	315
Short-term investments	50	
Cash in hand	2	1
	592	418
	1,222	948
Equity and liabilities		
Share capital ($1 ordinary shares)	200	150
Share premium account	160	150
Revaluation surplus	100	91
Retained earnings	160	100
	620	491
Non-current liabilities		
Long-term loan	100	
Current liabilities		
Trade payables	127	119
Bank overdraft	85	98
Taxation	290	240
	502	457
	1,222	948

The following information is available.

(a)   The proceeds of the sale of non-current asset investments amounted to $30,000.

(b)   Fixtures and fittings, with an original cost of $85,000 and a carrying value of $45,000, were sold for $32,000 during the year.

(c)   The current asset investments fall within the definition of cash equivalents under IAS 7.

(d)   The following information relates to property, plant and equipment.

	31.12.20X2 $'000	31.12.20X1 $'000
Cost	720	595
Accumulated depreciation	340	290
Carrying value	380	305

(e)   50,000 $1 ordinary shares were issued during the year at a premium of 20c per share.

Required

Prepare a statement of cash flows for the year to 31 December 20X2 using the format laid out in IAS 7, together with the relevant notes to the statement.   **(15 marks)**

17.7 Sioux

The following information is available for Sioux, a limited liability company:

Statements of financial position

		31 December		
		20X4		20X3
	$'000	$'000	$'000	$'000
Non-current assets				
Cost or valuation		11,000		8,000
Accumulated depreciation		(5,600)		(4,800)
Carrying value		5,400		3,200
Current assets				
Inventories	3,400		3,800	
Receivables	3,800		2,900	
Cash at bank	400	7,600	100	6,800
		13,000		10,000
Equity and liabilities				
Capital and reserves				
Ordinary share capital	1,000		1,000	
Revaluation surplus	1,500		1,000	
Retained earnings	3,100	5,600	2,200	4,200
Non-current liabilities				
10% Loan notes		3,000		2,000
Current liabilities				
Trade payables	3,700		3,200	
Income tax	700	4,400	600	3,800
		13,000		10,000

Summarised statement of profit or loss for the year ended 31 December 20X4

	$'000
Profit from operations	2,650
Finance cost (loan note interest)	(300)
	2,350
Income tax expense	(700)
Net profit for the year	1,650

Notes

1   During the year non-current assets which had cost $800,000, with a carrying value of $350,000, were sold for $500,000.

2   The revaluation surplus arose from the revaluation of some land that was not being depreciated.

3   The 20X3 income tax liability was settled at the amount provided for at 31 December 20X3.

4   The additional loan notes were issued on 1 January 20X4. Interest was paid on 30 June 20X4 and 31 December 20X4.

5   Dividends paid during the year amounted to $750,000.

Required

Prepare the company's statement of cash flows for the year ended 31 December 20X4, using the indirect method, adopting the format in IAS 7 *Statement of cash flows*.   **(15 marks)**

17.8 Snowdrop

The following information has been extracted from the draft financial statements of Snowdrop, a limited liability company.

SNOWDROP
STATEMENTS OF FINANCIAL POSITION AS AT 31 MAY

	20X4		20X5	
	$'000	$'000	$'000	$'000
Non-current assets		4,600		2,700
Current assets				
Inventory	580		500	
Trade receivables	360		230	
Bank	0		170	
		940		900
Total assets		5,540		3,600
Equity and liabilities				
Equity				
Ordinary share capital		3,500		2,370
Share premium		300		150
Retained earnings		1,052		470
		4,852		2,990
Non-current liabilities				
10% Loan note				
(redeemable 31 May 20X5)		0		100
Current liabilities				
Trade payables	450		365	
Taxation	180		145	
Bank overdraft	58		0	
		688		510
		5,540		3,600

Additional information

(a)   The statement of profit or loss for the year ended 31 May 20X5 shows the following.

	$'000
Operating profit	1,042
Interest payable	(10)
Profit before taxation	1,032
Taxation	(180)
Profit for financial year	852

(b)   During the year dividends paid were $270,000.

(c)   Profit before taxation had been arrived at after charging $700,000 for depreciation on non-current assets.

(d)   During the year non-current assets with a net book value of $200,000 were sold for $180,000.

Required

Prepare a statement of cash flows for Snowdrop for the year ended 31 May 20X5 in accordance with IAS 7 *Statement of cash flows*, using the indirect method.   **(15 marks)**

17.9 Geofost

Geofost is preparing its statement of cash flows for the year ended 31 October 20X7. You have been presented with the following information.

GEOFOST
STATEMENT OF PROFIT OR LOSS FOR THE YEAR ENDED 31 OCTOBER 20X7

	$'000
Profit from operations	15,730
Finance cost	(730)
Profit before tax	15,000
Taxation	(4,350)
Profit for the year	10,650

STATEMENTS OF FINANCIAL POSITION AS AT 31 OCTOBER

	20X7		20X6	
	$'000	$'000	$'000	$'000
Non-current assets		44,282		26,574
Current assets				
Inventory	3,560		9,635	
Trade receivables	6,405		4,542	
Cash	559		1,063	
		10,524		15,240
Total assets		54,806		41,814
Equity and liabilities				
Equity				
Ordinary share capital		16,000		15,000
Share premium account		3,365		2,496
Retained earnings		15,629		6,465
		34,994		23,961
Non-current liabilities				
9% loan notes		8,000		10,300
Current liabilities				
Bank overdraft	1,230		429	
Trade payables	7,442		4,264	
Interest payable	120		100	
Taxation	3,020		2,760	
		11,812		7,553
Total equity and liabilities		54,806		41,814

Additional information

(a) During the year dividends paid were $1,486,000.

(b) Summary schedule of changes to non-current assets during 20X7.

	Cost	Accumulated depreciation	Carrying value
	$'000	$'000	$'000
Balance b/f	33,218	6,644	26,574
Additions	24,340		24,340
Disposals	(2,964)	(990)	(1,974)
Depreciation		4,658	(4,658)
Balance c/f	54,594	10,312	44,282

(c) The total proceeds from the disposal of non-current assets were $2,694,000.

Required

Prepare a statement of cash flows for Geofost for the year ended 31 October 20X7 in accordance with IAS 7 *Statement of cash flows*, using the indirect method. **(15 marks)**

(Total = 135 marks)

18 Incomplete records

38 mins

18.1 A business has compiled the following information for the year ended 31 October 20X2:

	$
Opening inventory	386,200
Purchases	989,000
Closing inventory	422,700

The gross profit as a percentage of sales is always 40%

Based on these figures, what is the sales revenue for the year?

A $1,333,500
B $1,587,500
C $2,381,250
D The sales revenue figure cannot be calculated from this information **(2 marks)**

18.2 Which of the following calculations could produce an acceptable figure for a trader's net profit for a period if no accounting records had been kept?

A Closing net assets plus drawings minus capital introduced minus opening net assets
B Closing net assets minus drawings plus capital introduced minus opening net assets
C Closing net assets minus drawings minus capital introduced minus opening net assets
D Closing net assets plus drawings plus capital introduced minus opening net assets

(2 marks)

18.3 A sole trader fixes his prices to achieve a gross profit percentage on sales revenue of 40%. All his sales are for cash. He suspects that one of his sales assistants is stealing cash from sales revenue.

His trading account for the month of June 20X3 is as follows:

	$
Recorded sales revenue	181,600
Cost of sales	114,000
Gross profit	67,600

Assuming that the cost of sales figure is correct, how much cash could the sales assistant have taken?

A $5,040
B $8,400
C $22,000
D It is not possible to calculate a figure from this information **(2 marks)**

The following information is relevant for questions 18.4 and 18.5

A is a sole trader who does not keep full accounting records. The following details relate to her transactions with credit customers and suppliers for the year ended 30 November 20X3.

	$
Trade receivables, 1 December 20X2	130,000
Trade payables, 1 December 20X2	60,000
Cash received from customers	686,400
Cash paid to suppliers	302,800
Discounts allowed	1,400
Discounts received	2,960
Irrecoverable debts	4,160
Amount due from a customer who is also a supplier offset against an amount due for goods supplied by him	2,000
Trade receivables, 30 November 20X3	181,000
Trade payables, 30 November 20X3	84,000

18.4   Based on the above information, what figure should appear in A's statement of profit or loss for the year
       ended 30 November 20X3 for sales revenue?

       A $748,960
       B $748,800
       C $744,960
       D $743,560   (2 marks)

18.5   Based on the above information, what figure should appear in A's statement of profit or loss for the year
       ended 30 November 20X3 for purchases?

       A $283,760
       B $325,840
       C $329,760
       D $331,760   (2 marks)

18.6   A sole trader fixes her prices by adding 50 per cent to the cost of all goods purchased. On 31 October
       20X3 a fire destroyed a considerable part of the inventory and all inventory records.

       Her trading account for the year ended 31 October 20X3 included the following figures:

	$	$
Sales		281,250
Opening inventory at cost	183,600	
Purchases	249,200	
	432,800	
Closing inventory at cost	204,600	
		228,200
Gross profit		53,050

       Using this information, what inventory loss has occurred?

       A $61,050
       B $87,575
       C $40,700
       D $110,850   (2 marks)

18.7   A fire on 30 September 20X2 destroyed some of a company's inventory and its inventory records.

       The following information is available:

	$
Inventory 1 September 20X2	318,000
Sales for September 20X2	612,000
Purchases for September 20X2	412,000
Inventory in good condition at 30 September 20X2	214,000

       Standard gross profit percentage on sales is 25%

       Based on this information, what is the value of the inventory lost?

       A $96,000
       B $271,000
       C $26,400
       D $57,000   (2 marks)

18.8 A business's bank balance increased by $750,000 during its last financial year. During the same period it issued shares of $1 million and repaid a loan note of $750,000. It purchased non-current assets for $200,000 and charged depreciation of $100,000. Working capital (other than the bank balance) increased by $575,000.

What was its profit for the year?

A $1,175,000
B $1,275,000
C $1,325,000
D $1,375,000   (2 marks)

18.9 A sole trader's business made a profit of $32,500 during the year ended 31 March 20X8. This figure was after deducting $100 per week wages for himself. In addition, he put his home telephone bill through the business books, amounting to $400 plus sales tax at 17.5%. He is registered for sales tax and therefore has charged only the net amount to his statement of profit or loss and other comprehensive income.

His capital at 1 April 20X7 was $6,500. What was his capital at 31 March 20X8?

A $33,730
B $33,800
C $38,930
D $39,000   (2 marks)

18.10 Senji does not keep proper accounting records, and it is necessary to calculate her total purchases for the year ended 31 January 20X3 from the following information:

	$
Trade payables: 31 January 20X2	130,400
31 January 20X3	171,250
Payment to suppliers	888,400
Cost of goods taken from inventory by Senji for her personal use	1,000
Refunds received from suppliers	2,400
Discounts received	11,200

What is the figure for purchases that should be included in Senji's financial statements?

A $914,650
B $937,050
C $939,050
D $941,850

                                                                                         (2 marks)

18.11 Aluki fixes prices to make a standard gross profit percentage on sales of 20%.

The following information for the year ended 31 January 20X3 is available to compute her sales total for the year.

	$
Inventory: 1 February 20X2	243,000
31 January 20X3	261,700
Purchases	595,400
Purchases returns	41,200

What is the sales figure for the year ended 31 January 20X3?

A $669,375
B $702,600
C $772,375
D $741,480   (2 marks)

18.12 The following information is relevant to the calculation of the sales figure for Alpha, a sole trader who does not keep proper accounting records:

	$
Opening accounts receivable	29,100
Cash received from credit customers and paid into the bank	381,600
Expenses paid out of cash received from credit customers before banking	6,800
Irrecoverable debts written off	7,200
Refunds to credit customers	2,100
Discounts allowed to credit customers	9,400
Cash sales	112,900
Closing accounts receivable	38,600

Which of the following should appear in Alpha's trading account for sales?

A $525,300
B $511,700
C $529,500
D $510,900   **(2 marks)**

18.13 A sole trader who does not keep full accounting records wishes to calculate her sales revenue for the year.

The information available is:

1	Opening inventory	$17,000
2	Closing inventory	$24,000
3	Purchases	$91,000
4	Standard gross profit percentage on sales revenue	40%

Which of the following is the sales figure for the year calculated from these figures?

A $117,600
B $108,000
C $210,000
D $140,000   **(2 marks)**

18.14 On 31 December 20X0 the inventory of V was completely destroyed by fire. The following information is available:

1   Inventory at 1 December 20X0 at cost $28,400
2   Purchases for December 20X0 $49,600
3   Sales for December 20X0 $64,800
4   Standard gross profit percentage on sales revenue 30%

Based on this information, which of the following is the amount of inventory destroyed?

A $45,360
B $32,640
C $40,971
D $19,440   **(2 marks)**

18.15 The following information is available for the year ended 31 December 20X4 for a trader who does not keep proper accounting records:

	$
Inventories at 1 January 20X4	38,000
Inventories at 31 December 20X4	45,000
Purchases	637,000

Gross profit percentage on sales = 30%

Based on this information, what was the trader's sales figure for the year?

A $900,000
B $819,000
C $920,000
D $837,200   **(2 marks)**

18.16 Wanda keeps no accounting records. The following information is available about her position and transactions for the year ended 31 December 20X4:

	$
Net assets at 1 January 20X4	210,000
Drawings during 20X4	48,000
Capital introduced during 20X4	100,000
Net assets at 31 December 20X4	400,000

Based on this information, what was Wanda's profit for 20X4?

A $42,000
B $242,000
C $138,000
D $338,000   **(2 marks)**

(Total = 32 marks)

19 Company financial statements   53 mins

19.1 The issued share capital of Alpha, a limited liability company, is as follows:

	$
Ordinary shares of 10c each	1,000,000
8% Redeemable preference shares of 50c each	500,000

In the year ended 31 October 20X2, the company has paid the preference dividend for the year and an interim dividend of 2c per share on the ordinary shares. A final ordinary dividend of 3c per share was proposed, before the reporting date.

What would be recognised for dividends in the equity section of the statement of financial position at 31 October 20X2?

A $580,000
B $90,000
C $130,000
D $200,000   **(2 marks)**

19.2 When a company makes a rights issue of equity shares which of the following effects will the issue have?

1   Assets are increased
2   Retained earnings are reduced
3   Share premium account is reduced
4   Investments are increased

A   1 only
B   1 and 2
C   3 only
D   1 and 4   **(2 marks)**

19.3 Which of the following items may appear as current liabilities in a company's statement of financial position?

1   Revaluation surplus
2   Loan due for repayment within one year
3   Taxation
4   Preference dividend payable on redeemable preference shares

A   1, 2 and 3
B   1, 2 and 4
C   1, 3 and 4
D   2, 3 and 4   **(2 marks)**

19.4 A company made an issue for cash of 1,000,000 50c shares at a premium of 30c per share.

Which one of the following journal entries correctly records the issue?

		Debit	Credit
		$	$
A	Share capital	500,000	
	Share premium	300,000	
	Bank		800,000
B	Bank	800,000	
	Share capital		500,000
	Share premium		300,000
C	Bank	1,300,000	
	Share capital		1,000,000
	Share premium		300,000
D	Share capital	1,000,000	
	Share premium		300,000
	Bank		1,300,000	**(2 marks)**

19.5 Which of the following might appear as an item in a company's statement of changes in equity?

1   Profit on disposal of properties
2   Surplus on revaluation of properties
3   Equity dividends proposed after the reporting date
4   Issue of share capital

A   1, 3 and 4 only
B   2 and 4 only
C   1 and 2 only
D   3 and 4 only   **(2 marks)**

19.6 At 31 December 20X2 the following matters require inclusion in a company's financial statements:

1   On 1 January 20X2 the company made a loan of $12,000 to an employee, repayable on 30 April 20X3, charging interest at 2 per cent per year. On the due date she repaid the loan and paid the whole of the interest due on the loan to that date.

2   The company has paid insurance $9,000 in 20X2, covering the year ending 31 August 20X3.

3   In January 20X3 the company received rent from a tenant $4,000 covering the six months to 31 December 20X2.

For these items, what total figures should be included in the company's statement of financial position at 31 December 20X2?

	Receivables and prepayments	Payables and accruals	
	$	$	
A	22,000	240	
B	22,240	NIL	
C	10,240	NIL	
D	16,240	6,000	(2 marks)

19.7 At 31 December 20X1 the capital structure of a company was as follows:

	$
Ordinary share capital	
100,000 shares of 50c each	50,000
Share premium account	180,000

During 20X2 the company made a bonus issue of 1 share for every 2 held, using the share premium account for the purpose, and later issued for cash another 60,000 shares at 80c per share.

What is the company's capital structure at 31 December 20X2?

	Ordinary share capital	Share premium account	
	$	$	
A	130,000	173,000	
B	105,000	173,000	
C	130,000	137,000	
D	105,000	137,000	
			(2 marks)

19.8 An organisation's year end is 30 September. On 1 January 20X6 the organisation took out a loan of $100,000 with annual interest of 12%. The interest is payable in equal instalments on the first day of April, July, October and January in arrears.

How much should be charged to the statement of profit or loss (SPL) for the year ended 30 September 20X6, and how much should be accrued on the statement of financial position (SOFP)?

	SPL	SOFP	
A	$12,000	$3,000	
B	$9,000	$3,000	
C	$9,000	NIL	
D	$6,000	$3,000	(2 marks)

19.9 Which of the following statements about company financial statements is/are correct, according to International Financial Reporting Standards?

1 Dividends paid on ordinary shares should be included in the statement of profit or loss and other comprehensive income.

2 Dividends paid on redeemable preference shares are treated in the same way as dividends paid on ordinary shares.

3 The statement of profit or loss and other comprehensive income shows the gain on revaluation of non-current assets for the period.

A 1, 2 and 3
B 2 and 3
C 3 only
D All three statements are correct   **(2 marks)**

19.10 Which of the following items are required to be disclosed in a limited liability company's financial statements according to International Financial Reporting Standards?

1 Share capital
2 Finance costs
3 Dividends proposed
4 Depreciation and amortisation

A 1, 2 and 3 only
B 2, 3 and 4 only
C 1, 2 and 4 only
D All four items   **(2 marks)**

19.11 At 30 June 20X2 a company's capital structure was as follows:

	$
Ordinary share capital	
500,000 shares of 25c each	125,000
Share premium account	100,000

In the year ended 30 June 20X3 the company made a rights issue of 1 share for every 2 held at $1 per share and this was taken up in full. Later in the year the company made a bonus issue of 1 share for every 5 held, using the share premium account for the purpose.

What was the company's capital structure at 30 June 20X3?

	Ordinary share capital	*Share premium account*
	$	$
A	450,000	25,000
B	225,000	250,000
C	225,000	325,000
D	212,500	262,500

(2 marks)

19.12 At 30 June 20X2 a company had $1m 8% loan notes in issue, interest being paid half-yearly on 30 June and 31 December.

On 30 September 20X2 the company redeemed $250,000 of these loan notes at par, paying interest due to that date.

On 1 April 20X3 the company issued $500,000 7% loan notes, interest payable half-yearly on 31 March and 30 September.

What figure should appear in the company's statement of profit or loss for interest payable in the year ended 30 June 20X3?

A $88,750
B $82,500
C $65,000
D $73,750   **(2 marks)**

19.13 Which of the following statements about the financial statements of limited liability companies are correct according to International Financial Reporting Standards?

1   In preparing a statement of cash flows, either the direct or the indirect method may be used. Both lead to the same figure for net cash from operating activities.

2   Loan notes can be classified as current or non-current liabilities.

3   Financial statements must disclose a company's total expense for depreciation, if material.

4   A company must disclose by note details of all adjusting events allowed for in the financial statements.

A   1, 2 and 3 only
B   2 and 4 only
C   3 and 4 only
D   All four items   **(2 marks)**

19.14 Which of the following could appear as separate items in the statement of changes in equity required by IAS 1 *Presentation of Financial Statements* as part of a company's financial statements?

1   Dividends on equity shares paid during the period
2   Loss on sale of investments
3   Proceeds of an issue of ordinary shares
4   Dividends proposed after the year end

A   1, 3 and 4 only
B   1, 2 and 4 only
C   1 and 3 only
D   All four items   **(2 marks)**

19.15 A limited liability company issued 50,000 ordinary shares of 25c each at a premium of 50c per share. The cash received was correctly recorded but the full amount was credited to the ordinary share capital account.

Which one of the following journal entries is needed to correct this error?

		Debit $	Credit $
A	Share premium account	25,000	
	Share capital account		25,000
B	Share capital account	25,000	
	Share premium account		25,000
C	Share capital account	37,500	
	Share premium account		37,500
D	Share capital account	25,000	
	Cash		25,000

(2 marks)

19.16 Which one of the following journal entries could correctly record a bonus issue of shares?

		Debit $	Credit $
A	Cash	100,000	
	Ordinary share capital		100,000
B	Ordinary share capital	100,000	
	Share premium		100,000
C	Share premium	100,000	
	Ordinary share capital		100,000
D	Investments	100,000	
	Cash		100,000

(2 marks)

19.17 Which of these statements about limited liability companies is/are correct?

1   A company might make a bonus issue of shares to raise funds for expansion.

2   No cash is received when a company makes a rights issue of shares, instead other reserves (usually share premium) are capitalised and reclassified as share capital.

3   A rights issue of shares dilutes the shareholding of existing shareholders if they do not take up their rights.

A   1 and 3
B   2 and 3
C   1 and 2
D   3 only

(2 marks)

19.18 Which one of the following items does not appear under the heading 'equity and reserves' on a company statement of financial position?

A   Share premium account
B   Retained earnings
C   Revaluation surplus
D   Loan stock

(2 marks)

19.19 Which one of the following statements regarding a limited liability company statement of profit or loss and other comprehensive income is correct?

A   Accounting standards define the expenses which are reported under 'cost of sales'.

B   'Depreciation' appears as a separate heading.

C   Interest payable is deducted from profit after taxation.

D   Irrecoverable debts will be included under one of the expense headings (usually administrative expenses).

(2 marks)

19.20 At 1 January 20X0 the capital structure of Q, a limited liability company, was as follows:

	$
Issued share capital 1,000,000 ordinary shares of 50c each	500,000
Share premium account	300,000

On 1 April 20X0 the company made an issue of 200,000 50c shares at $1.30 each, and on 1 July the company made a bonus (capitalisation) issue of one share for every four in issue at the time, using the share premium account for the purpose.

Which of the following correctly states the company's share capital and share premium account at 31 December 20X0?

	Share capital	Share premium account
A	$750,000	$230,000
B	$875,000	$285,000
C	$750,000	$310,000
D	$750,000	$610,000

(2 marks)

19.21 According to the illustrative financial structure in IAS 1 Presentation of financial statements, where should dividends paid during the year should be disclosed?

A   Statement of profit or loss and other comprehensive income
B   Statement of changes in equity
C   Statement of financial position
D   None of these   **(2 marks)**

19.22 Which of the following statements about limited liability companies' accounting is/are correct?

1   A revaluation surplus arises when a non-current asset is sold at a profit.

2   The authorised share capital of a company is the maximum nominal value of shares and loan notes the company may issue.

3   IAS 10 Events after the reporting period requires all non-adjusting events to be disclosed in the notes to the financial statements.

A   1 and 2 only
B   2 only
C   3 only
D   None of the statements are correct   **(2 marks)**

(Total = 44 marks)

20   Disclosure notes   24 mins

20.1   Which of the following best describes the purpose of disclosure notes in the financial statements?

A   To provide more detail for the users of accounts about the information in the main financial statements.

B   To allow companies to present their financial results in a more favourable way by only disclosing some things in the notes and not on the main financial statements.

C   To give all the detail of all the transactions that occurred during the period because the main financial statements only present a summary.

D   To explain the accounting treatment adopted where management have chosen not to apply accounting standards.   **(2 marks)**

20.2 For which class or classes of assets should a company disclose in the notes to the financial statements a reconciliation of the opening carrying amount to the closing carrying amount, showing the movements in the period?

1   Cash
2   Intangible assets
3   Tangible non-current assets
4   Trade receivables

A   3 only
B   2 and 3 only
C   1 and 4 only
D   1 only   **(2 marks)**

20.3 Which of the following should be disclosed in the note to the financial statements for inventories?

1   The date the inventories were purchased or manufactured and/or how long they have been held as inventories

2   The amount of inventories carried at net realisable value

3   The accounting policies adopted in measuring inventories

4   The useful life of the inventories

A   3 only
B   2 and 3 only
C   1 and 4 only
D   1 only   **(2 marks)**

20.4 Which of the following should be disclosed for tangible non-current assets according to IAS 16 *Property, plant and equipment*?

1   Depreciation methods used and the total depreciation allocated for the period

2   A reconciliation of the carrying amount of non-current assets at the beginning and end of the period

3   For revalued assets, whether an independent valuer was involved in the valuation

4   For revalued assets, the effective date of the revaluation

A   1, 2 and 4 only
B   1 and 2 only
C   1, 2, 3 and 4
D   1, 3 and 4 only   **(2 marks)**

20.5 Which of the following should be disclosed in the note to the financial statements for intangible assets?

1   The method of amortisation used
2   A reconciliation of the carrying amount at the beginning and end of the period
3   The useful life of the assets
4   The net realisable value of any deferred development costs capitalised

A   1, 2 and 3 only
B   2 and 3 only
C   2, 3 and 4 only
D   2 only   **(2 marks)**

20.6 Which of the following statements is/are correct?

1 IAS 37 requires disclosure in the notes to the financial statements of the uncertainties affecting the outcome of a provision

2 IAS 10 requires disclosure of the nature and financial effect of a non-adjusting event after the reporting period in the notes to the financial statements

A 1 only
B 2 only
C Both 1 and 2
D Neither 1 or 2 **(2 marks)**

20.7 A certain IFRS requires that the following disclosure is made in a note to the financial statements:

(i) A brief description of its nature

(ii) Where practicable an estimate of the financial effect

(iii) An indication of the uncertainties relating to the amount or timing of any outflow

(iv) The possibility of any reimbursement

Which of the following does the above disclosure apply to?

A Provisions
B Contingent liabilities
C Contingent assets
D Events after the reporting period **(2 marks)**

20.8 Which of the following should be disclosed in the note to the financial statements for tangible non-current assets?

1 The market value of all assets classified as tangible non-current assets, whether they have been revalued or not

2 A reconciliation of the carrying amount of non-current assets at the beginning and end of the period

3 For revalued assets, the methods and significant assumptions applied in estimating the value

4 For revalued assets, the carrying amount of each class of assets that would have been included in the financial statements had the assets been carried at cost less depreciation

A 1, 2 and 3 only
B 2 and 3 only
C 2, 3 and 4 only
D 2 only **(2 marks)**

20.9 Which of the following are required as disclosures by IAS2 *Inventories*?

1. The amount of write-downs of inventories in the period that have been recognised as an expense

2 The original cost of inventories that are carried at net realisable value

3 The carrying amount of inventories classified by type (for example, raw materials, work in progress)

A 1 and 2 only
B 1 and 3 only
C 2 and 3 only
D 1, 2 and 3 **(2 marks)**

20.10 Which one of the following is a disclosure about non-adjusting events required by IAS10 *Events after the reporting period*?

A   Dividends declared before the end of the reporting period and paid after the end of the reporting period

B   The nature of both material and non-material non-adjusting events

C   The date that the non-adjusting event occurred

D   An estimate of the financial effect of the event, unless a reasonable estimate cannot be made

(2 marks)

(Total = 20 marks)

21   Events after the reporting period   19 mins

21.1   Which of the following material events after the reporting period and before the financial statements are approved by the directors should be adjusted for in those financial statements?

1   A valuation of property providing evidence of impairment in value at the reporting period

2   Sale of inventory held at the end of the reporting period for less than cost

3   Discovery of fraud or error affecting the financial statements

4   The insolvency of a customer with a debt owing at the end of the reporting period which is still outstanding

A   All of them
B   1, 2 and 4 only
C   3 and 4 only
D   1, 2 and 3 only   **(2 marks)**

21.2   The draft financial statements of a limited liability company are under consideration. The accounting treatment of the following material events after the reporting period needs to be determined.

1   The bankruptcy of a major customer, with a substantial debt outstanding at the end of the reporting period

2   A fire destroying some of the company's inventory (the company's going concern status is not affected)

3   An issue of shares to finance expansion

4   Sale for less than cost of some inventory held at the end of the reporting period

According to IAS 10 *Events after the reporting period*, which of the above events require an adjustment to the figures in the draft financial statements?

A   1 and 4 only
B   1, 2 and 3 only
C   2 and 3 only
D   2 and 4 only   **(2 marks)**

21.3 In finalising the financial statements of a company for the year ended 30 June 20X4, which of the following material matters should be adjusted for?

1   A customer who owed $180,000 at the end of the reporting period went bankrupt in July 20X4.

2   The sale in August 20X4 for $400,000 of some inventory items valued in the statement of financial position at $500,000.

3   A factory with a value of $3,000,000 was seriously damaged by a fire in July 20X4. The factory was back in production by August 20X4 but its value was reduced to $2,000,000.

4   The company issued 1,000,000 ordinary shares in August 20X4.

A   All four items
B   1 and 2 only
C   1 and 4 only
D   2 and 3 only   **(2 marks)**

21.4 IAS 10 *Events after the reporting period* regulates the extent to which events after the reporting period should be reflected in financial statements.

Which one of the following lists of such events consists only of items that, according to IAS 10, should normally be classified as non-adjusting?

A   Insolvency of an account receivable which was outstanding at the end of the reporting period, issue of shares or loan notes, an acquisition of another company

B   Issue of shares or loan notes, changes in foreign exchange rates, major purchases of non-current assets

C   An acquisition of another company, destruction of a major non-current asset by fire, discovery of fraud or error which shows that the financial statements were incorrect

D   Sale of inventory which gives evidence about its value at the end of the reporting period, issue of shares or loan notes, destruction of a major non-current asset by fire   **(2 marks)**

21.5 Which of the following events occurring after the reporting period are classified as adjusting, if material?

1   The sale of inventories valued at cost at the end of the reporting period for a figure in excess of cost

2   A valuation of land and buildings providing evidence of an impairment in value at the year end

3   The issue of shares and loan notes

4   The insolvency of a customer with a balance outstanding at the year end

A   1 and 3
B   2 and 4
C   2 and 3
D   1 and 4   **(2 marks)**

21.6 The accounts of Overexposure Inc for the year ended 31 December 20X1 are to be approved on 31 March 20X2. Before they are approved, the following events take place.

1 On 14 February 20X2 the directors took the strategic decision to sell their investment in Quebec Inc despite the fact that this investment generated material revenues.

2 On 15 March 20X2, a fire occurred in the eastern branch factory which destroyed a material amount of inventory. It is estimated that it will cost $505,000 to repair the significant damage done to the factory.

3 On 17 March 20X2, a customer of Overexposure Inc went into liquidation. Overexposure has been advised that it is unlikely to receive payment for any of the outstanding balances owed by the customer at the year end.

How should these events reflected in the financial statements at 31 December 20X1?

	Adjust	Disclose	Do nothing
A	3	2, 3	1
B	2, 3	1	-
C	3	1, 2	-
D	2	3, 1	

(2 marks)

21.7 Which of the following events between the reporting date and the date the financial statements are authorised for issue must be adjusted in the financial statements?

1 Declaration of equity dividends
2 Decline in market value of investments
3 The announcement of changes in tax rates
4 The announcement of a major restructuring

A 1 only
B 2 and 4
C 3 only
D None of them   (2 marks)

21.8 Which of the following is the correct definition of an adjusting event after the reporting period?

A An event that occurs between the reporting date and the date on which the financial statements are authorised for issue that provides further evidence of conditions that existed at the reporting date

B An event that occurs between the reporting date and the date on which the financial statements are authorised for issue that provides evidence of conditions that arose subsequent to the reporting date

C An event that occurs after the date the financial statements are authorised for issue that provides further evidence of conditions that existed at the reporting date

D An event that occurs after the date the financial statements are authorised for issue that provides evidence of conditions that arose subsequent to the reporting date   (2 marks)

(Total = 16 marks)

22 Statements of cash flows   38 mins

22.1 Which of the following items could appear in a company's statement of cash flows?

1   Surplus on revaluation of non-current assets
2   Proceeds of issue of shares
3   Proposed dividend
4   Irrecoverable debts written off
5   Dividends received

A   1, 2 and 5 only
B   2, 3, 4, 5 only
C   2 and 5 only
D   3 and 4 only   **(2 marks)**

22.2 Part of the process of preparing a company's statement of cash flows is the calculation of cash inflow from operating activities.

Which of the following statements about that calculation (using the indirect method) are correct?

1   Loss on sale of operating non-current assets should be deducted from net profit before taxation.
2   Increase in inventory should be deducted from operating profits.
3   Increase in payables should be added to operating profits.
4   Depreciation charges should be added to net profit before taxation.

A   1, 2 and 3
B   1, 2 and 4
C   1, 3 and 4
D   2, 3 and 4   **(2 marks)**

22.3 In the course of preparing a company's statement of cash flows, the following figures are to be included in the calculation of net cash from operating activities.

	$
Depreciation charges	980,000
Profit on sale of non-current assets	40,000
Increase in inventories	130,000
Decrease in receivables	100,000
Increase in payables	80,000

What will the net effect of these items be in the statement of cash flows?

		$	
A	Addition to operating profit	890,000	
B	Subtraction from operating profit	890,000	
C	Addition to operating profit	1,070,000	
D	Addition to operating profit	990,000	**(2 marks)**

22.4 Part of a company's draft statement of cash flows is shown below:

	$'000
Net profit before tax	8,640
Depreciation charges	(2,160)
Proceeds of sale of non-current assets	360
Increase in inventory	(330)
Increase in accounts payable	440

The following criticisms of the above extract have been made:

1   Depreciation charges should have been added, not deducted.

2   Increase in inventory should have been added, not deducted.

3   Increase in accounts payable should have been deducted, not added.

4   Proceeds of sale of non-current assets should not appear in this part of the statement of cash flows.

Which of these criticisms are valid?

A   2 and 3 only
B   1 and 4 only
C   1 and 3 only
D   2 and 4 only   **(2 marks)**

22.5 In preparing a company's statement of cash flows complying with IAS 7, which, if any, of the following items could form part of the calculation of cash flow from financing activities?

1   Proceeds of sale of premises
2   Dividends received
3   Bonus issue of shares

A   1 only
B   2 only
C   3 only
D   None of them   **(2 marks)**

22.6 Which of the following assertions about statement of cash flows is/are correct?

1   A statement of cash flows prepared using the direct method produces a different figure for operating cash flow from that produced if the indirect method is used.

2   Rights issues of shares do not feature in statements of cash flows.

3   A surplus on revaluation of a non-current asset will not appear as an item in a statement of cash flows.

4   A profit on the sale of a non-current asset will appear as an item under Cash Flows from Investing Activities in a statement of cash flows.

A   1 and 4
B   2 and 3
C   3 only
D   2 and 4   **(2 marks)**

22.7 An extract from a statement of cash flows prepared by a trainee accountant is shown below.

Cash flows from operating activities

	$m
Net profit before taxation	28
Adjustments for: Depreciation	(9)
Operating profit before working capital changes	19
Decrease in inventories	13
Increase in receivables	(4)
Increase in payables	(8)
Cash generated from operations	10

Which of the following criticisms of this extract are correct?

1 Depreciation charges should have been added, not deducted
2 Decrease in inventories should have been deducted, not added.
3 Increase in receivables should have been added, not deducted.
4 Increase in payables should have been added, not deducted

A 2 and 4
B 2 and 3
C 1 and 3
D 1 and 4 **(2 marks)**

22.8 Which of the following items could appear in a company's statement of cash flows?

1 Proposed dividends
2 Rights issue of shares
3 Bonus issue of shares
4 Repayment of loan

A 1 and 3
B 2 and 4
C 1 and 4
D 2 and 3 **(2 marks)**

22.9 IAS 7 requires the statement of cash flows to open with the calculation of net cash from operating activities, arrived at by adjusting net profit before taxation.

Which one of the following lists consists only of items which could appear in such a calculation?

A Depreciation, increase in receivables, decrease in payables, proceeds from sale of equipment, increase in inventories

B Increase in payables, decrease in inventories, profit on sale of plant, depreciation, decrease in receivables

C Increase in payables, proceeds from sale of equipment, depreciation, decrease in receivables, increase in inventories

D Depreciation, interest paid, proceeds from sale of equipment, decrease in inventories. **(2 marks)**

22.10 The following extract is from the financial statements of Pompeii, a limited liability company at 31 October:

	20X9 $'000	20X8 $'000
Equity and liabilities		
Share capital	120	80
Share premium	60	40
Retained earnings	85	68
	265	188
Non-current liabilities		
Bank loan	100	150
	365	338

What is the cash flow from financing activities to be disclosed in the statement of cash flows for the year ended 31 October 20X9?

A $60,000 inflow
B $10,000 inflow
C $110,000 inflow
D $27,000 inflow   **(2 marks)**

22.11 A draft statement of cash flows contains the following calculation of cash flows from operating activities:

	$m
Profit before tax	13
Depreciation	2
Decrease in inventories	(3)
Decrease in trade and other receivables	5
Decrease in trade payables	4
Net cash inflow from operating activities	21

Which of the following corrections need to be made to the calculation?

1   Depreciation should be deducted, not added.
2   Decrease in inventories should be added, not deducted.
3   Decrease in receivables should be deducted, not added.
4   Decrease in payables should be deducted, not added.

A   1 and 3
B   2 and 3
C   1 and 4
D   2 and 4   **(2 marks)**

22.12 The following extract is taken from a draft version of company's statement of cash flows, prepared by a trainee accountant.

	$'000
Net cash flow from operating activities	
Profit before tax	484
Depreciation charges	327
Profit on sale of property, plant and equipment	35
Increase in inventories	(74)
Decrease in trade and other receivables	(41)
Increase in trade payables	29
Cash generated from operations	760

Four possible mistakes that may have been made by the trainee accountant are listed below.

1   The profit on sale of property, plant and equipment should be subtracted, not added.
2   The increase in inventories should be added, not subtracted.
3   The decrease in trade and other receivables should be added, not subtracted.
4   The increase in trade payables should be subtracted, not added.

Which of the four mistakes did the trainee accountant make when preparing the draft statement?

A   1 and 2 only
B   1 and 3 only
C   2 and 4 only
D   3 and 4 only   **(2 marks)**

22.13 Which, if any, of the following items could be included in 'cash flows from financing activities' in a statement of cash flows that complies with IAS7 *Statements of Cash Flows*?

1   Interest received
2   Taxation paid
3   Proceeds from sale of property

A   1 only
B   2 only
C   3 only
D   None of them   **(2 marks)**

22.14 Which one of the following statements is correct, with regard to the preparation of a statement of cash flows that complies with IAS7 *Statements of Cash Flows*?

A   A statement of cash flows prepared using the direct method produces the same figure for net cash from operating activities as a statement produced by the indirect method.

B   An increase in a bank overdraft during the accounting period is included within cash flows from financing activities.

C   A profit on the sale of equipment is included within cash flows from investing activities.

D   A surplus on the revaluation of property will appear within cash flows from investing activities.

(2 marks)

22.15 The following information is available about the plant, property and equipment of Lok Co, for the year to 31 December 20X3.

	$'000
Carrying value of assets at beginning of the year	462
Carrying value of assets at end of the year	633
Increase in revaluation reserve during the year	50
Disposals during the year, at cost	110
Accumulated depreciation on the assets disposed of	65
Depreciation charge for the year	38

What will be included in cash flows from investing activities for the year, in a statement of cash flows that complies with IAS7 *Statements of Cash Flows*?

A $104,000
B $159,000
C $166,000
D $204,000   **(2 marks)**

22.16 A company sold warehouse premises at a loss during a financial period. How would this transaction be included in a statement of cash flows for the period that complies with IAS7 *Statements of Cash Flows* and that uses the indirect method to present cash flows from operating activities?

	Loss on disposal	*Proceeds from sale*
A	Deduct as an adjustment in the calculation of cash flows from operating activities	Include in cash flows from investing activities
B	Deduct as an adjustment in the calculation of cash flows from operating activities	Include in cash flows from operating activities
C	Add as an adjustment in the calculation of cash flows from operating activities	Include in cash flows from investing activities
D	Add as an adjustment in the calculation of cash flows from operating activities	Include in cash flows from operating activities

(2 marks)

(Total = 32 marks)

Do you know? – Preparing simple consolidated financial statements

Check that you can fill in the blanks in the statements below before you attempt any questions. If in doubt, you should go back to your BPP Interactive Text and revise first.

- .... means presenting the results, assets and liabilities of a group of companies as if they were one company.

- A .... is an entity controlled by another entity.

- An .... is an entity over which another entity exerts significant influence.

- .... are accounted for in the consolidated statements of a group using the **e**......... method.

- A **t**......... **i**............ is a simple investment in the shares of another entity that is not an associate or a subsidiary.

- .... financial statements present the results of the **g**........., they do not replace the separate financial statements of the individual group companies.

- Basic consolidation consists of two procedures:

  - .... which appear as an asset in one company and a liability in another

  - then adding together all the .... assets and liabilities on a line by line basis.

- .... arising on consolidation is recognised as an .... asset in the consolidated statement of financial position.

- The **n**....-**c**............ **i**......... shows the extent to which net assets controlled by the group are owned by other parties.

- A consolidation adjustment is required to remove .... profit on intra-group trading and transfer of non-current assets.

- When a parent company acquires a subsidiary part way through the year, the profits for the period need to be apportioned between **p**..... and **p**...... acquisition. Only **p**..... acquisition profits are included in the group's consolidated statement of financial position.

- The .... statement of profit or loss is prepared by combining the statements of profit or loss of each group company on a line-by-line basis.

- Intra-group .... and .... are eliminated from the consolidated statement of profit or loss.

- If a .... is acquired during the year, only the post-acquisition element of statement of profit or loss balances are included on consolidation.

- The .... statement of ....is produced using the consolidated statement of profit or loss as a basis.

BPP
LEARNING MEDIA

Did you know? – Preparing simple consolidated financial statements

Could you fill in the blanks? The answers are in bold. Use this page for revision purposes as you approach the exam.

- **Consolidation** means presenting the results, assets and liabilities of a group of companies as if they were one company.

- A **subsidiary** is an entity controlled by another entity.

- An **associate** is an entity over which another entity exerts significant influence.

- **Associates** are accounted for in the consolidated statements of a group using the **equity** method.

- A **trade investment** is a simple investment in the shares of another entity that is not an associate or a subsidiary.

- **Consolidated** financial statements present the results of the **group**, they do not replace the separate financial statements of the individual group companies.

- Basic consolidation consists of two procedures:

    - **cancelling out items** which appear as an asset in one company and a liability in another
    - then adding together all the **uncancelled** assets and liabilities on a line by line basis.

- **Goodwill** arising on consolidation is recognised as an **intangible** asset in the consolidated statement of financial position.

- The **non-controlling interest** (**NCI**) shows the extent to which net assets controlled by the group are owned by other parties.

- A consolidation adjustment is required to remove **unrealised** profit on intra-group trading and transfer of non-current assets.

- When a parent company acquires a subsidiary part way through the year, the profits for the period need to be apportioned between **pre** and **post** acquisition. Only **post** acquisition profits are included in the group's consolidated statement of financial position.

- The **consolidated** statement of profit or loss is prepared by combining the statements of profit or loss of each group company on a line-by-line basis.

- Intra-group **sales** and **purchases** are eliminated from the consolidated statement of profit or loss.

- If a **subsidiary** is acquired during the year, only the post-acquisition element of statement of profit or loss balances are included on consolidation.

- The **consolidated** statement of **profit or loss** and other comprehensive income is produced using the consolidated statement of profit or loss as a basis.

23 | 15 mark questions: preparing simple consolidated financial statements | 72 mins

23.1 Swing and Cat

Swing purchased 80% of Cat's equity on 1 January 20X8 for $120,000 when Cat's retained earnings were $50,000. The fair value of the non-controlling interest on that date was $40,000. During the year, Swing sold goods which cost $80,000 to Cat, at an invoiced cost of $100,000. Cat had 50% of the goods still in inventories at the year end. The two companies' draft financial statements as at 31 December 20X8 are shown below.

STATEMENTS OF PROFIT OR LOSS FOR THE YEAR ENDED 31 DECEMBER 20X8

	Swing $'000	Cat $'000
Revenue	5,000	1,000
Cost of sales	2,900	600
Gross profit	2,100	400
Other expenses	1,700	320
Net profit	400	80
Income tax	130	25
Profit for the year	270	55

STATEMENTS OF FINANCIAL POSITION AT 31 DECEMBER 20X8

	Swing $'000	Cat $'000
Non-current assets		
Investment in Cat	120	-
Tangible non-current assets	1,880	200
	2,000	200
Current assets		
Inventory	500	120
Trade receivables	650	40
Bank and cash	390	35
	1,540	195
	3,540	395
Equity and liabilities		
Equity		
Share capital	2,000	100
Retained earnings	400	200
	2,400	300
Current liabilities		
Trade payables	910	30
Tax	230	65
	1,140	95
	3,540	395

Required

Prepare the draft consolidated statement of profit or loss and draft consolidated statement of financial position for the Swing group at 31 December 20X8. **(15 marks)**

23.2 Black and Bury

The following are the financial statements relating to Black, a limited liability company, and its subsidiary company Bury.

STATEMENTS OF PROFIT OR LOSS
FOR THE YEAR ENDED 31 OCTOBER 20X5

	Black	Bury
	$'000	$'000
Sales revenue	245,000	95,000
Cost of sales	(140,000)	(52,000)
Gross profit	105,000	43,000
Distribution costs	(12,000)	(10,000)
Administrative expenses	(55,000)	(13,000)
Dividend income from Bury	7,000	–
Profit before tax	45,000	20,000
Tax	(13,250)	(5,000)
Profit for the year	31,750	15,000

STATEMENTS OF FINANCIAL POSITION
AS AT 31 OCTOBER 20X5

	Black		Bury	
	$'000	$'000	$'000	$'000
Assets				
Non-current assets				
Property, plant and equipment		110,000		40,000
Investments				
21,000,000 $1 ordinary shares in Bury at cost		21,000		–
		131,000		40,000
Current assets				
Inventory, at cost	13,360		3,890	
Trade receivables and dividend receivable	14,640		6,280	
Bank	3,500		2,570	
Total assets		31,500		12,740
		162,500		52,740
Equity and liabilities				
Equity				
$1 Ordinary shares		100,000		30,000
Retained earnings		33,500		10,280
		133,500		40,280
Current liabilities				
Payables	9,000		2,460	
Dividend	20,000		10,000	
Total equity and liabilities		29,000		12,460
		162,500		52,740

Additional information

(a)   Black purchased its $1 ordinary shares in Bury on 1 November 20X0. At that date the balance on Bury's retained earnings was $2 million. The fair value of the non-controlling interest at the date of acquisition was $11,800,000.

(b)   During the year ended 31 October 20X5 Black sold goods which originally cost $12 million to Bury. Black invoiced Bury at cost plus 40%. Bury still has 30% of these goods in inventory at 31 October 20X5.

(c)   Bury owed Black $1.5 million at 31 October 20X5 for some of the goods Black supplied during the year.

Required

(a)   Calculate the goodwill arising on the acquisition of Bury.   (3 marks)

(b)   Prepare the following financial statements for Black.

    (i)   The consolidated statement of profit or loss for the year ended 31 October 20X5.

                                                                         (6 marks)

    (ii)   The consolidated statement of financial position as at 31 October 20X5.   (6 marks)

Disclosure notes are not required.   **(15 marks)**

23.3 Prestend

Prestend is the parent company of Northon. The following are the statements of financial position for both companies as at 31 October 20X7.

	Prestend		Northon	
	$'000	$'000	$'000	$'000
Assets				
Non-current assets				
Property, plant and equipment		4,200		3,300
Investments: shares in Northon at cost		3,345		–
Current assets				
Inventory	1,500		800	
Receivables	1,800		750	
Bank	600		350	
		3,900		1,900
Total assets		11,445		5,200
Equity and liabilities				
Equity				
$1 ordinary shares		9,000		4,000
Retained earnings		525		200
		9,525		4,200
Current liabilities				
Payables		1,220		200
Tax		700		800
Total equity and liabilities		11,445		5,200

The following information is also available.

(a)   Prestend purchased 2,800,000 shares in Northon a year ago when Northon had retained earnings of $60,000. The fair value of the non-controlling interest at the date of acquisition was $1,415,000.

(b)   During the year Prestend sold goods with an invoice value of $240,000 to Northon. These goods were invoiced at cost plus 20%. Half of the goods are still in Northon's inventory at the year end.

(c)   Northon owes Prestend $30,000 at 31 October 20X7 for goods it purchased during the year.

Required

(a)   Calculate the goodwill on acquisition.   (5 marks)

(b)   Prepare the consolidated statement of financial position for the Prestend group as at 31 October 20X7.

    Note. A working should be included for group retained earnings. Disclosure notes are not required.

                                                                     (10 marks)

                                                                            (15 marks)

23.4 Liverton and Everpool

The summarised statements of profit or loss of two companies, Liverton and Everpool, for the year ended 31 May 20X6 are provided below. Liverton acquired 3,000,000 ordinary shares in Everpool for $3,500,000 on 1 June 20X4. At that time, the retained earnings of Everpool were $200,000 and the fair value of the non-controlling interest in Everpool was $1,000,000.

STATEMENTS OF PROFIT OR LOSS FOR THE YEAR ENDED 31 MAY 20X6

	Liverton	Everpool
	$'000	$'000
Sales revenue	6,400	2,600
Cost of sales	(3,700)	(1,450)
Gross profit	2,700	1,150
Distribution costs	(1,100)	(490)
Administrative expenses	(700)	(320)
Profit from operations	900	340
Dividends received from Everpool	150	–
Profit before tax	1,050	340
Tax	(400)	(80)
Profit for the year	650	260

The following information is also available.

(a)   Everpool's total share capital consists of 4,000,000 ordinary shares of $1 each.

(b)   During the year ended 31 May 20X6 Liverton sold goods costing $110,000 to Everpool for $200,000. At 31 May 20X6, 60% of these goods remained in Everpool's inventory.

Required

(a)   Calculate the total goodwill arising on the acquisition of Everpool.   (5 marks)
(b)   Prepare the consolidated statement of profit or loss for Liverton for the year ended 31 May 20X6.
                                                                                            (10 marks)

                                                                                     (15 marks)

                                                                            (Total = 60 marks)

---

24   Consolidated financial statements   58 mins

The following information is relevant for questions 24.1 to 24.3

On 1 January 20X0 Alpha Co purchased 90,000 ordinary $1 shares in Beta Co for $270,000. At that date Beta Co's retained earnings amounted to $90,000 and the fair values of Beta Co's assets at acquisition were equal to their book values.

Three years later, on 31 December 20X2, the statements of financial position of the two companies were:

	Alpha Co	Beta Co
	$	$
Sundry net assets	230,000	260,000
Shares in Beta	180,000	–
	410,000	260,000
Share capital		
Ordinary shares of $1 each	200,000	100,000
Retained earnings	210,000	160,000
	410,000	260,000

The share capital of Beta Co has remained unchanged since 1 January 20X0. The fair value of the non-controlling interest at acquisition was $42,000.

24.1 What amount should appear in the group's consolidated statement of financial position at 31 December 20X2 for goodwill?

    A $52,000
    B $80,000
    C $122,000
    D $212,000   **(2 marks)**

24.2 What amount should appear in the group's consolidated statement of financial position at 31 December 20X2 for non-controlling interest?

    A $49,000
    B $58,000
    C $51,000
    D $42,000   **(2 marks)**

24.3 What amount should appear in the group's consolidated statement of financial position at 31 December 20X2 for retained earnings?

    A $280,000
    B $291,000
    C $354,000
    D $273,000   **(2 marks)**

24.4 Which of the following companies are subsidiaries of Gamma Co?

Zeta Co: Gamma Co owns 51% of the non-voting preference shares of Zeta Co Iota Co: Gamma Co has 3 representatives on the board of directors of Iota Co. Each director can cast 10 votes each out of the total of 40 votes at board meetings.

Kappa Co: Gamma Co owns 75% of the ordinary share capital of Kappa Co, however Kappa Cois located overseas and is subject to tax in that country.

    A   Zeta Co, Iota Co and Kappa Co
    B   Zeta Co and Kappa Co
    C   Iota Co and Kappa Co
    D   Zeta Co and Iota Co   **(2 marks)**

The following information is relevant for questions 24.5 and 24.6

Hilton Co acquired 80% of the share capital of Shrew Co on 1 January 20X3 for $280,000.

The statements of financial position of the two companies at 31 December 20X3 were as follows:

STATEMENTS OF FINANCIAL POSITION

	Hilton Co $	Shrew Co $
Sundry assets	660,000	290,000
Investment in Shrew	280,000	–
	940,000	290,000
Issued share capital	400,000	140,000
Share premium account	320,000	50,000
Retained earnings		
As at 1 Jan 20X3	140,000	60,000
Profit for 20X3	80,000	40,000
	940,000	290,000

There have been no changes in the share capital or share premium account of either company since 1 January 20X3. The fair value of the non-controlling interest on acquisition was $65,000.

24.5 What figure for goodwill on consolidation should appear in the consolidated statement of financial position of the Hilton group at 31 December 20X3?

A $30,000
B $55,000
C $95,000
D $(10,000)   (2 marks)

24.6 What figure for non-controlling interest should appear in the consolidated statement of financial position of the Hilton group at 31 December 20X3?

A $77,000
B $85,000
C $73,000
D $105,000   (2 marks)

24.7 Fanta Co acquired 100% of the ordinary share capital of Tizer Co on 1 October 20X7.

On 31 December 20X7 the share capital and retained earnings of Tizer Co were as follows:

	$'000
Ordinary shares of $1 each	400
Retained earnings at 1 January 20X7	100
Retained profit for the year ended 31 December 20X7	80
	580

The profits of Tizer Co have accrued evenly throughout 20X7. Goodwill arising on the acquisition of Tizer Co was $30,000.

What was the cost of the investment in Tizer Co?

A $400,000
B $580,000
C $610,000
D $590,000   (2 marks)

24.8 Evergreen Co owns 35% of the ordinary shares of Deciduous Co. What is the correct accounting treatment of the revenues and costs of Deciduous Co for reporting period in the consolidated statement of profit or loss of the Evergreen group?

A   The revenues and costs of Deciduous Co are added to the revenues and costs of Evergreen on a line by line basis.

B   35% of the profit after tax of Deciduous Co should be added to Evergreen's consolidated profit before tax.

C   35% of the revenues and costs of Deciduous Co are added to the revenues and costs of Evergreen on a line by line basis.

D   The revenues and costs of Deciduous Co are added to the revenues and costs of Evergreen Co on a line by line basis, then 65% of the profit after tax is deducted so that only Evergreen Co's share remains in the consolidated accounts.   (2 marks)

24.9 Mercedes Co has owned 100% of Benz Co since incorporation. At 31 March 20X9 extracts from their individual statements of financial position were as follows.

	Mercedes Co	Benz Co
	$	$
Share capital	100,000	50,000
Retained earnings	450,000	120,000
	550,000	170,000

During the year ended 31 March 20X9, Benz Co had sold goods to Mercedes Co for $50,000. Mercedes Co still had these goods in inventory at the year end. Benz Co uses a 25% mark up on all goods.

What were the consolidated retained earnings of Mercedes Group at 31 March 20X9?

A $560,000
B $580,000
C $570,000
D $557,500 **(2 marks)**

24.10 Micro Co acquired 90% of the $100,000 ordinary share capital of Minnie Co for $300,000 on 1 January 20X9 when the retained earnings of Minnie Co were $156,000. At the date of acquisition the fair value of plant held by Minnie Co was $20,000 higher than its carrying value. The fair value of the non-controlling interest at the date of acquisition was $75,000.

What is the goodwill arising on the acquisition of Minnie Co?

A $119,000
B $99,000
C $139,000
D $24,000 **(2 marks)**

24.11 On 1 April 20X7 Possum Co acquired 60% of the share capital of Koala Co for $120,000. During the year Possum Co sold goods to Koala Co for $30,000, including a profit margin of 25%. 40% of these goods were still in inventory at the year end.

The following extract was taken from the financial statements of Possum Co and Koala Co at 31 March 20X8.

	Possum Co	Koala Co
	$'000	$'000
Revenue	750	400
Cost of sales	(420)	(100)
Gross profit	330	300

What is the consolidated gross profit of the Possum group at 31 March 20X8?

A $627,600
B $633,000
C $622,500
D $627,000 **(2 marks)**

24.12 Which of the following statements is/are incorrect?

1   A Co owns 25% of the ordinary share capital of B Co, which means that B Co is an associate of A Co.

2   C Co can appoint 4 out of 6 directors to the board of D Co, which means that C Co has control over D Co.

3   E Co has the power to govern the financial and operating policies of F Co, which means that F Co is an associate of E Co.

4   G Co owns 19% of the share capital of H Co, but by agreement with the majority shareholder, has control over the financial and operating policies of H Co, so H Co is an associate of G Co.

A   1 and 2 only
B   1, 2 and 3 only
C   3 and 4 only
D   4 only   **(2 marks)**

24.13 Clementine Co has owned 21% of the ordinary shares of Tangerine Co for several years. Clementine Co does not have any investments in any other companies. How should the investment in Tangerine Co be reflected in the financial statements of Clementine Co?

A   The revenues and costs and assets and liabilities of Tangerine Co are added to the revenues and costs and assets and liabilities of Clementine Co on a line by line basis.

B   An amount is shown in the statement of financial position for 'investment in associate' being the original cost paid for the investment plus Clementine Co's share of the profit after tax of Tangerine Co. 21% of the profit after tax of Tangerine Co should be added to Clementine Co's profit before tax in the statement of profit or loss each year.

C   An amount is shown in the statement of financial position under 'investments' being the original cost paid for the investment, this amount does not change. Dividends received from Tangerine are recognised in the statement of profit or loss of Clementine Co.

D   An amount is shown in the statement of financial position under 'investments' being the original cost paid for the investment, this amount does not change. 21% of the profit after tax of Tangerine Co should be added to Clementine Co's profit after tax in the statement of profit or loss each year.

        (2 marks)

24.14 Which of the following statements relating to parent companies and subsidiaries are correct?

1   A parent company could consolidate a company in which it holds less than 50% of the ordinary share capital in certain circumstances.

2   Goodwill on consolidation will appear as an item in the parent company's individual statement of financial position.

3   Consolidated financial statements ignore the legal form of the relationship between parents and subsidiaries and present the results and position of the group as if it was a single entity.

A   1 and 2 only
B   1 and 3 only
C   2 and 3 only
D   3 only   **(2 marks)**

24.15 P Co, the parent company of a group, owns shares in three other companies. P Co's holdings are:

Q   Shares giving control of 60% of the voting rights in Q Co

R   Shares giving control of 20% of the voting rights in R Co. P Co also has the right to appoint or remove all the directors of R Co

S   Shares giving control of 10% of the voting rights in S Co, plus 90% of the non-voting preference shares

Which of these companies are subsidiaries of P Co?

A   Q Co, R Co and S Co
B   Q Co and S Co only
C   R Co and S Co only
D   Q Co and R Co only   **(2 marks)**

24.16 Which of the following should be accounted for in the consolidated financial statements of Company A using equity accounting?

1   An investment in 51% of the ordinary shares of W Co

2   An investment in 20% of the preference (non-voting) shares of X Co

3   An investment in 33% of the ordinary shares of Y Co

4   An investment in 20% of the ordinary shares of Z Co, and an agreement with other shareholders to appoint the majority of the directors to the board of Z Co

A   1 and 4 only
B   2 only
C   3 only
D   3 and 4 only   **(2 marks)**

24.17 Breakspear Co purchased 600,000 of the voting equity shares of Fleet Co when the value of the non-controlling interest in Fleet Co is $150,000.

The following information relates to Fleet at the acquisition date.

	At acquisition $'000
Share capital, $0.5 ordinary shares	500
Retained earnings	150
Revaluation surplus	50
	700

The goodwill arising on acquisition is $70,000. What was the consideration paid by Breakspear Co for the investment in Fleet Co?

A $420,000
B $770,000
C $620,000
D $570,000   **(2 marks)**

24.18 Date Co owns 100% of the ordinary share capital of Prune Co. The following balances relate to Prune Co.

	At acquisition $'000	At 31.12.X8 $'000
Tangible non-current assets		
Freehold land	500	500
Plant and equipment	350	450
	850	950

At acquisition, the fair value of Prune Co's land was $50,000 more than shown in the financial statements of Prune Co. At 31 December 20X8, Date Co's financial statements show a total tangible non-current asset balance of $1,250,000.

What amount should be included in the consolidated financial statements of the Date group at 31 December 20X8 for tangible non-current assets?

A $2,250,000
B $1,000,000
C $1,850,000
D $2,200,000   **(2 marks)**

24.19 Six Co owns 80% of the equity share capital of Seven Co. At 31 December 20X4, the trade receivables and trade payables of the two companies were as follows:

	Six Co	Seven Co
Trade receivables	$64,000	$39,000
Trade payables	$37,000	$48,000

These figures include $30,000 that is owed by Seven Co to Six Co for the purchase of goods, for which Six Co has not yet paid. These goods were sold by Six Co for a profit of $15,000 and 50% of them were still held as inventory by Seven Co at 31 December 20X4.

What should be the amounts for trade receivables and trade payables in the consolidated statement of financial position as at 31 December 20X4?

A   Trade receivables $73,000, Trade payables $55,000
B   Trade receivables $88,000, Trade payables $70,000
C   Trade receivables $95,000, Trade payables $77,000
D   Trade receivables $103,000, Trade payables $85,000   **(2 marks)**

24.20 Tempo Co acquired 100% of the equity shares capital of Lento Co. This consisted of 40,000 shares of $0.50 each. It paid for the acquisition by issuing 60,000 new shares of $1 each in Tempo Co, and exchanging three new shares in Tempo Co for every 2 shares in Lento Co.

The market value of Tempo Co shares at the time of the acquisition was $3.50 per share. The fair value of the net assets acquired in Lento Co was $50,000.

What was the goodwill arising on the acquisition of the shares in Lento Co by Tempo Co?

A $10,000
B $40,000
C $140,000
D $160,000   **(2 marks)**

24.21 Donna Co acquired 80% of the equity share capital of Blitsen Co on 1 January 20X4 when the retained earnings of Blitsen Co were $40,000. The fair value of the non-controlling interest at this date was $25,000. At 31 December 20X4, the equity capital of Blitsen Co was as follows:

	$'000
Share capital	40
Share premium	10
Retained earnings	60
	110

During the year Blitsen Co sold goods to Donna Co for $20,000. This price included a mark-up of $12,000 for profit. At 31 December 20X4, 50% of these goods remained unsold in the inventory of Donna Co.

What is the value of the non-controlling interest in the Donna Group at 31 December 20X4, for the purpose of preparing the consolidated statement of financial position?

A $20,800
B $27,800
C $26,600
D $29,000 **(2 marks)**

24.22 Volcano Co acquired 75% of the equity share capital of Lava Co on 1 September 20X3. The retained profits of the two individual companies at the beginning and end of their financial year were as follows.

	Volcano Co	Lava Co
	$'000	$'000
Retained earnings at 1 January 20X3	596	264
Retained earnings at 31 December 20X3	650	336

What is the parent company's share of consolidated retained earnings that should be reported in the consolidated statement of financial position of the Volcano Group at 31 December 20X3?

A $668,000
B $674,000
C $704,000
D $722,000 **(2 marks)**

24.23 Tin Co acquired 90% of the equity share capital of Drum Co on 1 April 20X3. The following information relates to the financial year to 31 December 20X3 for each company.

	Tin Co	Drum Co
	$'000	$'000
Retained earnings at 1 January 20X3	840	170
Profit for the year	70	60
Retained earnings at 31 December 20X3	910	230

Neither company paid any dividends during the year.

What profit is attributable to the parent company in the consolidated statement of profit or loss of the Tin Group for the year to 31 December 20X3?

A $83,500
B $110,500
C $115,000
D $124,000 **(2 marks)**

FFA/F3 FINANCIAL ACCOUNTING

24.24 Sand Co acquired 80% of the equity share capital of Sun Co several years ago. In the year to 31 December 20X4, Sand Co made a profit after taxation of $120,000 and Sun Co made a profit after taxation of $35,000. During the year Sun Co sold goods to Sand Co at a price of $40,000. The profit mark-up was 40% on the sales price. At 31 December 20X4, 25% of these goods were still held in the inventory of Sand Co.

What profit is attributable to the parent company in the consolidated statement of profit or loss of the Sand Group for the year to 31 December 20X4?

A $144,000
B $148,000
C $144,800
D $151,000

(2 marks)

(Total = 48 marks)

LEARNING MEDIA

Do you know? – Interpretation of financial statements

Check that you can fill in the blanks in the statements below before you attempt any questions. If in doubt, you should go back to your BPP Interactive Text and revise first.

- Users of financial statements can gain a better understanding of the **s**.............. of the information in financial statements by comparing it with other **r**.............. information.

- Ratios provide information through ....

- **P**.................. ratios include:

    –   Return on capital employed
    –   Net .... as a percentage of sales
    –   .... turnover ratio
    –   **G**......... profit as a percentage of sales

- Liquidity and working capital ratios include:

    –   .... ratio
    –   .... ratio
    –   Accounts .... collection period
    –   Accounts .... payment period
    –   .... inventory .... period

- Debt and **g**.................. /leverage ratios include:

    –   Debt ratios
    –   **G**................. ratio/leverage
    –   **I**................. cover

Did you know? – Interpretation of financial statements

Could you fill in the blanks? The answers are in bold. Use this page for revision purposes as you approach the exam.

- Users of financial statements can gain a better understanding of the **significance** of the information in financial statements by comparing it with other **relevant** information.

- Ratios provide information through **comparison**.

- **Profitability** ratios include:

  - Return on capital employed
  - Net **profit** as a percentage of sales
  - **Asset** turnover ratio
  - **Gross** profit as a percentage of sales

- Liquidity and working capital ratios include:

  - **Current** ratio
  - **Quick** ratio
  - Accounts **receivable** collection period
  - Accounts **payable** payment period
  - **Average** inventory **turnover** period

- Debt and **gearing**/leverage ratios include:

  - Debt ratios
  - **Gearing** ratio/leverage
  - **Interest** cover

25 15 mark question: interpretation of financial statements 18 mins

25.1 Binky and Smokey

Two companies Binky and Smokey trade in the same market. Their financial statements for the year ended 31 October 20X6 are summarised below:

STATEMENTS OF PROFIT OR LOSS FOR THE YEAR ENDED 31 OCTOBER 20X6

	Binky		Smokey	
	$'000	$'000	$'000	$'000
Sales revenue		284		305
Cost of sales		(155)		(151)
Gross profit		129		154
Expenses				
Administrative	24		37	
Selling and distribution	35		53	
Depreciation	9		12	
Loan note interest	–		5	
		(68)		(107)
Net profit		61		47

STATEMENTS OF FINANCIAL POSITION AS AT 31 OCTOBER 20X6

	Binky		Smokey	
Assets	$'000	$'000	$'000	$'000
Non-current assets				
At cost	320		515	
Accumulated depreciation	(75)		(96)	
		245		419
Current assets				
Inventory	91		293	
Receivables	46		75	
Bank	64		15	
		201		383
		446		802
Equity and liabilities				
Share capital and reserves				
Share capital		150		250
Retained earnings		108		177
10% Loan note		–		50
Current liabilities		188		325
Total equity and liabilities		446		802

Required

(a) Calculate the following ratios for Binky and Smokey:

(State the formulae used for calculating the ratios.)

Profitability ratios
Gross profit percentage
Net profit percentage
Asset turnover ratio

Liquidity ratios
Current ratio
Quick ratio (acid test ratio)
Receivables collection period (6 marks)

(b)   Compare and comment on the performance of the companies as indicated by the ratios you have
        calculated in part (a).   (9 marks)

                                                                                            (15 marks)

26 Interpretation of financial statements   31 mins

26.1   Which one of the following would help a company with high gearing to reduce its gearing ratio?

        A   Making a rights issue of equity shares
        B   Issuing further long-term loan notes
        C   Making a bonus issue of shares
        D   Paying dividends on its equity shares   **(2 marks)**

26.2   Which one of the following would cause a company's gross profit percentage on sales to fall?

        A   Sales volume has declined.
        B   Closing inventory is lower than opening inventory.
        C   Some closing inventory items were included at less than cost.
        D   Selling and distribution costs have risen.   **(2 marks)**

26.3   A company's gross profit as a percentage of sales increased from 24% in the year ended 31 December
        20X1 to 27% in the year ended 31 December 20X2.

        Which of the following events is most likely to have caused the increase?

        A   An increase in sales volume
        B   A purchase in December 20X1 mistakenly being recorded as happening in January 20X2
        C   Overstatement of the closing inventory at 31 December 20X1
        D   Understatement of the closing inventory at 31 December 20X1   **(2 marks)**

26.4   Which of the following transactions would result in an increase in capital employed?

        A   Selling inventory at a profit
        B   Writing off a bad debt
        C   Paying a payable in cash
        D   Increasing the bank overdraft to purchase a non-current asset   **(2 marks)**

26.5   From the following information regarding the year to 31 August 20X6, what is the accounts payable
        payment period? You should calculate the ratio using purchases as the denominator.

	$
Sales	43,000
Cost of sales	32,500
Opening inventory	6,000
Closing inventory	3,800
Trade accounts payable at 31 August 20X6	4,750

        A   40 days
        B   50 days
        C   53 days
        D   57 days   **(2 marks)**

26.6 The draft statement of financial position of B at 31 March 20X8 is set out below.

	$	$
Non-current assets		450
Current assets: Inventory	65	
Receivables	110	
Prepayments	30	
	205	
Current liabilities: Payables	30	
Bank overdraft (Note)	50	
	80	
		125
		575
Non-current liability: Loan		(75)
		500
Ordinary share capital		400
Statement of profit or loss		100
		500

Note: The bank overdraft first occurred on 30 September 20X7.

What is the gearing of the company? You should calculate gearing using capital employed as the denominator.

A   13%
B   16%
C   20%
D   24%   **(2 marks)**

26.7 Which of the following is *not* a ratio which is used to explain how well the operations of a business have been managed?

A   Asset turnover
B   Profit margin
C   Gearing
D   Return on capital employed   **(2 marks)**

26.8 An increase in selling prices may lead to which of the following effects?

A   Asset turnover will increase
B   Profit margins will fall
C   Profit margins may increase subject to a fall in asset turnover
D   Return on capital employed will increase   **(2 marks)**

26.9 A business operates on a gross profit margin of $33^1/_3$%. Gross profit on a sale was $800, and expenses were $680.

What is the net profit margin?

A   3.75%
B   5%
C   11.25%
D   22.67%   **(2 marks)**

26.10 Which of the following would cause a company's gearing ratio to rise?

A   A decrease in long-term loans is *less* than a decrease in shareholders' funds
B   A decrease in long-term loans is *more* than a decrease in shareholders' funds
C   Interest rates rose
D   Dividends were paid   **(2 marks)**

26.11 A company has the following details extracted from its statement of financial position:

	$'000
Inventories	1,900
Receivables	1,000
Bank overdraft	100
Payables	1,000

Which of the following could describe the company's liquidity position?

A   Very well-controlled because its current assets far outweigh its current liabilities

B   Poorly-controlled because its quick assets are less than its current liabilities

C   Poorly-controlled because its current ratio is significantly higher than the industry norm of 1.8

D   Poorly-controlled because it has a bank overdraft   **(2 marks)**

26.12 A company sells large, expensive items of plant and consequently has a slow inventory turnover. The company has the following current assets and liabilities at 31 October 20X8:

		$'000
Current assets	inventory	970
	receivables	380
	bank	40
		1,390
Current liabilities	payables	420

When measured against accepted 'norms', which of the following is correct?

A   The company can be said to have a high current ratio and an ideal acid test ratio.

B   The company can be said to have an ideal current ratio and a low acid test ratio.

C   The company can be said to have a high current ratio and a low acid test ratio.

D   The company can be said to have ideal current and acid test ratios.   **(2 marks)**

26.13 Why is analysis of financial statements carried out?

A   So that the analyst can determine a company's accounting policies

B   So that the significance of financial statements can be better understood through comparisons with historical performance and with other companies

C   To get back to the 'real' underlying figures, without the numbers being skewed by the requirements of International Financial Reporting Standards

D   To produce a report that can replace the financial statements, so that the financial statements no longer need to be looked at   **(2 marks)**

(Total = 26 marks)

27 Mixed bank 1   48 mins

27.1 The following information is available for a sole trader who keeps no accounting records:

	$
Net business assets at 1 July 20X4	186,000
Net business assets at 30 June 20X5	274,000

During the year ended 30 June 20X5:

	$
Cash drawings by proprietor	68,000
Additional capital introduced by proprietor	50,000
Business cash used to buy a car for the proprietor's wife, who takes no part in the business	20,000

Using this information, what is the trader's profit for the year ended 30 June 20X5?

A $126,000
B $50,000
C $86,000
D $90,000   **(2 marks)**

27.2 Evon, a limited liability company, issued 1,000,000 ordinary shares of 25 cents each at a price of $1.10 per share, all received in cash.

What should be the accounting entries to record this issue?

A	Debit:	Cash	$1,100,000
	Credit:	Share capital	$250,000
	Credit:	Share premium	$850,000

B	Debit:	Share capital	$250,000
	Debit:	Share premium	$850,000
	Credit:	Cash	$1,100,000

C	Debit:	Cash	$1,100,000
	Credit:	Share capital	$1,100,000

D	Debit:	Cash	$1,100,000
	Credit:	Share capital	$250,000
	Credit:	Retained earnings	$850,000

                                       (2 marks)

27.3 Which of the following statements apply when producing a consolidated statement of financial position?

(i)   All inter-company balances should be eliminated.
(ii)   Inter-company profit in year-end inventory should be eliminated.
(iii)   Closing inventory held by subsidiaries needs to be included at fair value.

A   (i) only
B   (i), (ii) and (iii)
C   (i) and (ii) only
D   (iii) only   **(2 marks)**

27.4 At 1 July 20X4 a limited liability company's capital structure was as follows:

	$
Share capital 1,000,000 shares of 50c each	500,000
Share premium account	400,000

In the year ended 30 June 20X5 the company made the following share issues:

1 January 20X5:

A bonus issue of one share for every four in issue at that date, using the share premium account.

1 April 20X5

A rights issue of one share for every ten in issue at that date, at $1.50 per share.

What will be the balances on the company's share capital and share premium accounts at 30 June 20X5 as a result of these issues?

	Share capital	Share premium account
	$	$
A	687,500	650,000
B	675,000	375,000
C	687,500	150,000
D	687,500	400,000

(2 marks)

27.5 Which of the following journal entries are correct, according to their narratives?

		Dr	Cr
		$	$
1	Suspense account	18,000	
	Rent received account		18,000
	Correction of error in posting $24,000 cash received for rent to the rent received account as $42,000		
2	B receivables ledger account	22,000	
	A receivables ledger account		22,000
	Correction of error: cash received from A wrongly entered to B's account		
3	Share premium account	400,000	
	Share capital account		400,000
	1 for 3 bonus issue on share capital of 1,200,000 50c shares		
4	Shares in X	750,000	
	Share capital account		250,000
	Share premium account		500,000
	500,000 50c shares issued at $1.50 per share in exchange for shares in X		

A   1 and 3
B   2 and 3
C   1 and 4
D   2 and 4

(2 marks)

27.6 The receivables ledger control account below contains several incorrect entries.

RECEIVABLES LEDGER CONTROL ACCOUNT

	$		$
Opening balance	138,400	Credit sales	80,660
		Contras against credit balances	
		in payables ledger	1,000
Cash received from credit customers	78,420	Discounts allowed to credit customers	1,950
		Irrecoverable debts written off	3,000
		Dishonoured cheques from credit	
		customers	850
		Closing balance	129,360
	216,820		216,820

What should the closing balance be when all the errors are corrected?

- A $133,840
- B $135,540
- C $137,740
- D $139,840 **(2 marks)**

27.7 A limited liability company's trial balance does not balance. The totals are:

Debit $384,030
Credit $398,580

A suspense account is opened for the difference.

Which of the following pairs of errors could clear the balance on the suspense account when corrected?

- A   Debit side of cash book undercast by $10,000; $6,160 paid for rent correctly entered in the cash book but entered in the rent account as $1,610.

- B   Debit side of cash book overcast by $10,000; $1,610 paid for rent correctly entered in the cash book but entered in the rent account as $6,160.

- C   Debit side of cash book undercast by $10,000; $1,610 paid for rent correctly entered in the cash book but entered in the rent account as $6,160.

- D   Debit side of cash book overcast by $10,000; $6,160 paid for rent correctly entered in the cash book but entered in the rent account as $1,610. **(2 marks)**

27.8 Which of the following items could appear in a company's statement of cash flows?

- (i)   Surplus on revaluation of non-current assets
- (ii)   Repayment of long-term borrowing
- (iii) Bonus issue of shares
- (iv)   Interest received

- A   (i) and (ii)
- B   (iii) and (iv)
- C   (i) and (iii)
- D   (ii) and (iv) **(2 marks)**

27.9 The following information is available for Orset, a sole trader who does not keep full accounting records:

	$
Inventory 1 July 20X4	138,600
30 June 20X5	149,100
Purchases made for year ended 30 June 20X5	716,100

Orset makes a standard gross profit of 30 percent on sales.

Based on these figures, what is Orset's sales figure for the year ended 30 June 20X5?

A $2,352,000
B $1,038,000
C $917,280
D $1,008,000   **(2 marks)**

27.10 At 1 July 20X4 a company had prepaid insurance of $8,200. On 1 January 20X5 the company paid $38,000 for insurance for the year to 30 September 20X5.

What figures should appear for insurance in the company's financial statements for the year ended 30 June 20X5?

	SPLOCI	SOFP
A	$27,200	Prepayment $19,000
B	$39,300	Prepayment $9,500
C	$36,700	Prepayment $9,500
D	$55,700	Prepayment $9,500

(2 marks)

27.11 Which of the following statements are correct?

(i)   A liability is a present obligation, arising from past events, the settlement of which is expected to result in an outflow of economic resources.

(ii)   An uncertain liability may be called a provision.

(iii) A contingent liability is recognised in the financial statements.

A   (i) only
B   (i) and (ii) only
C   (ii) and (iii) only
D   (i), (ii) and (iii)   **(2 marks)**

27.12 Alpha buys goods from Beta. At 30 June 20X5 Beta's account in Alpha's records showed $5,700 owing to Beta. Beta submitted a statement to Alpha as at the same date showing a balance due of $5,200.

Which one of the following could account fully for the difference?

A   Alpha has sent a cheque to Beta for $500 which has not yet been received by Beta.
B   The credit side of Beta's account in Alpha's records has been undercast by $500.
C   An invoice for $250 from Beta has been treated in Alpha's records as if it had been a credit note.
D   Beta has issued a credit note for $500 to Alpha which Alpha has not yet received.

(2 marks)

27.13 Which of the following statements about intangible assets are correct?

1　　If certain criteria are met, research expenditure must be recognised as an intangible asset.

2　　The notes to the financial statements should disclose the gross carrying amount and the accumulated amortisation at the beginning and the end of the period for each class of intangible asset.

3　　Intangible assets must be amortised over their useful life.

A　　2 and 3 only
B　　1 and 3 only
C　　1 and 2 only
D　　All three statements are correct.　　　　　　　　　　　　　　**(2 marks)**

27.14 Which of the following material events that took place after the reporting date, but before the financial statements were approved, are non-adjusting when applying IAS 10 *Events after the reporting period*?

(i)　　Inventory held at the reporting date was sold for less than cost.

(ii)　　Capital raised by issuing shares at a premium.

(iii)　　A company reorganisation which results in discontinuing a line of activity producing 25% of its profit.

(iv)　　The settlement of a claim for compensation from a former employee wrongly dismissed just before the reporting date.

A　　(i) and (ii)
B　　(i), (iii) and (iv)
C　　(i) and (iii) only
D　　(ii) and (iii)　　　　　　　　　　　　　　　　　　　　**(2 marks)**

27.15 A company sublets part of its office accommodation. In the year ended 30 June 20X5 cash received from tenants was $83,700.

Details of rent in arrears and in advance at the beginning and end of the year were:

	In arrears	In advance
	$	$
30 June 20X4	3,800	2,400
30 June 20X5	4,700	3,000

All arrears of rent were subsequently received.

What figure for rental income should be included in the company's statement of profit or loss for the year ended 30 June 20X5?

A　　$84,000
B　　$83,400
C　　$80,600
D　　$85,800　　　　　　　　　　　　　　　　　　　　　　**(2 marks)**

27.16 At 30 June 20X4 a company's allowance for receivables was $39,000. At 30 June 20X5 trade receivables totalled $517,000. It was decided to write off debts totalling $37,000 and to adjust the allowance for receivables to the equivalent of 5 per cent of the trade receivables based on past events.

What figure should appear in the statement of profit or loss for these items?

A　　$61,000
B　　$22,000
C　　$24,000
D　　$23,850　　　　　　　　　　　　　　　　　　　　　　**(2 marks)**

27.17 IAS 2 *Inventories* defines the extent to which overheads are included in the cost of inventories of finished goods.

Which of the following statements about the IAS 2 requirements in this area are correct?

1   Finished goods inventories may be valued on the basis of labour and materials cost only, without including overheads.

2   Carriage inwards, but not carriage outwards, should be included in overheads when valuing inventories of finished goods.

3   Factory management costs should be included in fixed overheads allocated to inventories of finished goods.

A   All three statements are correct
B   1 and 2 only
C   1 and 3 only
D   2 and 3 only   **(2 marks)**

27.18 A limited liability company sold a building at a profit.

How will this transaction be treated in the company's statement of cash flows?

	Proceeds of sale	*Profit on sale*
A	Cash inflow under financing activities	Add to profit in calculating cash flow from operating activities
B	Cash inflow under investing activities	Deducted from profit in calculating cash flow from operating activities
C	Cash inflow under investing activities	Added to profit in calculating cash flow from operating activities
D	Cash inflow under financing activities	Deducted from profit in calculating cash flow from operating activities

(2 marks)

27.19 Which of the following items may appear in a company's statement of changes in equity, according to IAS 1 *Presentation of financial statements*?

1   Unrealised revaluation gains
2   Dividends paid
3   Proceeds of equity share issue
4   Profit for the period

A   2, 3 and 4 only
B   1, 3 and 4 only
C   All four items
D   1, 2 and 4 only   **(2 marks)**

27.20 Sigma's bank statement shows an overdrawn balance of $38,600 at 30 June 20X5. A check against the company's cash book revealed the following differences:

1   Bank charges of $200 have not been entered in the cash book.
2   Lodgements recorded on 30 June 20X5 but credited by the bank on 2 July $14,700.
3   Cheque repayments entered in cash book but not presented for payment at 30 June 20X5 $27,800.
4   A cheque payment to a supplier of $4,200 charged to the account in June 20X5 recorded in the cash book as a receipt.

Based on this information, what was the cash book balance **before** any adjustments?

A $43,100 overdrawn
B $16,900 overdrawn
C $60,300 overdrawn
D $34,100 overdrawn   **(2 marks)**

(Total = 40 marks)

138

28 Mixed bank 2 · 48 mins

28.1 The plant and machinery cost account of a company is shown below. The company's policy is to charge depreciation at 20% on the straight line basis, with proportionate depreciation in years of acquisition and disposal.

PLANT AND MACHINERY - COST

20X5	$	20X5	$
1 Jan Balance b/f	280,000	30 June Transfer disposal	14,000
1 Apr Cash	48,000		
1 Sept Cash	36,000	31 Dec Balance c/f	350,000
	364,000		364,000

What should be the depreciation charge for the year ended 31 December 20X5?

A $67,000
B $70,000
C $64,200
D $68,600

(2 marks)

28.2 Which of the following are correct?

1 The statement of financial position value of inventory should be as close as possible to net realisable value.

2 The valuation of finished goods inventory must include production overheads.

3 Production overheads included in valuing inventory should be calculated by reference to the company's normal level of production during the period.

4 In assessing net realisable value, inventory items must be considered separately, or in groups of similar items, not by taking the inventory value as a whole.

A 1 and 2 only
B 3 and 4 only
C 1 and 3 only
D 2, 3 and 4

(2 marks)

28.3 A business sublets part of its office accommodation.

The rent is received quarterly in advance on 1 January, 1 April, 1 July and 1 October. The annual rent has been $24,000 for some years, but it was increased to $30,000 from 1 July 20X5.

What amounts for this rent should appear in the company's financial statements for the year ended 31 January 20X6?

	SPLOCI	SOFP
A	$27,500	$5,000 in sundry receivables
B	$27,000	$2,500 in sundry receivables
C	$27,000	$2,500 in sundry payables
D	$27,500	$5,000 in sundry payables

(2 marks)

28.4 The figures shown in the table below are an extract from the accounts of Ridgeway (capital employed is $1.5m).

	$
Revenue	1,000,000
Cost of sales	400,000
Gross profit	600,000
Distribution expenses and administration cost	300,000
Profit before interest and tax	300,000
Finance cost	50,000
Profit before tax	250,000
Income tax expense	100,000
Profit after tax	150,000

What is the return on capital employed (ROCE)?

A   7%
B   10%
C   40%
D   20%   **(2 marks)**

28.5 Which of the following events after the reporting period would normally qualify as adjusting events according to IAS 10 *Events after the reporting period*?

1   The bankruptcy of a credit customer with a balance outstanding at the end of the reporting period

2   A decline in the market value of investments

3   The declaration of an ordinary dividend

4   The determination of the cost of assets purchased before the end of the reporting period

A   1, 3, and 4
B   1 and 2 only
C   2 and 3 only
D   1 and 4 only   **(2 marks)**

28.6 Ordan received a statement from one of its suppliers, Alta, showing a balance due of $3,980. The amount due according to the payables ledger account of Alta in Ordan's records was only $230. Comparison of the statement and the ledger account revealed the following differences:

1   A cheque sent by Ordan for $270 has not been allowed for in Alta's statement.

2   Alta has not allowed for goods returned by Ordan $180.

3   Ordan made a contra entry, reducing the amount due to Alta by $3,200, for a balance due from Alta in Ordan's receivables ledger. No such entry has been made in Alta's records.

What difference remains between the two companies' records after adjusting for these items?

A $460
B $640
C $6,500
D $100   **(2 marks)**

28.7   A company's trial balance failed to agree, and a suspense account was opened for the difference.

Subsequent checking revealed that discounts allowed $13,000 had been credited to discounts received account and an entry on the credit side of the cash book for the purchase of some machinery $18,000 had not been posted to the plant and machinery account.

Which two of the following journal entries would correct the errors?

		Debit	Credit
		$	$
(1)	Discounts allowed	13,000	
	Discounts received		13,000
(2)	Discounts allowed	13,000	
	Discounts received	13,000	
	Suspense account		26,000
(3)	Suspense account	26,000	
	Discounts allowed		13,000
	Discounts received		13,000
(4)	Plant and machinery	18,000	
	Suspense account		18,000
(5)	Suspense account	18,000	
	Plant and machinery		18,000

A   1 and 4
B   2 and 5
C   2 and 4
D   3 and 5   (2 marks)

The following information is relevant for questions 28.8 and 28.9.

A company's draft financial statements for 20X5 showed a profit of $630,000. However, the trial balance did not agree, and a suspense account appeared in the company's draft statement of financial position. Subsequent checking revealed the following errors:

(1)   The cost of an item of plant $48,000 had been entered in the cash book and in the plant register as $4,800. Depreciation at the rate of 10% per year ($480) had been charged.

(2)   Bank charges of $440 appeared in the bank statement in December 20X5 but had not been entered in the company's records.

(3)   One of the directors of the company paid $800 due to a supplier in the company's payables ledger by a personal cheque. The bookkeeper recorded a debit in the supplier's ledger account but did not complete the double entry for the transaction. (The company does not maintain a payables ledger control account).

(4)   The payments side of the cash book had been understated by $10,000.

28.8   Which of the above items would require an entry to the suspense account in correcting them?

A   All four items
B   3 and 4 only
C   2 and 3 only
D   1, 2 and 4 only   (2 marks)

28.9   What would the company's profit become after the correction of the above errors?

A $634,760
B $624,760
C $624,440
D $625,240   (2 marks)

28.10 Which of the following statements are correct?

1   A company might make a rights issue if it wished to raise more equity capital.

2   A rights issue might increase the share premium account whereas a bonus issue is likely to reduce it.

3   A bonus issue will generate cash for a company.

4   A rights issue will always increase the number of shareholders in a company whereas a bonus issue will not.

A   1 and 2
B   1 and 3
C   2 and 3
D   2 and 4   **(2 marks)**

28.11 Which of the following statements are correct?

1   Contingent assets are included as assets in financial statements if it is probable that they will arise.

2   Contingent liabilities must be provided for in financial statements if it is probable that they will arise.

3   Details of all adjusting events after the reporting period must be given in notes to the financial statements.

4   Material non-adjusting events are disclosed by note in the financial statements.

A   1 and 2
B   2 and 4
C   3 and 4
D   1 and 3   **(2 marks)**

28.12 At 1 January 20X5 a company had an allowance for receivables of $18,000

At 31 December 20X5 the company's trade receivables were $458,000.

It was decided:

(a)   To write off debts totalling $28,000 as irrecoverable

(b)   To adjust the allowance for receivables to the equivalent of 5% of the remaining receivables based on past experience

What figure should appear in the company's statement of profit or loss for the total of debts written off as irrecoverable and the movement in the allowance for receivables for the year ended 31 December 20X5?

A $49,500
B $31,500
C $32,900
D $50,900   **(2 marks)**

28.13 The following payables ledger control account contains some errors. All goods are purchased on credit.

PAYABLES LEDGER CONTROL ACCOUNT

	$		$
Purchases	963,200	Opening balance	384,600
Discounts received	12,600	Purchases returns	17,400
Contras with amounts		Cash paid to suppliers	988,400
receivable in receivables ledger	4,200		
Closing balance	410,400		
	1,390,400		1,390,400

What should the closing balance be when the errors have been corrected?

A	$325,200	
B	$350,400	
C	$358,800	
D	$376,800	**(2 marks)**

28.14 Which one of the following journal entries is required to record goods taken from inventory by the owner of a business?

A   Debit Drawings
     Credit Purchases

B   Debit Sales
     Credit Drawings

C   Debit Drawings
     Credit Inventory

D   Debit Purchases
     Credit Drawings   **(2 marks)**

28.15 The following information is available about the transactions of Razil, a sole trader who does not keep proper accounting records:

	$
Opening inventory	77,000
Closing inventory	84,000
Purchases	763,000
Gross profit as a percentage of sales	30%

Based on this information, what is Razil's sales revenue for the year?

A	$982,800	
B	$1,090,000	
C	$2,520,000	
D	$1,080,000	**(2 marks)**

28.16 Which of the following statements are correct?

1   All non-current assets must be depreciated.

2   If property accounted for in accordance with *IAS 16 Property, plant and equipment* is revalued, the gain on revaluation is shown in the statement of profit or loss.

3   If a tangible non-current asset is revalued, all tangible assets of the same class should be revalued.

4   In a company's published statement of financial position, tangible assets and intangible assets must be shown separately.

A	1 and 2	
B	2 and 3	
C	3 and 4	
D	1 and 4	**(2 marks)**

28.17 The following bank reconciliation statement has been prepared by a trainee accountant at 31 December 20X5.

	$
Balance per bank statement (overdrawn)	38,640
Add: lodgements not credited	19,270
	57,910
Less: unpresented cheques	14,260
Balance per cash book	43,650

What should the final cash book balance be when all the above items have been properly dealt with?

A $43,650   overdrawn
B $33,630   overdrawn
C $5,110   overdrawn
D $72,170   overdrawn

(2 marks)

28.18 On 1 January 20X5 a company purchased some plant.

The invoice showed

	$
Cost of plant	48,000
Delivery to factory	400
One year warranty covering breakdown during 20X5	800
	49,200

Modifications to the factory building costing $2,200 were necessary to enable the plant to be installed.

What amount should be capitalised for the plant in the company's records?

A $51,400
B $48,000
C $50,600
D $48,400

(2 marks)

28.19 A business had an opening inventory of $180,000 and a closing inventory of $220,000 in its financial statements for the year ended 31 December 20X5.

Which of the following entries for these opening and closing inventory figures are made when completing the financial records of the business?

		Debit	Credit
		$	$
A	Inventory account	180,000	
	Statement of profit or loss (SPL)		180,000
	Statement of profit or loss (SPL)	220,000	
	Inventory account		220,000
B	Statement of profit or loss (SPL)	180,000	
	Inventory account		180,000
	Inventory account	220,000	
	Statement of profit or loss (SPL)		220,000
C	Inventory account	40,000	
	Purchases account		40,000
D	Purchases account	40,000	
	Inventory account		40,000

(2 marks)

28.20 Tinsel Co has 5 million $1 issued ordinary shares. At 1 May 20X0 Fairy Co purchased 60% of Tinsel Co's $1 ordinary shares for $4,000,000. At that date Tinsel Co had net assets with a fair value of $4,750,000 and a share price of $1.10. Fairy Co valued the non-controlling interest in Tinsel Co at acquisition as $2,200,000.

What is the total goodwill on acquisition at 1 May 20X0?

A $1,150,000
B $1,750,000
C $ 750,000
D $1,450,000

(2 marks)

(Total = 40 marks)

29 Mixed bank 3   48 mins

29.1 On 1 September 20X6, a business had inventory of $380,000. During the month, sales totalled $650,000 and purchases $480,000. On 30 September 20X6 a fire destroyed some of the inventory. The undamaged goods in inventory were valued at $220,000. The business operates with a standard gross profit margin of 30%.

Based on this information, what is the cost of the inventory destroyed in the fire?

A $185,000
B $140,000
C $405,000
D $360,000   **(2 marks)**

29.2 A company had the following transactions:

1   Goods in inventory that had cost $1,000 were sold for $1,500 cash.
2   A credit customer whose $500 debt had been written off paid the amount in full.
3   The company paid credit suppliers $1,000

What will be the combined effect of these transactions on the company's total net assets (current assets less current liabilities)?

A   Increase of $1,000
B   Net assets remains unchanged
C   Increase of $2,000
D   Increase of $3,000   **(2 marks)**

29.3 Which of the following should appear as separate items in a company's statement of changes in equity?

1   Profit for the financial year
2   Income from investments
3   Dividends paid on redeemable preference shares
4   Dividends paid on equity shares

A   1, 3 and 4
B   1 and 4 only
C   2 and 3 only
D   1, 2 and 3   **(2 marks)**

29.4 The following information is available about a company's dividends:

		$
20X5		
Sept.	Final dividend for the year ended 30 June 20X5 paid (declared August 20X5)	100,000
20X6		
March	Interim dividend for the year ended 30 June 20X6 paid	40,000
Sept.	Final dividend for the year ended 30 June 20X6 paid (declared August 20X6)	120,000

What figures, if any, should be disclosed in the company's statement of profit or loss and other comprehensive income for the year ended 30 June 20X6 and its statement of financial position as at that date?

	SPLOCI for the period	SOFP liability
A	$160,000 deduction	$120,000
B	$140,000 deduction	nil
C	nil	$120,000
D	nil	nil

                                                           (2 marks)

29.5 Goose Co has a 49% shareholding in each of the following three companies.

1   Turkey Co: Goose Co has the right to appoint or remove a majority of the directors of Turkey Co.

2   Duck Co: Goose Co has more than half the voting rights in Duck Co as a result of an agreement with other investors.

3   Partridge Co: Goose Co has the power to govern the financial and operating policies of Partridge Co.

Which of these companies are subsidiaries of Goose Co for financial reporting purposes?

A   Turkey Co and Duck Co only
B   Partridge Co and Duck Co only
C   Partridge Co and Turkey Co only
D   Partridge Co, Turkey Co and Duck Co   (2 marks)

29.6 At 1 July 20X5 a company's allowance for receivables was $48,000.

At 30 June 20X6, trade receivables amounted to $838,000. It was decided to write off $72,000 of these debts and adjust the allowance for receivables to $60,000.

What are the final amounts for inclusion in the company's statement of financial position at 30 June 20X6?

	Trade receivables	Allowance for receivables	Net balance
	$	$	$
A	838,000	60,000	778,000
B	766,000	60,000	706,000
C	766,000	108,000	658,000
D	838,000	108,000	730,000

(2 marks)

29.7 Which of the following statements about inventory valuation for statement of financial position purposes are correct?

1   According to IAS 2 *Inventories*, average cost and FIFO (first in, first out) are both acceptable methods of arriving at the cost of inventories.

2   Inventories of finished goods may be valued at labour and materials cost only, without including overheads.

3   Inventories should be valued at the lowest of cost, net realisable value and replacement cost.

4   It may be acceptable for inventories to be valued at selling price less estimated profit margin.

A   1 and 3
B   2 and 3
C   1 and 4
D   2 and 4   (2 marks)

29.8 A business received a delivery of goods on 29 June 20X6, which was included in inventory at 30 June 20X6. The invoice for the goods was recorded in July 20X6.

What effect will this have on the business?

1   Profit for the year ended 30 June 20X6 will be overstated.
2   Inventory at 30 June 20X6 will be understated.
3   Profit for the year ending 30 June 20X7 will be overstated.
4   Inventory at 30 June 20X6 will be overstated.

A   1 and 2
B   2 and 3
C   1 only
D   1 and 4   (2 marks)

29.9 What is the acid test ratio of Edward Co given the information below?

EDWARD CO TRIAL BALANCE (EXTRACT)

	$
Receivables	176,000
Inventories	20,000
Trade payables	61,000
Bank overdraft	79,000
Long term loan	10,000
Retained earnings	5,000

A   1.13:1
B   1.40:1
C   1.35:1
D   1.26:1   **(2 marks)**

29.10 Which of the following characteristics of financial information are included in the IASB's *Conceptual Framework for Financial Reporting*?

1   Comparability
2   Relevance
3   Timeliness
4   Faithful representation

A   All four items
B   1, 2 and 3 only
C   1, 2 and 4 only
D   2, 3 and 4 only   **(2 marks)**

29.11 Details of a company's insurance policy are shown below:

Premium for year ended 31 March 20X6 paid April 20X5 $10,800
Premium for year ending 31 March 20X7 paid April 20X6 $12,000

What figures should be included in the company's financial statements for the year ended 30 June 20X6?

	SPL	SOFP
	$	$
A	11,100	9,000 prepayment (Dr)
B	11,700	9,000 prepayment (Dr)
C	11,100	9,000 accrual (Cr)
D	11,700	9,000 accrual (Cr)

       (2 marks)

29.12 Which of the following statements about bank reconciliations are correct?

1   In preparing a bank reconciliation, unpresented cheques must be deducted from a balance of cash at bank shown in the bank statement.

2   A cheque from a customer paid into the bank but dishonoured must be corrected by making a debit entry in the cash book.

3   An error by the bank must be corrected by an entry in the cash book.

4   An overdraft is a debit balance in the bank statement.

A   1 and 3
B   2 and 3
C   1 and 4
D   2 and 4   **(2 marks)**

29.13 At 30 June 20X5 the capital and reserves of Meredith, a limited liability company, were:

	$m
Share capital	
Ordinary shares of $1 each	100
Share premium account	80

During the year ended 30 June 2006, the following transactions took place:

1 September 20X5   A bonus issue of one ordinary share for every two held, using the share premium account.

1 January 20X6   A fully subscribed rights issue of two ordinary shares for every five held at that date, at $1.50 per share.

What would the balances on each account be at 30 June 20X6?

	Share capital	*Share premium*
	$m	$m
A	210	110
B	210	60
C	240	30
D	240	80

(2 marks)

29.14 Which of the following statements about the requirements of IAS 37 *Provisions, Contingent Liabilities and Contingent Assets* are correct?

1   Contingent assets and liabilities should not be recognised in the financial statements.

2   A contingent asset should only be disclosed in the notes to a financial statement where an inflow of economic benefits is probable.

3   A contingent liability may be ignored if the possibility of the transfer of economic benefits is remote.

A   All three statements are correct
B   1 and 2 only
C   1 and 3 only
D   2 and 3 only

(2 marks)

29.15 Which of the following errors would cause a trial balance not to balance?

1   An error in the addition in the cash book.
2   Failure to record a transaction at all.
3   Cost of a motor vehicle debited to motor expenses account. The cash entry was correctly made.
4   Goods taken by the proprietor of a business recorded by debiting purchases and crediting drawings account.

A   1 only
B   1 and 2 only
C   3 and 4 only
D   All four items

(2 marks)

29.16 Manchester has 10 million $1 issued ordinary shares. At 1 May 20X9 Bristol purchased 70% of Manchester's $1 ordinary shares for $8,000,000. At that date Manchester had net assets with a fair value of $8,750,000 and its share price was $1.20. The non-controlling interest is valued using the share price at the date of acquisition.

What was the total goodwill arising on acquisition at 1 May 20X9?

A $4,400,000
B $350,000
C $750,000
D $2,850,000

(2 marks)

29.17 All the sales made by a retailer are for cash, and her sale prices are fixed by doubling cost. Details recorded of her transactions for September 20X6 are as follows:

		$
1 Sept	Inventories	40,000
30 Sept	Purchases for month	60,000
	Cash banked for sales for month	95,000
	Inventories	50,000

Which two of the following conclusions could separately be drawn from this information?

1   $5,000 cash has been stolen from the sales revenue prior to banking.
2   Goods costing $5,000 have been stolen.
3   Goods costing $2,500 have been stolen.
4   Some goods costing $2,500 had been sold at cost price.

A   1 and 2
B   1 and 3
C   2 and 4
D   3 and 4   **(2 marks)**

29.18 A company owns a number of properties which are rented to tenants. The following information is available for the year ended 30 June 20X6:

	Rent in advance $	Rent in arrears $
30 June 20X5	134,600	4,800
30 June 20X6	144,400	8,700

Cash received from tenants in the year ended 30 June 20X6 was $834,600.

All rent in arrears was subsequently received.

What figure should appear in the company's statement of profit or loss for rent receivable in the year ended 30 June 20X6?

A $840,500
B $1,100,100
C $569,100
D $828,700   **(2 marks)**

29.19 The payables ledger control account below contains a number of errors:

PAYABLES LEDGER CONTROL ACCOUNT

	$		$
Opening balance (amounts owed to suppliers)	318,600	Purchases	1,268,600
Cash paid to suppliers	1,364,300	Contras against debit balances in receivables ledger	48,000
Purchases returns	41,200	Discounts received	8,200
Refunds received from suppliers	2,700	Closing balance	402,000
	$1,726,800		$1,726,800

All items relate to credit purchases.

What should the closing balance be when all the errors are corrected?

A $128,200
B $509,000
C $224,200
D $144,600   **(2 marks)**

29.20 The carrying value of a company's non-current assets was $200,000 at 1 August 20X0. During the year ended 31 July 20X1, the company sold non current assets for $25,000 on which it made a loss of $5,000. The depreciation charge of the year was $20,000. What was the carrying value of non current assets at 31 July 20X1?

A $150,000
B $155,000
C $170,000
D $175,000   **(2 marks)**

(Total = 40 marks)

30   Mixed bank 4   48 mins

30.1   A company issued one million ordinary $1 shares at a premium of 50c per share. The proceeds were correctly recorded in the cash book, but were incorrectly credited to the sales account.

Which one of the following journal entries will correct the error?

		Debit $	Credit $
A	Sales	1,500,000	
	Share capital		1,000,000
	Share premium		500,000
B	Share capital	1,000,000	
	Share premium		500,000
	Sales		1,500,000
C	Sales	1,500,000	
	Share capital		1,500,000
D	Share capital	1,500,000	
	Sales		1,500,000

(2 marks)

30.2   After proposing a final dividend, Kenilworth Co has a current ratio of 2.0 and a quick ratio of 0.8.

If the company now uses its positive cash balance to pay that final dividend, what will be the effect upon these two ratios?

A   Increase current ratio and decrease quick ratio
B   Increase current ratio and increase quick ratio
C   Decrease current ratio and decrease quick ratio
D   Decrease current ratio and increase quick ratio   **(2 marks)**

30.3   Making an allowance for receivables and valuing inventory on the same basis in each accounting period are examples of which accounting concepts?

	Allowance for receivables	Inventory valuation
A	Accruals	Consistency
B	Accruals	Going concern
C	Prudence	Consistency
D	Prudence	Going concern

(2 marks)

30.4 A property company received cash for rent totalling $838,600 in the year ended 31 December 20X6.

Figures for rent in advance and in arrears at the beginning and end of the year were:

	31 December 20X5 $	31 December 20X6 $
Rent received in advance	102,600	88,700
Rent in arrears (all subsequently received)	42,300	48,400

What amount should appear in the company's statement of profit or loss for the year ended 31 December 20X6 for rental income?

A $818,600
B $738,000
C $939,200
D $858,600   (2 marks)

30.5 Which one of the following journal entries is correct according to its narrative?

		Debit $	Credit $
A	Mr Smith personal account	100,000	
	Directors' remuneration		100,000

Bonus allocated to account of managing director (Mr Smith)

		Debit $	Credit $
B	Purchases	14,000	
	Wages	24,000	
	Repairs to buildings		38,000

Transferring cost of repairs to buildings carried out by company's own employees, using materials from inventory.

		Debit $	Credit $
C	Discounts allowed	2,800	
	Discounts received		2,800

Correction of error: discounts allowed total incorrectly debited to discounts received account

		Debit $	Credit $
D	Suspense account	20,000	
	Rent receivable		10,000
	Rent payable		10,000

Correction of error: rent received credited in error to rent payable account.   (2 marks)

30.6 IAS 37 deals with accounting for contingencies. What is the correct accounting treatment for the following?

1   A probable loss (a constructive obligation exists, for which the amount can be reliably estimated)

2   A probable gain

	Probable loss	Probable gain
A	Accrued	Disclosed
B	Accrued	Not disclosed
C	Disclosed, but not accrued	Disclosed
D	Disclosed, but not accrued	Not disclosed

(2 marks)

30.7 A company has occupied rented premises for some years, paying an annual rent of $120,000. From 1 April 20X6 the rent was increased to $144,000 per year. Rent is paid quarterly in advance on 1 January, 1 April, 1 July and 1 October each year.

What figures should appear for rent in the company's financial statements for the year ended 30 November 20X6?

	SPLOCI		SOFP	
	$			$
A	136,000	Prepayment	12,000	
B	136,000	Prepayment	24,000	
C	138,000		Nil	
D	136,000	Accrual	12,000	**(2 marks)**

30.8 At 1 January 20X6 a company had an allowance for receivables of $49,000.

At 31 December 20X6 the company's trade receivables were $863,000 and it was decided to write off balances totalling $23,000 and to adjust the allowance for receivables to the equivalent of 5% of the remaining receivables based on past experience.

What total figure should appear in the company's statement of profit or loss for receivables expense?

A $16,000
B $65,000
C $30,000
D $16,150   **(2 marks)**

30.9 At 1 January 20X6, a company's capital structure was as follows:

	$
Ordinary share capital	
2,000,000 shares of 50c each	1,000,000
Share premium account	1,400,000

In January 20X6 the company issued 1,000,000 shares at $1·40 each.

In September 20X6 the company made a bonus issue of 1 share for every 3 held using the share premium account.

What were the balances on the company's share capital and share premium accounts after these transactions?

	Share capital	Share premium
	$	$
A	4,000,000	800,000
B	3,200,000	600,000
C	2,000,000	1,800,000
D	2,000,000	1,300,000

(2 marks)

30.10 Which of the following statements about the treatment of inventory and work in progress in financial statements are correct?

  1   Inventory should be valued at the lowest of cost, net realisable value and replacement cost.

  2   In valuing work in progress, materials costs, labour costs and variable and fixed production overheads must be included.

  3   Inventory items can be valued using either first in, first out (FIFO) or weighted average cost.

  4   A company's financial statements must disclose the accounting policies used in measuring inventories.

  A   All four statements are correct.
  B   1, 2 and 3 only
  C   2, 3 and 4 only
  D   1 and 4 only   **(2 marks)**

30.11 The plant and equipment account in the records of a company for the year ended 31 December 20X6 is shown below.

PLANT AND EQUIPMENT - COST

20X6	$	20X6	$
1 Jan Balance	960,000		
1 July Cash	48,000	30 Sept Transfer disposal account	84,000
		31 Dec Balance	924,000
	1,008,000		1,008,000

The company's policy is to charge depreciation on the straight line basis at 20% per year, with proportionate depreciation in the years of purchase and sale.

What should be the charge for depreciation in the company's statement of profit or loss for the year ended 31 December 20X6?

  A $184,800
  B $192,600
  C $191,400
  D $184,200   **(2 marks)**

30.12 The trial balance of a company did not balance, and a suspense account was opened for the difference.

Which of the following errors would require an entry to the suspense account in correcting them?

  (1)   A cash payment to purchase a motor van had been correctly entered in the cash book but had been debited to the motor expenses account.

  (2)   The debit side of the wages account had been undercast.

  (3)   The total of the discounts allowed column in the cash book had been credited to the discounts received account.

  (4)   A cash refund to a customer had been recorded by debiting the cash book and crediting the customer's account.

  A   1 and 2
  B   2 and 3
  C   3 and 4
  D   2 and 4   **(2 marks)**

30.13 A trader took goods that had cost $2,000 from inventory for personal use.

Which one of the following journal entries would correctly record this?

		Debit $	Credit $	
A	Drawings	2,000		
	Inventory		2,000	
B	Purchases	2,000		
	Drawings		2,000	
C	Sales	2,000		
	Drawings		2,000	
D	Drawings	2,000		
	Purchases		2,000	**(2 marks)**

30.14 Mulroon, a publishing company, is being sued for $1 million in a libel action in respect of a book published in January 20X6. On 31 October 20X6, the reporting date, the directors believed that it was possible that the claim would be successful.

What amount should be provided in the financial statements to 31 October 20X6?

A   Nil
B $100,000
C $300,000
D $1,000,000   **(2 marks)**

30.15 Nasty is a wholly owned subsidiary of Ugly. Inventories in their individual statements of financial position at the year end are shown as:

Ugly $40,000
Nasty $20,000

Sales by Ugly to Nasty during the year were invoiced at $15,000 which included a profit by Ugly of 25% on cost. Two thirds of these goods were included in inventories at the year end.

At what value should inventories appear in the consolidated statement of financial position?

A $50,000
B $57,000
C $57,500
D $58,000   **(2 marks)**

30.16 Where in the financial statements should tax on profit for the current period, and profit for the period, be separately disclosed?

	Statement of profit or loss and other comprehensive income	Statement of changes in equity
A	Tax on profit and profit for the period	Tax on profit
B	Profit for the period	Tax on profit and profit for the period
C	Tax on profit	Profit for the period
D	Tax on profit and profit for the period	Profit for the period **(2 marks)**

30.17 When is the reducing balance method of depreciating non-current assets more appropriate than the straight-line method?

    A   When the expected life of the asset is short

    B   When the asset is expected to decrease in value by a fixed percentage of cost each year

    C   When the expected life of the asset is not capable of being estimated accurately

    D   When the asset is expected to decrease in value less in later years than in the early years of its life   **(2 marks)**

30.18 A draft statement of cash flows contains the following:

	$m
Profit before tax	22
Depreciation	8
Increase in inventories	(4)
Decrease in receivables	(3)
Increase in payables	(2)
Net cash inflow from operating activities	21

Which of the following corrections need to be made to the calculation?

1   Depreciation should be deducted, not added
2   Increase in inventories should be added, not deducted
3   Decrease in receivables should be added, not deducted
4   Increase in payables should be added, not deducted

    A   1 and 2
    B   1 and 3
    C   2 and 4
    D   3 and 4   **(2 marks)**

30.19 Your inexperienced colleague, Paul Jones, has attempted to extract and total the individual balances in the receivables ledger. He provides you with the following listing which he has prepared.

	$
Bury Inc	7,500
P Fox & Son (Swindon) Co	2,000
Frank Wrendlebury & Co	4,297
D Richardson & Co	6,847
Ultra Co	783
Lawrenson Co	3,765
Walkers Inc	4,091
P Fox & Son (Swindon) Co	2,000
Whitchurch Co	8,112
Ron Bradbury & Co	5,910
Anderson Co	1,442
	46,747

Subsequent to the drawing up of the list, the following errors have so far been found.

(a)   A sales invoice for $267 sent to Whitchurch Co had been correctly entered in the day book but had not then been posted to the account for Whitchurch Co in the receivables ledger.

(b)   One of the errors made by Paul Jones was to omit the $2,435 balance of Rectofon Co from the list.

(c)   A credit note for $95 sent to Bury Inc had been correctly entered in the day book but was entered in the account in the receivables ledger as $75.

What is the revised balance of the receivables ledger after correcting these errors?

    A $45,665
    B $47,449
    C $47,429
    D $45,645   **(2 marks)**

30.20 A payables ledger control account showed a credit balance of $768,420. The payables ledger balances totalled $781,200.

Which one of the following possible errors could account in full for the difference?

A   A contra against a receivables ledger debit balance of $6,390 has been entered on the credit side of the payables ledger control account.

B   The total of discount allowed $28,400 was entered to the debit of the payables ledger control account instead of the correct figure for discount received of $15,620.

C $12,780 cash paid to a supplier was entered on the credit side of the supplier's account in the payables ledger.

D   The total of discount received $6,390 has been entered on the credit side of the payables ledger control account.   **(2 marks)**

(Total = 40 marks)

31 Mixed bank 5   48 mins

31.1 A firm has the following transactions with its product R

1 January 20X1	Opening inventory: nil
1 February 20X1	Buys 10 units at $300 per unit
11 February 20X1	Buys 12 units at $250 per unit
1 April 20X1	Sells 8 units at $400 per unit
1 August 20X1	Buys 6 units at $200 per unit
1 December 20X1	Sells 12 units at $400 per unit

The firm uses FIFO to value its inventory. What is the inventory value at the end of the year?

A $nil
B $1,700
C $2,400
D $2,007.2   **(2 marks)**

31.2 Which of the following provides advice to the International Accounting Standards Board (IASB) as well as informing the IASB of the implications of proposed standards for users and preparers of financial statements?

A   The IFRS Advisory Council
B   The IFRS Interpretations Committee
C   The IFRS Foundation
D   The Trustees   **(2 marks)**

31.3 Samantha has extracted a trial balance and created a suspense account with a credit balance of $759 to make it balance.

Samantha found the following:

1   A sales invoice for $4,569 has not been entered in the accounting records.
2   A payment of $1,512 has been posted correctly to the payables control account but no other entry has been made.
3   A credit sale of $131 has only been credited to the sales account.

What is the remaining balance on the suspense account after these errors have been corrected?

A $3,810 debit
B $2,140 credit
C $890 credit
D $622 debit   **(2 marks)**

31.4 Which of the following errors should be identified by performing a receivables control account reconciliation?

    A   A sales invoice of $500 has been omitted from the sales daybook.

    B   A sales return of $45 was entered as $54 in the sales returns daybook.

    C   Purchases of $72 were entered as sales returns in the sales returns daybook and the individual account.

    D   The total of the sales daybook was miscast by $200.   **(2 marks)**

31.5 Carol had receivables of $598,600 at 30 November 20X8. Her allowance for receivables at 1 December 20X7 was $12,460 and she wishes to change that to 2% of receivables at 30 November 20X8. On 29 November 2008 she received $635 in full settlement of a debt that she had written off in the year ended 30 November 20X7.

What total amount should be recognised for receivables in the statement of profit or loss for the year ended 30 November 20X8?

    A $488 credit
    B $11,972 debit
    C $1,123 credit
    D $147 debit   **(2 marks)**

31.6 Joanna has prepared her draft accounts for the year ended 30 April 2008, and needs to adjust them for the following items:

    1   Rent of $10,500 was paid and recorded on 2 January 2007 for the period 1 January to 31 December 2007. The landlord has advised that the annual rent for 2008 will be $12,000 although it has not been invoiced or paid yet.

    2   Property and contents insurance is paid annually on 1 March. Joanna paid and recorded $6,000 on 1 March 2008 for the year from 1 March 2008 to 28 February 2009.

What should the net effect on profit be in the draft accounts for the year ended 30 April 2008 of adjusting for the above items?

    A $1,000 decrease
    B $1,500 increase
    C $1,000 increase
    D $1,500 decrease   **(2 marks)**

31.7 Carter, a limited liability company, has non-current assets with a carrying value of $2,500,000 on 1 December 20X7.

During the year ended 30 November 20X8, the following occurred:

    –   Depreciation of $75,000 was charged to the statement of profit or loss
    –   Land and buildings with a carrying value of $1,200,000 were revalued to $1,700,000
    –   An asset with a carrying value of $120,000 was disposed of for $150,000
    –   The carrying value of non-current assets at 30 November 20X8 was $4,200,000.

In accordance with IAS7 *Statement of Cash Flows*, what net cash flows from the above transactions would be included within 'net cash flows from investing activities' for the year ended 30 November 20X8?

    A $(1,395,000)
    B $(1,365,000)
    C $150,000
    D $(1,245,000)   **(2 marks)**

31.8 Steven's receivables ledger control account does not agree with the total of the receivables ledger. He discovered the following errors:

1   A sales invoice has been entered into the sales day book as $895 rather than $859

2   The receivables column of the cash received day book has been undercast by $600

3   A contra of $400 against the purchase ledger has only been entered in the control account

Which of the above errors would cause a difference between the receivables control account and the total of the receivables ledger?

A   2 and 3 only
B   1 and 3 only
C   1 and 2 only
D   1, 2 and 3   **(2 marks)**

31.9 Luis sold goods to Pedro in May 2009 with a list price of $98,000. Luis allowed a trade discount of 10%. Pedro returned goods with a list price of $3,000 on 31 May and returned a further $5,000 of goods at list price on 6 June as they were found to be unsuitable.

How much should Luis record in the sales returns account at 31 May?

A $2,700
B $3,000
C $8,000
D $7,200   **(2 marks)**

31.10 A newly-registered company is considering the accounting policies it should adopt.

Policies under consideration are:

1   Research and development expenditure should be capitalised and amortised over the years in which the resultant product is sold or used.

2   Inventory should be valued at the lower of cost and net realisable value.

3   Goodwill arising in a business combination should be written off immediately to the statement of profit or loss.

Which of these possible accounting policies would, if adopted, contravene International Financial Reporting Standards?

A   1 and 2 only
B   2 and 3 only
C   1 and 3 only
D   1, 2 and 3   **(2 marks)**

31.11 You have recently been appointed as assistant accountant of PQR Co. You have assisted in preparing a forecast set of final accounts for the company whose year end is 31 December 20X7. The forecast shows that the company is expected to make a loss during the year to 31 December 20X7.

The managing director is concerned that the company's shareholders would be unhappy to hear that the company had made a loss. He is determined to avoid making a loss if at all possible. He has made the following suggestions in order to remedy the situation.

1   Value inventory using the LIFO basis as prices are rising so this will reduce inventory costs in the statement of profit or loss.

2   Create a provision against future losses in case this happens again in the future.

3   Stop amortising all capitalised development expenditure.

Which of these suggestions do you agree with?

A   1 and 2 only
B   3 only
C   2 only
D   None of the statements   **(2 marks)**

31.12 Which of the following journal entries may be accepted as being correct according to their narratives?

		DR $	CR $
1	Wages account	38,000	
	Purchases account	49,000	
	Buildings account		87,000

Labour and materials used in construction of extension to factory

			DR $	CR $
2	Directors' personal accounts:	A	30,000	
		B	40,000	
	Directors' remuneration			70,000

Directors' bonuses transferred to their accounts

		DR $	CR $
3	Suspense account	10,000	
	Sales account		10,000

Correction of error in addition – total of credit side of sales account $10,000 understated

- A 1 and 3
- B 1 and 2
- C 3 only
- D 2 and 3 **(2 marks)**

31.13 Which of the following costs should be included in valuing inventories of finished goods held by a manufacturing company, according to IAS 2 *Inventories*?

1 Carriage inwards
2 Carriage outwards
3 Depreciation of factory plant
4 Accounts department costs relating to wages for production employees

- A All four items
- B 2 and 3 only
- C 1, 3 and 4 only
- D 1 and 4 only **(2 marks)**

31.14 Frog acquired 100% of the ordinary share capital of Toad on 1 October 20X7.

On 31 December 20X7 retained earnings of Toad and Frog were as follows:

	Frog $'000	Toad $'000
Retained earnings at 1 January 20X7	500	100
Retained profit for the year ended 31 December 20X7	150	60
	650	160

The profits of Toad have accrued evenly throughout 20X7.

What figure for retained earnings should be included in the consolidated financial statements of the Frog group at 31 December 20X7?

- A $150,000
- B $175,000
- C $665,000
- D $810,000 **(2 marks)**

31.15 The following extract is from the statement of profit or loss of Gearing Co for the year ended 30 April 20X8.

	$
Profit before tax	68,000
Tax	(32,000)
Profit for the year	36,000

In addition to the profit above:

1   Gearing Co paid a dividend of $21,000 during the year.
2   A gain on revaluation of land resulted in a surplus of $18,000.

What total amount will be added to retained earnings at the end of the financial year?

A $36,000
B $33,000
C $47,000
D $15,000   **(2 marks)**

31.16 What does an increase in the allowance for receivables result in?

A   A decrease in current liabilities
B   An increase in net profit
C   An increase in working capital
D   A decrease in working capital   **(2 marks)**

31.17 A company's telephone bill consists of two elements. One is a quarterly rental charge, payable in advance; the other is a quarterly charge for calls made, payable in arrears. At 1 April 20X9, the previous bill dated 1 March 20X9 had included line rental of $90. Estimated call charges during March 20X9 were $80.

During the following 12 months, bills totalling $2,145 were received on 1 June, 1 September, 1 December 20X9 and 1 March 20Y0, each containing rental of $90 as well as call charges. Estimated call charges for March 20Y0 were $120.

What is the amount to be charged to the statement of profit or loss for the year ended 31 March 20Y0?

A $2,185
B $2,205
C $2,155
D $2,215   **(2 marks)**

31.18 Which *three* of the following sets of items all appear on the same side of the trial balance?

1   Sales, interest received and accruals
2   Receivables, drawings and discount received
3   Non current assets, cost of sales and carriage outwards
4   Capital, trade payables and other operating expenses
5   Sundry expenses, prepayments and purchases

A   1, 4 and 5
B   1, 3 and 5
C   1, 2 and 3
D   3, 4 and 5   **(2 marks)**

31.19 The increase in net assets is $173, drawings are $77 and capital introduced is $45.

What is the net profit for the year?

A $295
B $205
C $51
D $141   **(2 marks)**

31.20 Capital introduced is $50. Profits brought forward at the beginning of the year amount to $100 and liabilities are $70. Assets are $90.

What is the retained profit for the year?

A $130 profit
B $130 loss
C $10 profit
D $10 loss   **(2 marks)**

(Total = 40 marks)

32 Mixed bank 6   48 mins

32.1 If there is a debit balance of $1,250 on X's account in the books of Y, what does this mean?

A   X owes $1,250 to Y
B   Y owes $1,250 to X
C   X has returned goods worth $1,250 to Y
D   X is owed $1,250 by Y   **(2 marks)**

32.2 You are an employee of Exelan Co and have been asked to help prepare the end of year statements for the period ended 30 November 20X9 by agreeing the figure for the total receivables.

The following figures, relating to the financial year, have been obtained from the books of original entry.

	$
Purchases for the year	361,947
Sales	472,185
Returns inwards	41,226
Returns outwards	16,979
Irrecoverable debts written off	1,914
Discounts allowed	2,672
Discounts received	1,864
Cheques paid to suppliers	342,791
Cheques received from customers	429,811
Customer cheques dishonoured	626

You discover that at the close of business on 30 November 20X8 the total of the receivables amounted to $50,241. What is the balance on the receivables ledger control account at 30 November 20X9?

A $47,429
B $52,773
C $51,257
D $48,237   **(2 marks)**

32.3 On 10 January 20X9, Jane Smith received her monthly bank statement for December 20X8. The statement showed the following.

SOUTHERN BANK INC

J Smith: Statement of Account

Date 20X8	Particulars	Debits $	Credits $	Balance $
Dec 1	Balance			1,862
Dec 5	417864	243		1,619
Dec 5	Dividend		26	1,645
Dec 5	Bank Giro Credit		212	1,857
Dec 8	417866	174		1,683
Dec 10	417867	17		1,666
Dec 11	Sundry Credit		185	1,851
Dec 14	Standing Order	32		1,819
Dec 20	417865	307		1,512
Dec 20	Bank Giro Credit		118	1,630
Dec 21	417868	95		1,535
Dec 21	417870	161		1,374
Dec 24	Bank charges	18		1,356
Dec 27	Bank Giro Credit		47	1,403
Dec 28	Direct Debit	88		1,315
Dec 29	417873	12		1,303
Dec 29	Bank Giro Credit		279	1,582
Dec 31	417871	25		1,557

Her cash book for the corresponding period showed:

CASH BOOK

20X8		$	20X8		Cheque no	$
Dec 1	Balance b/d	1,862	Dec 1	Electricity	864	243
Dec 4	J Shannon	212	Dec 2	P Simpson	865	307
Dec 9	M Lipton	185	Dec 5	D Underhill	866	174
Dec 19	G Hurst	118	Dec 6	A Young	867	17
Dec 26	M Evans	47	Dec 10	T Unwin	868	95
Dec 27	J Smith	279	Dec 14	B Oliver	869	71
Dec 29	V Owen	98	Dec 16	Rent	870	161
Dec 30	K Walters	134	Dec 20	M Peters	871	25
			Dec 21	L Philips	872	37
			Dec 22	W Hamilton	873	12
			Dec 31	Balance c/d		1,793
		2,935				2,935

What is the revised cash book balance at 31 December 20X8?

A $1,655
B $1,866
C $1,681
D $1,713

(2 marks)

32.4 Sandilands Co uses a computer package to maintain its accounting records. A printout of its cash book for the month of May 20X3 was extracted on 31 May and is summarised below.

	$		$
Balance b/d	546	Payments	5,966
Receipts	6,293	Balance c/d	873
	6,839		6,839

The company's chief accountant provides you with the following information.

(a) Bank charges of $630 shown on the bank statement have not been entered in the company's cash book.

(b) Three standing orders entered on the bank statement have not been recorded in the company's cash book: a subscription for trade journals of $52, an insurance premium of $360 and a business rates payment of $2,172.

(c) A cheque drawn by Sandilands Co for $693 and presented to the bank on 26 May has been incorrectly entered in the cash book as $936.

After correcting the errors above, what is the revised balance on the cash book?

A $2,098 debit
B $2,584 debit
C $3,868 credit
D $3,382 credit   **(2 marks)**

32.5 A company purchases a machine with an expected useful life of 6 years for $9,000. After two years of use, management revised the expected useful life to 8 years. The machine is to be depreciated at 30% per annum on the reducing balance basis. A full year's depreciation is charged in the year of purchase, with none in the year of sale. During year 4, it is sold for $3,000.

What is the profit or loss on disposal?

A $1,000 profit
B $87 loss
C $1,410 profit
D $840 profit   **(2 marks)**

32.6 Which one of the following does a business aim to ensure by charging depreciation in the accounts?

A   The cost of non current assets is spread over the accounting periods which benefit from their use.
B   There are sufficient funds set aside to replace the assets when necessary.
C   Profits are not understated.
D   Assets are shown at their realisable value.   **(2 marks)**

32.7 A business purchased an asset on 1 January 20X1 at a cost of $160,000. The asset had an expected life of eight years and a residual value of $40,000. The straight-line method is used to measure depreciation. The financial year ends on 31 December.

At 31 December 20X3, the estimated remaining life of the asset from that date is now expected to be only three more years, but the residual value is unchanged.

What will be the net book value of the asset as at 31 December 20X3, for inclusion in the statement of financial position?

A $97,500
B $100,000
C $107,500
D $115,000   **(2 marks)**

32.8 The debit side of a trial balance totals $400 more than the credit side.

Which one of the following errors would fully account for the difference?

A $200 paid for building repairs has been correctly entered in the cashbook and credited to the building non-current asset account.

B Discount received $200 has been debited to the discount allowed account.

C A receipt of $400 for commission receivable has been omitted from the records.

D An invoice for $400 has been entered into the sales day book but omitted from the receivables ledger. **(2 marks)**

32.9 Under IAS 1 *Presentation of financial statements*, which of the following **must** be disclosed on the *face* of the statement of profit or loss and other comprehensive income?

A Profit before tax
B Gross profit
C Revenue
D Dividends **(2 marks)**

32.10 The following bank reconciliation has been prepared:

	$
Balance per bank statement (overdrawn)	73,680
Add: Outstanding lodgements	102,480
Less: Outstanding cheques	(87,240)
Balance per cash book (credit)	88,920

Assuming the amounts stated for items other than the cash book balance are correct, what should the cash book balance be?

A $88,920 credit (as stated)
B $120,040 credit
C $58,440 debit
D $58,440 credit **(2 marks)**

32.11 In relation to statements of cash flows, which, if any, of the following are correct?

1 The direct method of calculating net cash from operating activities leads to a different figure from that produced by the indirect method, but this is balanced elsewhere in the statement of cash flows.

2 A company making high profits must necessarily have a net cash inflow from operating activities.

3 Profits and losses on disposals of non-current assets appear as items under cash flows from investing activities in the statement of cash flows or a note to it.

A Item 1 only
B Items 2 and 3
C None of the items
D All of the items **(2 marks)**

32.12 Panther owns her own business selling Gladiator dolls to department stores. At 30 June 20X2 she had the following balances in her books:

	$
Trade receivables	31,450
Allowance for receivables (General)	(450)
(as at 1 July 20X1)	
	31,000

A balance of $1,000 due from Selfrodges Co is considered irrecoverable and is to be written off. Horrids Co was in financial difficulty and Panther wished to allow for 60% of their balance of $800. She also decided to make a general allowance of 10% on her remaining trade receivables. What was the allowance for receivables in her statement of financial position at 30 June 20X2?

A $3,477
B $3,765
C $3,445
D $3,545   (2 marks)

32.13 Which of the following items could appear on the credit side of a sales ledger control account?

1   Cash received from customers
2   Irrecoverable debts written off
3   Increase in the allowance for receivables
4   Discounts allowed
5   Sales
6   Credits for goods returned by customers
7   Cash refunds to customers

A   1, 2, 4, and 6
B   1, 2, 4 and 7
C   3, 4, 5 and 6
D   3, 4, 6 and 7   (2 marks)

32.14 A business has compiled the following information for the year ended 31 October 20X2:

	$
Opening inventories	386,200
Purchases	989,000
Closing inventories	422,700

The gross profit percentage of sales is 40%

What is the sales revenue for the year?

A $1,333,500
B $1,587,500
C $2,381,250
D   The sales revenue is impossible to calculate from this information.   (2 marks)

32.15 On 30 September 20X1 part of the inventory of a company was completely destroyed by fire.

The following information is available:

−   Inventory at 1 September 20X1 at cost $49,800
−   Purchases for September 20X1 $88,600
−   Sales for September 20X1 $130,000
−   Inventory at 30 September 20X1 – undamaged items $32,000
−   Standard gross profit percentage on sales 30%

Based on this information, what is the cost of the inventory destroyed?

A $17,800
B $47,400
C $15,400
D $6,400   (2 marks)

32.16 Catt sells goods at a margin of 50%. During the year to 31 March 20X3 the business made purchases totalling $134,025 and sales totalling $240,000. Inventories in hand at 31 March 20X3, valued at cost, was $11,385 higher than the corresponding figure at 1 April 20X2.

What was the cost of the goods Catt had drawn out?

A $2,640
B $14,590
C $25,410
D $37,360   **(2 marks)**

32.17 Thatch plc's current ratio this year is 1.33:1 compared to that of 1.25:1 last year. Which of the following would be possible explanations?

1   Thatch made an unusually large sale immediately prior to the year end.

2   Thatch paid its payables earlier than usual out of a bank overdraft.

3   Thatch made an unusually large purchase of goods for cash immediately prior to the year end and these goods remain in inventory.

4   Thatch paid its payables earlier than usual out of a positive cash balance.

A   1 and 2 only
B   2 and 3 only
C   1 and 3 only
D   1 and 4 only   **(2 marks)**

32.18 Lexus has owns 60% of voting equity of Nexus. The following information relates to the results of Lexus and Nexus for the year.

	Lexus $'000	Nexus $'000
Revenue	350	150
Cost of sales	200	60
Gross profit	150	90

During the year, Nexus sold goods to Lexus for $50,000. Lexus still had 40% of these goods in inventory at the year end. Nexus uses a 25% mark up on all goods.

What were the consolidated sales and cost of sales of the Lexus group at the year end?

	Sales	Cost of sales
A	$500,000	$210,000
B	$500,000	$214,000
C	$450,000	$210,000
D	$450,000	$214,000

(2 marks)

32.19 At 1 July 20X0 the share capital and share premium account of a company were as follows:

	$
Share capital – 300,000 ordinary shares of 25c each	75,000
Share premium account	200,000

During the year ended 30 June 20X1 the following events took place:

1   On 1 January 20X1 the company made a rights issue of one share for every five held, at $1.20 per share.

2   On 1 April 20X1 the company made a bonus (capitalisation) issue of one share for every three in issue at that time, using the share premium account to do so.

What are the correct balances on the company's share capital and share premium accounts at 30 June 20X1?

	Share capital	Share premium account
A	$460,000	$287,000
B	$480,000	$137,000
C	$120,000	$137,000
D	$120,000	$227,000

(2 marks)

32.20 A statement of cash flows prepared in accordance with IAS 7 *Statements of cash flows* opens with the calculation of cash flows from operating activities from the net profit before taxation.

Which of the following lists of items consists only of items that would be ADDED to net profit before taxation in that calculation?

A   Decrease in inventories, depreciation, profit on sale of non-current assets
B   Increase in trade payables, decrease in trade receivables, profit on sale of non-current assets
C   Loss on sale of non-current assets, depreciation, increase in trade receivables
D   Decrease in trade receivables, increase in trade payables, loss on sale of non-current assets

(2 marks)

(Total = 40 marks)

33   Mixed bank 7   48 mins

33.1 The following information was disclosed in the financial statements of Highfield Co for the year ended 31/12/20X2

	20X1	20X2
	$	$
Plant & Equipment cost	255,000	235,000
Accumulated depreciation	(100,000)	(110,000)

During 20X2, the following occurred in respect of Plant & Equipment:

	$
Purchases of plant and equipment	10,000
Depreciation charged on plant and equipment	25,000
Loss on disposal of plant and equipment	8,000

What were the sales proceeds received on disposal of the plant and equipment?

A $7,000
B $15,000
C $25,000
D $8,000

(2 marks)

33.2 The issued share capital of Maelstrom Co is as follows:

Ordinary shares of 10c each	$1,000,000
8% Preferred shares of 50c each (redeemable)	$500,000

In the year ended 31 October 20X2, the company has paid the preferred dividend for the year and an interim dividend of 2c per share on the ordinary shares. A final ordinary dividend of 3c per share is declared on 30 October 20X2.

What is the total amount of dividends recognised in the financial statements relating to the year ended 31 October 20X2?

A $580,000
B $90,000
C $130,000
D $500,000

(2 marks)

33.3 When a company makes a rights issue of equity shares which of the following effects will the issue have?

1   Working capital is increased
2   Liabilities are increased
3   Share premium account is reduced
4   Investments are increased

A   1 only
B   1 and 2
C   3 only
D   1 and 4   **(2 marks)**

33.4 Which of the following may appear as current liabilities in a company's statement of financial position?

1   a revaluation surplus
2   loan due for repayment within 1 year
3   income tax payable
4   preferred dividends payable on redeemable preference shares

A   1,2 and 3
B   1,2 and 4
C   1,3 and 4
D   2,3 and 4   **(2 marks)**

33.5 Which of the following errors would cause a trial balance imbalance?

(i)   The discounts received column of the cash payments book was overcast
(ii)   Cash paid for the purchase of office furniture was debited to the general expenses account
(iii)   Returns inwards were included on the credit side of the trial balance

A   (i) only
B   (i) and (ii)
C   (iii) only
D   (ii) and (iii)   **(2 marks)**

33.6 The following information is available about a company's dividends:

		$
2005		
Sept	Final dividend for the year ended 30 June 2005 paid (declared August 2005)	100,000
2006		
March	Interim dividend for the year ended 30 June 2006 paid	40,000
Sept	Final dividend for the year ended 30 June 2006 paid (declared August 2006)	20,000

What figures, if any, should be disclosed in the company's statement of profit or loss and other comprehensive income for the year ended 30 June 2006 and its statement of financial position as at that date?

	SPLOCI for the period	SOFP liability
A	$160,000 deduction	$120,000
B	$140,000 deduction	nil
C	nil	$120,000
D	nil	nil

     (2 marks)

33.7 Which, if any, of the following statements about intangible assets are correct?

 1   Deferred development expenditure must be amortised over a period not exceeding five years.
 2   If the conditions specified in IAS 38 *Intangible assets* are met, development expenditure may be capitalised, if the directors decide to do so.
 3   Trade investments must appear in a company's statement of financial position under the heading of intangible assets.

 A   1 and 2
 B   2 and 3
 C   1 and 3
 D   None of the statements is correct   **(2 marks)**

33.8 A company owns a number of properties which are rented to tenants. The following information is available for the year ended 30 June 2006:

	Rent in advance	Rent in arrears
	$	$
30 June 2005	134,600	4,800
30 June 2006	144,400	8,700

Cash received from tenants in the year ended 30 June 2006 was $834,600.

All rent in arrears was subsequently received.

What figure should appear in the company's statement of profit or loss for rent receivable in the year ended 30 June 2006?

 A $840,500
 B $1,100,100
 C $569,100
 D $828,700   **(2 marks)**

33.9 Which of the following transactions is a capital transaction?

 A   Depreciation of plant and equipment
 B   Expenditure on rent
 C   Payment of interest on loan stock
 D   Buying shares as an investment   **(2 marks)**

33.10 Which of the following transactions is revenue expenditure?

 A   Expenditure resulting in improvements to property
 B   Expenditure on heat and light
 C   Purchasing non-current assets
 D   Repaying a bank overdraft   **(2 marks)**

33.11 In October 2006 Utland sold some goods on sale or return terms for $2,500. Their cost to Utland was $1,500. The transaction has been treated as a credit sale in Utland's financial statements for the year ended 31 October 2006. In November 2006 the customer accepted half of the goods and returned the other half in good condition.

What adjustments, if any, should be made to the financial statements?

 A   Sales and receivables should be reduced by $2,500, and closing inventory increased by $1,500.
 B   Sales and receivables should be reduced by $1,250, and closing inventory increased by $750.
 C   Sales and receivables should be reduced by $2,500, with no adjustment to closing inventory.
 D   No adjustment is necessary.   **(2 marks)**

33.12 The payables ledger control account below contains a number of errors:

PAYABLES LEDGER CONTROL ACCOUNT

	$		$
Opening balance (amounts owed to suppliers)	318,600	Purchases	1,268,600
		Contras against debt balances in	
Cash paid to suppliers	1,364,300	receivables ledger	48,000
Purchases returns	41,200	Discounts received	8,200
Refunds received from suppliers	2,700	Closing balance	402,000
	1,726,800		1,726,800

All items relate to credit purchases.

What should the closing balance be when all the errors are corrected?

A $128,200
B $509,000
C $224,200
D $144,600   (2 marks)

33.13 What are the journal entries for an accrual of rent expenses of $500?

A   Debit prepayments $500, credit rent $500
B   Debit accrual $500, credit rent $500
C   Debit rent $500, credit accruals $500
D   Debit rent $500, credit prepayments $500   (2 marks)

33.14 A company (the parent company) acquires 85% of another company, which becomes its subsidiary. The non-controlling interest (NCI) is therefore 15%. How should the goodwill arising on consolidation be calculated?

A   Fair value of consideration transferred less the fair value of NCI at acquisition less the fair value of the net assets acquired.
B   Fair value of consideration transferred less the parent company's share (85%) of the fair value of the net assets acquired.
C   Fair value of consideration transferred plus the book value of NCI at acquisition less the fair value of the net assets acquired.
D   Fair value of consideration transferred plus the fair value of NCI at acquisition less the fair value of the net assets acquired.   (2 marks)

33.15 An electrical store and a cake shop both have the same mark up on cost. However, the gross profit margin of the electrical store is significantly higher than that of the cake shop.

Which of the following is a possible reason for this?

A   The cake shop has a higher turnover of inventory than the electrical store.
B   The electrical store takes advantage of trade-discounts for bulk buying.
C   The cake shop has a higher level of wastage of inventory than the electrical store.
D   The cake shop's revenue is increasing, while that of the electrical store is decreasing.   (2 marks)

33.16 Analysis of the statement of financial position of Charon for the year ended 20X9 reveals the following relationships:

Current ratio   2:1
Sales: current assets   5:1
Acid test ratio   1.5:1

If the sales for the year were $30 million, what is the value of inventory that will appear in the statement of financial position?

A $1.5m
B $10.5m
C $3.0m
D $4.5m   (2 marks)

33.17 Which of the following statements are correct?

    1   If company A has an investment in company B that gives it control over the company B, then the company B is classified as a subsidiary in the consolidated financial statements of company A.

    2   If a company has associates, but not subsidiaries, it will not prepare consolidated financial statements.

    3   If a company has a 21% investment in the voting equity of another company, it will account for its investment using the equity method.

    A   1 and 2
    B   2 and 3
    C   All three statements are correct
    D   None of the statements are correct   **(2 marks)**

33.18 XYX Co's non-current assets had written down values of $368,400 and $485,000 at the beginning and end of the year respectively. Depreciation for the year was $48,600. Assets originally costing $35,000, with a carrying amount of $18,100 were sold in the year for $15,000.

What were the additions to non-current assets in the year?

    A $183,300
    B $200,200
    C $49,900
    D $180,200   **(2 marks)**

33.19 At 1 November 20X9, Telway Co had an allowance for receivables of $90,000. At 31 October 20X0, its trade receivables were $1,232,000 of which $60,000 was identified as unrecoverable and was written off. Telway Co's allowance for receivables has now been adjusted to 5% of remaining trade receivables.

What amount should be recorded in the statement of profit or loss for the receivables expense for the year ended 31 October 20X0?

    A $58,600 debit
    B $28,600 debit
    C $31,400 credit
    D $118,600 debit   **(2 marks)**

33.20 Why do we prepare a trial balance?

    A   To test the accuracy of the double entry bookkeeping records
    B   To prepare management accounts
    C   To prepare financial accounts
    D   To clear the suspense account   **(2 marks)**

(Total = 40 marks)

Answers

1 The context and purpose of financial reporting

1.1   C   The role of the IASB is to develop and publish International Financial Reporting Standards.

1.2   B   A sole trader does not have any shareholders. The accounts are unlikely to be of interest to a financial analyst, they are more usually interested in the accounts of public companies.

1.3   B   (2) is the IASB's *Conceptual framework* description of the purpose of financial statements. (1) is false - although the shareholder needs to know the future prospects, he also needs to know that the current position of the company is secure. Similarly the supplier needs to know the future prospects to ensure that he will be paid.

1.4   A   (2) is incorrect – shareholders are only liable for the debts of the business up to the amount they have invested in shares, whereas sole traders are liable for all of the debts of the business.

1.5   B   Corporate governance is the system by which companies and other entities are directed and controlled.

1.6   A   The responsibility of the financial statements rests with the directors, whether or not those financial statements are audited. Some of the duties of directors are statutory duties, laid down in law, including the duty to act within their powers, promote the success of the company and exercise reasonable skill and care.

1.7   D   Providing information regarding the financial position and performance of a business are primary objectives of financial statements. All classes of users require information for decision making.

1.8   A   This information is needed by lenders.

1.9   D   (1) is incorrect, the presentation or classification can be changed if there is a significant change in the nature of operations, if an IFRS requires it or if a review of the accounts indicates a more appropriate presentation. (3) is incorrect. Companies should never make provisions in order to boost profits in more difficult times, provisions should only be made in accordance with IAS 37.

1.10   C   Unless a partnership is a limited liability partnership, the partners' individual exposure to debt is not limited because the partnership is not a separate legal entity from the partners themselves. Financial records must be maintained by a partnership, but there is no requirement to make them publicly available unless the partnership is a limited liability partnership.

1.11   C   A is the definition of a liability, B is the definition of an asset and D is the definition of income according to the *Conceptual framework*.

1.12   C   All three statements are true.

1.13   D   The IFRS Advisory Council is a forum for the IASB to consult with the outside world. The IASB produces IFRSs and is overseen by the IFRS Foundation.

1.14   B   The role of the IASB is to develop and publish international financial reporting standards.

2 The qualitative characteristics of financial information

2.1   D   The business entity concept.

2.2   C   The accruals concept.

2.3   C   The materiality concept.

2.4   C   Information has the quality of faithful representation when it is complete, neutral and free from material error.

2.5   D   Consistency. To maintain consistency, the presentation and classification of items in the financial statements should stay the same from one period to the next, unless a change is required by an IFRS or unless there is a significant change in the nature of operations or a review of the accounts indicates a more appropriate presentation.

2.6   D   Relevance and faithful representation.

2.7   C   The prudence concept does not require the understating of assets or the overstating of liabilities.

2.8   A   (a)   Materiality concerns whether an item in the financial statements can influence users decisions.

                (b)   Substance over form means that the commercial effect should be recognised not the strict legal form.

2.9   D   None of these statements are correct.

2.10   D   Comparability, verifiability, timeliness, understandability.

2.11   D   The accruals concept is not a qualitative characteristic of financial information. It is implied by the going concern concept.

3   Double entry bookkeeping I

3.1   C   Assets - liabilities = opening capital + profits - drawings

            Therefore, assets - liabilities - opening capital + drawings = profit

3.2   B   Closing capital – opening capital = increase (I) in net assets. This means that option B is equivalent to:

$$P = I + D - C_i$$

            This is the correct form of the business equation.

3.3   D $I = P + C_i - D$
                 $= \$(72,500 + 8,000 - 2,200)$
                 $= \$78,300$

            Therefore, closing net assets = $\$(101,700 + 78,300) = \$180,000$.

3.4   B $I = P + C_i - D$
                 $= \$(35,400 - 6,000 + 10,200)$
                 $= \$39,600$

            Therefore, opening capital = opening net assets = $\$(95,100 - 39,600) = \$55,500$.

3.5   B   The selling price is not relevant to this adjustment.

3.6   C   This will mean less cash coming into the bank.

3.7   A   Increase in net assets   =   Capital introduced + profit – drawings

            184,000 – 128,000   =   50,000 + profit – 48,000

            Profit   =   56,000 – 50,000 + 48,000

                                     = $\$54,000$

3.8   C   Dr Purchases $400
            Dr Trade Payables $250
            Cr Cash $650

            A payment is a credit to the cash account. The payment to J Bloggs is a cash purchase and so the double entry is Dr Purchases, Cr Cash. Remember that the purchase from J Doe has already been recorded as Dr Purchases, Cr Trade Payables, so the payment of cash to clear the invoice should now be recorded as Dr Trade Payables, Cr Cash.

3.9   A   Dr Receivables $150
                Dr Sales Returns $300
                Cr Sales $150
                Cr Cash $300

The double entry for the sale of goods on credit is Dr Receivables, Cr Sales $150. The return of goods previously sold for cash is Dr Sales Returns, Cr Cash $300.

3.10   A   A debit note is sent to a supplier with a return of goods. A debit note is in effect a request for a credit note.

3.11   B   The journal, cash book and sales day book are books of prime entry.

3.12   C   Debit notes sent to suppliers are recorded in the purchase returns day book.

3.13   D   Balance carried down from previous period shows debits exceed credits and so it is a debit balance brought down for the new period.

3.14   B   The opening balance on the ledger is $14,000 CR, this is the amount that would have appeared in the trial balance at 1 October 20X0.

3.15   B   Discounts allowed are recorded in the cash book. Credit notes received are to do with returned purchases (not sales). Trade discounts are not recorded, as they are deducted on the sales invoices and only the net sale is recorded.

3.16   C   A debit records an increase in assets or a decrease in liabilities. A credit records an increase in liabilities and/or capital. Therefore only C is true.

3.17   D   Remember that only credit purchases are listed in the purchases daybook.

4   Double entry bookkeeping II

4.1   A $544

SALES DAY BOOK

20X9		$
1 May	P Dixon	160
4 May	M Maguire	80
5 May	M Donald	304
		544

4.2   B $823

PURCHASES BOOK

20X9		$
2 May	A Clarke (W1)	323
4 May	D Daley	400
6 May	G Perkins	100
		823

W1 $380 \times \dfrac{85}{100} = \$323

4.3   C   Dr Purchases $450
                Dr Trade Payables $250
                Cr Purchase Returns $700

The purchase of goods on credit is recorded as Dr Purchases, Cr Trade payables $450. The return of goods which were purchased on credit is recorded as Dr Trade Payables, Cr Purchase Returns, combining both entries gives the answer above.

4.4 B Dr Cash
Cr Sales
Cr Trade Receivables

Cash received is a debit to the cash account. The cash received from R Singh is offset against the trade receivable balance due from R Singh: Dr Cash, Cr Trade Receivables. The cash received from S Kalu is a cash sale: Dr Cash, Cr Sales.

4.5 D Remember the receivables account is a memorandum account.

4.6 D When cash is received by a business, a debit entry is made in the cashbook. A receipt of cash decreases an overdraft and increases a bank balance.

4.7 C

TRADE PAYABLES ACCOUNT

	$		$
Cash at bank	100,750	Balance b/d	250,225
Balance c/d	474,485	Purchases	325,010
	575,235		575,235

4.8 C Credit sales = $80,000 – $10,000 + $9,000 = $79,000.

4.9 C A is incorrect as the debits and credits don't equal each other, B is incorrect as the debits and credits are the wrong way round and D are incorrect as the credit purchase has been ignored.

4.10 C You are recording the transaction in Steel Co's books – Steel Co is the seller, so the double entry is Dr receivables, Cr sales $250.

4.11 A $22,000

	$	$
Sales		40,000
Returns inwards		(2,000)
		38,000
Opening inventory	3,000	
Purchases	20,000	
Returns outwards	(4,000)	
Closing inventory	(3,000)	
		(16,000)
Gross profit		22,000

4.12 A The receivables allowance is deducted from trade receivables and the net figure of $71,192 ($75,943 – $4,751) is reported in the statement of financial position.

4.13 B Assets are represented by debit balances.

4.14 C The two balances must be separately disclosed.

4.15 D The debits are as follows:

	$
Opening inventory	9,649
Purchases	142,958
Expenses	34,835
Non-current assets	63,960
Receivables	31,746
Cash at bank	1,783
	284,931

4.16 A (5,754 + 11,745 + 150)

5 Sales tax

5.1 D A, B and C could all be reasons why the output tax does not equal 20% of sales. D is incorrect as it makes no difference whether the customer is registered for sales tax or not.

5.2 B

SALES TAX CONTROL ACCOUNT

	$		$
		b/d	4,540
Purchases ($64,000 × 15%)	9,600	Sales ($109,250 × 15%/115%)	14,250
∴ Cash	11,910	c/d	2,720
	21,510		21,510

5.3 D Dr Purchases $575 and Cr Payables $575.

Alana is not registered for sales tax purposes and therefore cannot reclaim the input sales tax of $75.

5.4 C The sales tax account is a personal account with the tax authorities.

5.5 D

	$
Assets	
Opening cash	1,000
Cash received $(1,000 + 200 sales tax)	1,200
Closing cash	2,200
Inventory $(800 – 400)	400
	2,600
Liabilities	
Opening liabilities	–
Sales tax payable $(200 – 160)	40
Purchase inventory $(800 + 160 sales tax)	960
Closing liabilities	1,000
Capital	
Opening capital	1,000
Profit on sale of inventory $(1,000 – 400)	600
Closing capital	1,600

5.6 A Receivables and payables include sales tax where applicable.

5.7 B The sales tax element of the invoices will go to the sales tax account in the statement of financial position.

5.8 B

	$
Output sales tax $27,612.50 × $\dfrac{17.5}{117.5}$	4,112.50
Input sales tax $18,000 × $\dfrac{17.5}{100}$	3,150.00
∴ Balance on sales tax a/c (credit)	962.50

6 Inventory

6.1 A $950,000 - 11,750 + 1,500 + (14,950 \times 100/115) = \$952,750$

6.2 C   Carriage outwards and storage are distribution costs.

6.3 A

	$
Original value	284,700
Coats − Cost 400 × $80	(32,000)
− NRV ($75 × 95%) × 400	28,500
	281,200

At 31 January 20X3 the skirts were correctly valued at costs incurred to date of $20 per skirt which was lower than the NRV of $22. Therefore no adjustment required.

6.4 A

	$
50 @ $190	9,500
500 @ $220	110,000
300 @ $230	69,000
	188,500

6.5 C   Statement 1) inventory should be valued at the lower of cost and NRV not the higher
Statement 2) production overheads based on a normal level of production should be included

6.6 D

	$
Inventory check balance	483,700
Less: goods from suppliers	(38,400)
Add: goods sold	14,800
Less: goods returned	(400)
Add: goods returned to supplier	1,800
	461,500

6.7 C   If closing inventory is understated, cost of sales will be overstated. Next year opening inventory will be understated and cost of sales will be understated.

6.8 A

	$	$
Original balance		386,400
Item 1) Cost	(18,000)	
NRV 15,000 − 800	14,200	
Write down		(3,800)
Inventory value		382,600

6.9 C

	$
Inventory count, 4 January 20X2	527,300
Purchases since end of year	(7,900)
Cost of sales since end of year (15,000 × 60%)	9,000
Purchase returns since end of year	800
Inventory at 31 December 20X1	529,200

6.10 A   Trade discounts should be deducted but not settlement discounts. IAS 2 does not allow the use of LIFO. Production overheads are part of the costs of conversion of finished goods and do form part of the valuation.

6.11 B

	$
Original inventory valuation	41,875
Cost of damaged items	(1,960)
NRV of damaged items (1,200 – 360)	840
	40,755

6.12 B

	Cost $	Net realisable value $	Lower of cost & NRV $	Units	Value $
Basic	6	8	6	200	1,200
Super	9	8	8	250	2,000
Luxury	18	10	10	150	1,500
					4,700

6.13 C

6.14 C

6.15 C

	$
	116,400
Line 1: (400 × $3) – $200	1,000
Line 2: (200 × $35) – $300 – $1,200	5,500
	122,900

6.16 A

	$
Inventory count value	836,200
Less: purchases	(8,600)
Add: sales (14,000 × 70/100)	9,800
Add: goods returned	700
Inventory figure	838,100

6.17 B The cost of materials used should be based on opening and closing valuations of inventory at AVCO.

	$
Opening inventory	56,200
Purchases	136,500
	192,700
Less: Closing inventory	(59,800)
Cost of materials used	132,900

6.18 C Continuous inventory in theory should remove the need for physical inventory counts, but in practice periodic counts are needed to ensure that the recorded quantities of inventory match the physical quantities that are held (and, for example, there have not been significant losses of inventory due to theft).

7 Tangible non-current assets I

7.1 A It is **never** B as funds are not set aside, nor C, this is revaluation, nor D – depreciation has nothing to do with the wearing out of assets, depreciation is an application of the matching concept and allocates the cost of the asset over the accounting periods expected to benefit from its use.

7.2 D ($5,000 – $1,000)/4 = $1,000 depreciation per annum ∴ carrying value = $2,000.

7.3   D

		$
Balance b/d		67,460
Less: Carrying value of non-current asset sold		
(4,000 + 1,250)		5,250
		62,210

7.4   A   If disposal proceeds were $15,000 and profit on disposal is $5,000, then carrying value must be $10,000, the difference between the asset register figure and the non-current asset account in the nominal ledger.

7.5   A   An expense has been posted as a non-current asset.

7.6   D

	$
December addition – 18,000 × 20% × 10/12	3,000
June disposal – 36,000 × 20% × 8/12	4,800
Balance – 345,200 × 20%	69,040
	76,840

7.7   C

	$
Valuation	210,000
Carrying value (170,000 × 16/20)	(136,000)
Revaluation surplus	74,000

7.8   A

	$
Repairs cost overstated	20,000
Depreciation understated ((20,000 – 4,000) × 20% × 6/12)	(1,600)
Profit understated	18,400

7.9   A

	$
Plant held all year (200,000 – 40,000) × 20%	32,000
Disposal 40,000 × 20% × 9/12	6,000
Additions 50,000 × 20% × 6/12	5,000
	43,000

7.10   D

	$
Plant held all year (240,000 – 60,000) × 20%	36,000
Addition 160,000 × 20% × 6/12	16,000
Disposal 60,000 × 20% × 3/12	3,000
	55,000

7.11   C   Cost less 4 months depreciation = 25,500 – 2,125 = $23,375

7.12   C

	$
Cost of machine	80,000
Installation	5,000
Testing	1,000
	86,000

Staff training cannot be capitalised as part of the cost of the asset.

7.13   C   Dr Non-current assets – cost, Cr Payables

7.14   A   Using T accounts:

PLANT AND MACHINERY ACCOUNT

	$		$
Balance b/d	100,000	Plant and machinery disposals a/c	100,000

PLANT AND MACHINERY ACCUMULATED DEPRECIATION

	$		$
Plant and machinery disposals	35,000	Balance b/d	35,000

PLANT AND MACHINERY DISPOSALS

	$		$
Plant and machinery account	100,000	Accumulated depreciation	35,000
		Cash	50,000
		SPL (loss on sale)	15,000
	100,000		100,000

7.15 B IAS 16 does not require the purchase date of each asset to be disclosed. The carrying amount of an asset = cost/valuation – accumulated depreciation. The useful life of an asset is determined upon acquisition and should be reviewed at least annually and depreciation rates adjusted for the current and future periods if expectations vary significantly from the original estimates. When an asset is revalued, IAS 16 permits entities to make a transfer from the revaluation surplus to retained earnings of the excess depreciation arising due to the revaluation.

7.16 B The depreciation charge is calculated based on the remaining useful life at the date of the revaluation: 1,000,000/20 years = $50,000

7.17 A The excess deprecation is the new depreciation amount of $50,000 less the old depreciation charge of $30,000 ($750,000/25 years) which is $20,000. This amount should be debited from the revaluation surplus and credited to retained earnings each year. Remember that both retained earnings and the revaluations surplus are credit balances in the trial balance.

8 Tangible non-current assets II

8.1 B

	$
Cost	10,000
20X0 Depreciation	2,500
	7,500
20X1 Depreciation	1,875
	5,625
20X2 Depreciation	1,406
	4,219
20X3 Part exchange	5,000
Profit	781

8.2 A

	$	$
Carrying value at 1st August 20X0		200,000
Less depreciation		(20,000)
Proceeds	25,000	
Loss	5,000	
Therefore carrying value		(30,000)
		150,000

8.3 B

DEBIT	Property, plant and equipment	$38,000
CREDIT	Plant repairs	$38,000
DEBIT	Dep'n expense	$1,900
CREDIT	Accumulated dep'n	$1,900

Profit is understated by $38,000 – $1,900 = $36,100

8.4 B $\dfrac{\$30,000 - \$6,000}{4 \text{ years}} \times \dfrac{5 \text{ months}}{12 \text{ months}} = \$2,500$

8.5 B Revaluation surplus – (1,000,000 – (800,000 – (800,000 × 2% × 10)) = $360,000
Depreciation charge – (1,000,000/40) = $25,000

8.6 D Improvements are capital expenditure, repairs and maintenance are not.

8.7　C　Correct, it is likely to be treated as capital expenditure. A replacement for a broken window is a repair, so it is revenue expenditure. Repainting the restaurant is a repair and renewal expense so it would be likely to be treated as revenue expenditure. Cleaning of the kitchen floors is a maintenance cost and therefore is revenue expenditure.

8.8　A　Number plates, radio and delivery costs are included in the capital cost of acquiring the car. Road tax is an annual charge against revenue.

8.9　B

	$
Water treatment equipment	39,800
Delivery	1,100
	40,900

8.10　C　A is a receivable, B and D are inventory.

8.11　C　Items (i) and (ii) are non-current assets. Only item (iii) is a current asset.

8.12　C　Assets which are expected to be converted into cash in the short term.

8.13　C　To record the purchase of the asset:
Dr Non-current assets – cost　　$15,000
Cr Payables　　$15,000
Depreciation charge is 15,000 × 15% × 2/12 = $375

8.14　D　$585,000

The revaluation surplus at 30 June 20Y8 was $600,000 ($1,600k – $1,000k). The old deprecation charge was $25,000 ($1,250,000/50 years) per year. The new depreciation charge is $40,000 ($1,600,000/40 years), so the excess depreciation is $15,000 per year. The balance on the revaluation surplus is therefore $600,000 – $15,000 = $585,000 at 30 June 20Y9.

8.15　A　At 1.1.X3, the carrying amount of the asset was $36,000 (depreciation charge in X1: 100,000 × 40% = $40,000, X2: (100,000 – 40,000) × 40% = $24,000). The depreciation charge is calculated as the carrying amount divided by the remaining useful life: $36,000/3 years = $12,000 per year. The carrying amount at 31.12.X3 is therefore $36,000 - $12,000 = $24,000.

8.16　B　$52,500
Carrying amount at 1.1.X3 = 100,000 – (100,000 × 2/5) = $60,000
New depreciation charge = Carrying amount/Revised useful life = $60,000/8 years = $7,500
Carrying amount at 31.12.X3 = $60,000 – $7,500 = $52,500

8.17　A　$7,000

Carrying amount at 1.10.X8: 34,000 – ((34,000 – 4,000) × 3/5) = $16,000

Revised depreciation charge: (Carrying amount – revised residual value)/remaining useful life

= (16,000 – 2,000)/2 = $7,000.

8.18　A　Dr Depreciation charge　　$6,000
Cr Accumulated depreciation　　$6,000

8.19　B　In the 5 years to 31 December 20X5, accumulated depreciation on the building is $1,600,000 × 2% × 5 years = $160,000.

On revaluation on 1 January 20X6:

	Debit	Credit
	$	$
Building (2,250,000 – 1,600,000)	650,000	
Accumulated depreciation	160,000	
Revaluation reserve		810,000

The annual depreciation charge from 1 January 20X6 = $2,250,000/45 years remaining = $50,000. This is $18,000 more than the annual depreciation charge based on the historical cost of the asset.

This excess depreciation charge is transferred each year from revaluation reserve to retained earnings, and the revaluation reserve at 31 December 20X6 = $810,000 - $18,000 = $792,000.

8.20   A   Annual depreciation was initially $1,000,000/50 years = $20,000.

After revaluation, annual depreciation is $1,200,000/48 years = $25,000.

		$
Valuation, 1 January 20X5		1,200,000
Accumulated depreciation to 30 June 20X5	(6/12 × $25,000)	12,500
Carrying amount at 30 June 20X5		1,187,500
Sale/disposal price		1,195,000
Profit on disposal in statement of profit or loss		7,500

Note: The balance on the revaluation reserve at 30 June will be transferred to realised profits (retained profits reserve), but this will not be reported as profit in the statement of profit or loss.

9   Intangible non-current assets

9.1   B   There is no requirement that development expenditure should be amortised over a period not exceeding five years.

9.2   C   1   Development expenditure must be capitalised if the criteria are met.
           3   There is no time scale given by IAS 38 for amortisation.

9.3   C   Development costs are amortised over the useful life of the project. This is not confined to five years.

9.4   A   3 only.

9.5   B   A factory is a tangible asset as it has physical form. The others are intangible assets.

9.6   A   Research expenditure is never capitalised.

9.7   D   Research expenditure is never capitalised.

9.8   A   Research expenditure is never capitalised, development expenditure is capitalised if it meets certain conditions per IAS 38. Intangible assets are amortised over their useful life, if the life of the asset is indefinite, then it does not have to be amortised.

9.9   A $123,000. Research expenditure $103,000 + depreciation of development costs $20,000.

9.10   A $219,000. Development costs b/f $180,000 + additions on project 910 $59,000 – depreciation $20,000.

9.11   B   The patent should be amortised over its useful life of 10 years, the balance at 30 November 20X5 is therefore $25,000 – (25,000 × 2/10) = $20,000

9.12   B   The amortisation charge is $15,000/3 years = $5,000 per annum. The double entry to record the amortisation is Dr expenses, Cr accumulated amortisation.

10 Accruals and prepayments

10.1 C

	$
Receipt	
1 October 20X1 ($7,500 × 1/3)	2,500
30 December 20X1	7,500
4 April 20X2	9,000
1 July 20X2	9,000
1 October 20X2 (9,000 × 2/3)	6,000 (3,000 Credit rent in advance)
Credit to statement of profit or loss	34,000

10.2 B

	$
February to March 20X2 (22,500 × 2/3)	15,000
April to June	22,500
July to September	22,500
October to December	30,000
January 20X3 (30,000 × 1/3)	10,000
Rent for the year	100,000

Accrual 30,000 × 1/3 = 10,000

10.3 D

	$
Payments made	34,600
Add: opening balance	8,200
Less: opening accrual	(3,600)
Less: closing balance	(9,300)
Add: closing accrual	3,200
	33,100

10.4 B

	$
Statement of profit or loss	
December to June 8,400 × 7/12	4,900
July to November 12,000 × 5/12	5,000
	9,900

Sundry payables 12,000 × 1/12 = 1,000 (December rent received in advance)

10.5 C

	$
August to September 60,000 × 2/12	10,000
October to July 72,000 × 10/12	60,000
	70,000

10.6 A $87,700

Diesel fuel payable account

	$
Balance b/fwd	(1,700)
Payments	85,400
Balance c/fwd	1,300
Purchases	85,000

Cost of fuel used

	$
Opening inventory	12,500
Purchases	85,000
Closing inventory	(9,800)
Transfer to SPL	87,700

10.7 C   ELECTRICITY ACCOUNT

			$			$
				Balance b/fwd		300
20X0:						
1 August	Paid bank		600			
1 November	Paid bank		720			
20X1:						
1 February	Paid bank		900			
30 June	Paid bank		840			
30 June	Accrual c/d					
	$840 × $^2/_3$		560	SPL		3,320
			3,620			3,620

10.8 A   GAS SUPPLIER ACCOUNT

		$			$
Balance b/fwd		200			
Bank $600 × 12		7,200	28 February	invoice	1,300
			31 May	invoice	1,400
			31 August	invoice	2,100
			30 November	invoice	2,000
			30 November	bal. c/d	600
		7,400			7,400

GAS ACCOUNT

		$			$
28 February	invoice	1,300			
31 May	invoice	1,400			
31 August	invoice	2,100			
30 November	invoice	2,000	30 November	SPL	6,800
		6,800			6,800

10.9 A $\dfrac{5 \text{ months}}{12 \text{ months}} \times \$24,000 = \$10,000$

$\dfrac{7 \text{ months}}{12 \text{ months}} \times \$30,000 = \$17,500$

Total rent: $10,000 + $17,500 = $27,500

10.10 D   RENTAL INCOME ACCOUNT

	$		$
Opening rent owing	16,900	Opening rent in advance	24,600
Rent income (balancing figure)	316,200	Cash received	318,600
Closing rent in advance	28,400	Closing rent owing	18,300
	361,500		361,500

10.11 A   Statement of profit or loss and other comprehensive income = $60,000 × 12/18 = $40,000

Statement of financial position = $60,000 × 3/18 prepayment = $10,000

10.12 B   Dr Expenses (SPL), Cr Liability (accruals in the SOFP)

10.13 A   An accrual should be made for $10,000 ($30,000/3 months). The double entry to record the accrual in the accounts is:

Dr Expenses (SPL) $10,000
Cr Accruals (SOFP) $10,000
This reduces profit from $25,000 to $15,000

An accrual is a liability and so will reduce the net asset position, from $275,000 to $265,000. Remember that net assets = assets – liabilities.

10.14 A   Dr Asset (prepayments in the SPL), Cr expenses (ie reduce expenses in the SPL)

10.15 B

	$
Original loss	(1,486)
Accrual	(1,625)
Prepayment	834
Revised loss	(2,277)

11 Receivables and payables

11.1 D

	$
Closing allowance required (400,000 – 38,000) × 10%	36,200
Opening allowance	50,000
Decrease in allowance	(13,800)
Irrecoverable debts written off	38,000
Statement of profit or loss charge	24,200

11.2 A

	$
Irrecoverable debts written off	14,600
Reduction in allowance	(2,000)
	12,600

11.3 D

	$
Irrecoverable debt written off	28,500
Increase in allowance ((868,500 – 28,500) × 5% – 38,000)	4,000
	32,500

11.4 C $146,000 + ($218,000 – $83,000) = $281,000

11.5 B   Because the debt has been previously written off, there is no receivable for which to offset the cash, therefore the double entry is Dr Cash, Cr Irrecoverable debts expense.

11.6 B

	$
Allowance required 5% × (864,000 – 13,000)	42,550
Existing allowance	(48,000)
Reduction in allowance	(5,450)
Irrecoverable debts written off	13,000
Statement of profit or loss charge	7,550

Net trade receivables   = $864,000 – 13,000 – 42,550
                  = $808,450

11.7 D   A decrease in the allowance is written back to profit or loss.

11.8 A   The debt needs to be written off. The allowance previously made will be adjusted at the year end.

11.9 C   An increase in the allowance for receivables will reduce profits and receivables. Gross profit will not be affected since allowances for receivables are dealt with in the net profit section.

11.10 D

	$	SPL charge $
Receivables allowance at 31.12.X1 (15% of $20,000)	1,000	
Receivables allowance at 1.1.X1	3,000	
Decrease in allowance		2,000
Irrecoverable debts written off		(1,000)
Debt recovered		800
Total credit to statement of profit or loss		1,800

11.11 D   Prudence. The provision prevents receivables being overstated.

11.12 C

		$	SPL charge $
Receivables allowance at year end		1,000	
Receivables allowance at beginning of year		850	
Increase in allowance			(150)
Irrecoverable debts written off			(500)
Total charge to statement of profit or loss			650

11.13 C An aged receivables analysis shows the outstanding balances owed by each customer analysed by how long they have been outstanding, usually 30, 60 and 90+ days. The receivables allowance is deducted from the receivables balance in the statement of financial position.

A credit limit is set by the credit control department of the business and is the maximum amount of credit each customer of that business can have. Credit limits are not applied to cash sales.

11.14 A The trade payables are due to be paid within 12 months, the overdraft is repayable on demand.

11.15 D A specific allowance should be made against the $3,500 that Jackson seems unlikely to pay.

11.16 A $10,000 + (2% x $490,000) = $19,800.

11.17 D

	$
Specific allowance for receivables at 1 January	20,000
General allowance: 2.5% of (380,000 – 20,000)	9,000
	29,000
General allowance at 31 December: 3% of 420,000	12,600
Reduction in allowance for receivables	(16,400)
Irrecoverable debt written off	28,000
Combined expense in statement of profit or loss	11,600

11.18 D An imprest system for petty cash helps with management of small cash expenditures are reduces the risk of fraud. The amount paid in to replenish petty cash at the beginning of each period should be the amount of petty cash spending in the previous period, which is the total of expenditures shown by petty cash vouchers for the previous period. The amount of petty cash at any time is the maximum petty cash balance minus the value of the petty cash vouchers for the period.

11.19 A The petty cash voucher is a record that cash has been issued for an approved item of expense. The receipt is evidence of the amount of the expense. The petty cash book is used to record the transaction in the book-keeping system.

12 Provisions and contingencies

12.1 C Contingent assets should not be recognised in the financial statements. However, they should be disclosed if it is probable that the economic benefits associated with the asset will flow to the entity. If it becomes probable that the a transfer of economic benefits associated with a contingent liability will happen, then the contingent liability is no longer contingent and a liability should be recognised in the financial statements.

12.2 A A possible transfer of economic benefits should be disclosed. Where transfer is probable a provision should be made.

12.3 C As the claim is unlikely to succeed, the potential settlement of $500,000 should be disclosed as a contingent liability note. However, given that the legal costs of $50,000 must be paid whether the claim is successful or not, this amount should be provided for in the company's financial statements.

12.4 A   A provision is required for the warranties sold, it should be calculated using the expected value approach. 2 is a contingent liability because it is possible that the company will have to pay out, if it was probable, then a provision would be required. If it was remote, no disclosure would be needed.

12.5 A   All 3 statements are correct.

12.6 C   The provision should be increased by $1,086, the double entry is therefore Dr Expenses, Cr Provision.

12.7 B   Doggard Co needs to reduce the provision by $500 ie a credit to the statement of profit or loss.

12.8 A   A provision is a liability of uncertain timing or amount. A contingent liability is a *possible* obligation of uncertain timing or amount.

12.9 C   The statement is the definition of a contingent liability.

12.10 C   Montague should include a provision of $3,000 in his year-end accounts as this is the best estimate of the amount he will probably have to pay out.

13   Control accounts

13.1 C   Credit sales = $80,000 – $10,000 + $9,000 = $79,000.

13.2 B   A, C and D would make the supplier's statement $150 *higher*.

13.3 A

	$
Opening balance	34,500
Credit purchases	78,400
Discounts	(1,200)
Payments	(68,900)
Purchase returns	(4,700)
	38,100

13.4 A $8,500 – (2 × $400) = $7,700.

13.5 A   Sales and refunds are posted on the *debit* side, changes in the allowance for receivables do not appear in the control account.

13.6 B

RECEIVABLES LEDGER CONTROL ACCOUNT

	$		$
Opening balance	180,000	Cash from credit customers	228,000
Credit sales	190,000	Irrecoverable debts written off	1,500
Cash refunds	3,300	Sales returns	8,000
		Discount allowed	4,200
		Contras	2,400
		Closing balance	129,200
	373,300		373,300

13.7 C

RECEIVABLES LEDGER CONTROL ACCOUNT

	$		$
Opening balance	284,680	Cash received	179,790
Credit sales	189,120	Discounts allowed	3,660
		Irrecoverable debts written off	1,800
		Sales returns	4,920
		Contras	800
		Closing balance	282,830
	473,800		473,800

13.8 C

RECEIVABLES LEDGER CONTROL ACCOUNT

	$		$
Opening balance	308,600	Cash received	147,200
Credit sales	154,200	Discounts allowed	1,400
Interest charged	2,400	Contra	4,600
		Irrecoverable debts	4,900
		Closing balance	307,100
	465,200		465,200

13.9 A

RECEIVABLES LEDGER CONTROL ACCOUNT

	$		$
Opening balance	614,000	Cash from customers	311,000
Credit sales	301,000	Discounts allowed	3,400
Interest charged on overdue		Irrecoverable debts written off	32,000
accounts	1,600	Contras	8,650
		Closing balance	561,550
	916,600		916,600

13.10 A

	Debit	Credit	$
Sales price			800
Less: 20% trade discount			120
Sale	PQ Co	Sales	640
Cash discount 5%	Discount allowed		32
Cash payment	Bank		608
		PQ Co	640

13.11 C

13.12 A

13.13 C

RECEIVABLES LEDGER CONTROL ACCOUNT

	$		$
Opening balance	318,650	Cash from customers	181,140
Credit sales	161,770	Discounts allowed	1,240
Interest on overdue accounts	280	Irrecoverable debts written off	1,390
		Sales returns	3,990
		Closing balance	292,940
	480,700		480,700

13.14 A $130,585

PAYABLES LEDGER CONTROL ACCOUNT

	$		$
Returns outwards	27,490	Balance b/f	142,320
Payments to payables	196,360	Credit purchases (183,800 × 1.175)	215,965
Discount received	1,430		
Contra	2,420		
Balance c/f	130,585		
	358,285		358,285
		Balance b/f	130,585

13.15 B   1, 4 and 5

JOURNAL ENTRIES

		$ DR	$ CR
Error 1	Payables ledger control	420	
	Receivables ledger control		420
Error 4	Irrecoverable debts	240	
	Receivables ledger control		240
Error 5	Sales	900	
	Receivables ledger control		900

13.16 C $16,495

BALANCES EXTRACTED FROM THE RECEIVABLES LEDGER

		+ $	– $	$
Total before corrections for errors				15,800
Error 2	Mahmood	90		
Error 3	Yasmin	780		
Error 6	Charles		300	
Error 7	Edward	125		
		995	300	695
				16,495

13.17 C $17,560

RECEIVABLES LEDGER CONTROL ACCOUNT

		$			$
∴ Balance b/f		17,560	Error 1	Ahmed	420
			Error 4	Thomas	240
			Error 5	Sales daybook total	900
					1,560
			Balance c/f		16,000
		17,560			17,560

13.18 C

Balance per ledger	$31,554	Cr
Discount	$53	Dr
Invoice	$622	Cr
Corrected balance	$32,123	

13.19 D

	Control account $	List of balances $
Balance/total	68,566	68,538
Credit balance omitted	–	127
Undercasting of day book	99	–
	68,665	68,665

13.20 D   Trade payables are a current liability

14   Bank reconciliations

14.1 B $(565)o/d – $92 dishonoured cheque = $(657) o/d

14.2 D

	$
Balance b/d	5,675 o/d
Less: standing order	(125)
Add: dishonoured cheque (450 × 2)	900
	6,450 o/d

14.3 A

	$
Opening bank balance	2,500
Payment ($1,000 – $200) × 90%	(720)
Receipt ($200 – $10)	190
Closing bank balance	1,970

14.4 B

	$
Balance per bank statement	(800)
Unpresented cheque	(80)
Dishonoured cheque (affects cash book only)	–
	(880)

14.5 B

	$
Original cash book figure	2,490
Adjustment re charges	(50)
Adjustment re dishonoured cheque	(140)
	2,300

14.6 D

	$
Bank statement	(36,840)
Deposits credited after date	51,240
Outstanding cheques	(43,620)
Balance per cash book (o/d)	(29,220)

14.7 A   Dishonoured cheques and bank charges must be entered in the cash book.

14.8 B   Bank charges, direct debits and dishonoured cheques will all be written into the cash book.

14.9 B

	$
Overdraft	(3,860)
Outstanding cheques	(9,160)
	(13,020)
Outstanding lodgements	16,690
Cash at bank	3,670

14.10 A   Bank charges not entered in the cash book can be entered, and the cash book balance adjusted.

14.11 B

Cash book	$	Bank statement	$
Balance	(8,970)	Balance	(11,200)
Bank charges	(550)	Credit in error	(425)
		Unpresented cheques	(3,275)
		Outstanding lodgements	5,380
	(9,520)		(9,520)

14.12 C   The bank is overdrawn.

	$
Overdraft	(38,600)
Outstanding lodgements	41,200
	2,600
Unpresented cheques	(3,300)
Overdraft	(700)

14.13 A   The other two items are part of the bank reconciliation.

14.14 B

	$
Overdraft per bank statement	39,800
Less: deposits credited after date	(64,100)
Add: outstanding cheques	44,200
Overdraft per cash book	19,900

14.15 B   Cash book 3, 5: bank reconciliation 1, 2, 4

15 Correction of errors

15.1 B The discount received should have been *credited* to discounts received, so the effect is doubled.

15.2 B Start by posting the adjustment in full:

	Debit $	Credit $
Discount allowed	3,840	2,960
Discount received	3,840	2,960
Suspense account		1,760

15.3 D Returns outwards are returns to suppliers, which should therefore reduce the purchases balance – ie it should be a credit balance.
Option A would result in credits being higher than debits in the trial balance. Options B and C would not cause an imbalance.

15.4 A B and C would make the credit side $50 higher. D would have no effect.

15.5 B This has debited a non-current asset to cost of sales which is an error of principle as it has broken the principles of accounting – ie that non-current assets should be capitalised.

15.6 C A transaction has been posted to the wrong account, but not the wrong class of account.

15.7 B This is an error of original entry.

15.8 C

	$
Draft net profit	83,600
Add: purchase price	18,000
Less: additional depreciation (18,000 × 25%)	(4,500)
Adjusted profit	97,100

15.9 B The cash book was credited with $210 reimbursement of petty cash. However, the nominal ledger was posted with only $200 of expenditure (debits). Therefore the credits are $10 higher than the debits.

15.10 D $10,200 + $3,000 + $1,400 = $14,600.

15.11 A Both errors will affect cost of sales and therefore gross profit, making a net effect of $40,000. Net profit will be further reduced by $10,000 missing from stationery expense.

15.12 D Debits will exceed credits by 2 × $48 = $96

15.13 D Errors of principle, such as recording a capital expenditure transaction as revenue expenditure, would not be revealed by a trial balance because it would not create an inequality between total debits and total credits. Transposition errors are errors where figures (digits) are written in the wrong order in either a credit or a debit entry. This would create an imbalance between credits and debts, and so the error would be indicated by extracting a trial balance.

15.14 C

	Debit $	Credit $
Non-current assets	85,000	
Receivables	7,000	
Trade payables		3,000
Bank loan		15,000
Allowance for depreciation, non-current assets		15,000
Inventory	4,000	
Accruals		1,000
Prepayments	2,000	
Bank overdraft		2,000
	98,000	36,000

15.15 A

Debit balances	$	$
Purchases	160,000	
Non-current assets	120,000	
Receivables	33,000	
Other expenses	110,000	
Bank	18,000	
		441,000
Credit balances		
Payables	27,000	
Capital	66,000	
Sales	300,000	
Purchase returns	2,000	
		395,000
Bank loan (credit balance)		46,000

16 Suspense accounts

16.1 D Error (5) will not cause a trial balance imbalance.

16.2 A

SUSPENSE ACCOUNT

	$		$
Share capital	3,000	Opening balance	3,460
Motor vehicles	9,000	Plant asset (2,800 × 2)	5,600
		Petty cash (TB)	500
		Closing balance	2,440
	12,000		12,000

16.3 B This results in a debit to the suspense account therefore reducing the balance.

Option A results in a credit to the suspense account and options C and D do not affect the suspense account at all.

16.4 B (1) This entry has been correctly debited but to the wrong account – no effect on trial balance
(4) Double entry has been carried out although the wrong way round – no effect on trial balance

16.5 A

SUSPENSE ACCOUNT

	$		$
Balance b/d	210	Gas bill (420 – 240)	180
Interest	70	Discount (2 × 500)	100
	280		280

16.6 C The transactions in 1 and 5 should both have been **debited.**

16.7 D

Suspense account	$	
Opening balance	16,500	credit
Discount allowed (debit discount allowed)	3,900	credit
Discount received (credit discount received)	(5,100)	debit
Transposition of cash received (credit RLCA)	(9,900)	debit
	5,400	credit

16.8 B Only errors 1 and 3 involve a suspense account entry to correct them.

16.9 D A and B will only affect the personal ledgers, C will cause an incorrect double entry.

16.10 B A would give a debit balance of $130, C would have no effect and D would not cause a trial balance imbalance.

17 | 15 mark questions: preparing financial statements

17.1 Mr Yousef

(a)

MR YOUSEF
STATEMENT OF PROFIT OR LOSS FOR THE YEAR ENDED 31 MAY 20X6

	$	$
Sales		138,078
Opening inventory	11,927	
Purchases (W1)	84,561	
	96,488	
Less closing inventory	13,551	
Cost of goods sold		82,937
Gross profit		55,141
Carriage out (W2)	2,933	
Rent and insurance (W3)	5,952	
Postage and stationery	3,001	
Advertising	1,330	
Salaries and wages	26,420	
Irrecoverable debts	877	
Depreciation charge (W4)	8,700	
Increase in allowance for receivables	40	
		49,253
Net profit		5,888

(b)

MR YOUSEF
STATEMENT OF FINANCIAL POSITION AS AT 31 MAY 20X6

	Cost $	Accumulated depreciation $	Carrying value $
Non-current assets			
Equipment	58,000	27,700	30,300
Current assets			
Inventory		13,551	
Receivables	12,120		
Less allowance for receivables	170		
		11,950	
Prepayment		880	
Cash		177	
Bank		1,002	
			27,560
			57,860
Capital			
At 1 June 20X5			53,091
Profit for year			5,888
			58,979
Drawings			(7,800)
At 31 May 20X6			51,179
Current liabilities			
Payables		6,471	
Accrual		210	
			6,681
			57,860

Workings

1   *Purchases*

		$
Per trial balance		82,350
Add carriage inwards		2,211
Per statement of profit or loss		84,561

2   Carriage out = $5,144 – $2,211 = $2,933.

3   *Rent, rates and insurance*

		$
Per trial balance		6,622
Add rent accrual		210
Less insurance prepayment		(880)
Per statement of profit or loss		5,952

4   Depreciation charge = 15% × $58,000 = $8,700

17.2 Shuswap

(a)   *Suspense account*

Proceeds of issue of 4m shares at $1.10	4,400
Proceeds of sale of plant (balance)	600
	5,000

Journal entries:		
DR Suspense a/c	5,000	
CR Issued share capital (4m x 50c)		2,000
Share premium (4m x 60c)		2,400
Disposal a/c		600

(b)

SHUSWAP
STATEMENT OF FINANCIAL POSITION AT 31 DECEMBER 20X4

	Cost or valuation $'000	Accumulated depreciation $'000	Carrying value $'000
Assets			
Non-current assets			
Land and buildings	12,000	–	12,000
Plant and equipment (W1)	19,600	7,950	11,650
			23,650
Current assets			
Inventories (3,000 – 140)			2,860
Receivables (2,600 – 200 – 106)			2,294
Cash at bank			1,900
Total assets			30,704
Equity and liabilities			
Equity			
Issued share capital (6,000 + 2,000 (part (a)))			8,000
Share premium (part (a))			2,400
Revaluation reserve (3,000 + 1,000)			4,000
Retained earnings (W2)			12,310
			26,710
Non-current liabilities			
Loan notes (redeemable 20Y0)			2,000
Current liabilities			
Trade payables (2,100 – 106)			1,994
Total equity and liabilities			30,704

Workings

1   *Plant and equipment*

		$'000
Disposal	– Cost	1,400
	– Depreciation	(700)
	– Carrying value	700
Proceeds (part (a))		(600)
Loss on sale		100

Cost adjustment 21,000 – 1,400 = 19,600

Accumulated depreciation adjustment (9,000 – 700 – (1,400 × 25%)) = 7,950

2   *Retained earnings*

	$'000
Per draft	12,400
Irrecoverable debts	(200)
Inventory write down (500 – 360)	(140)
Loss on disposal of plant (W1)	(100)
Depreciation adjustment (1,400 × 25%) (W1)	350
	12,310

17.3 Malright

(a)   MALRIGHT
       STATEMENT OF PROFIT OR LOSS FOR THE YEAR ENDED 31 OCTOBER 20X7

	$'000
Revenue (W4)	1,765
Cost of sales (W1)	(1,343)
Gross profit	422
Distribution costs (W1)	(80)
Administrative expenses (W1)	(192)
Profit before interest and tax	150
Finance cost: 50,000 × 10%	(5)
Profit before taxation	145
Income taxes	(45)
Profit for the year	100

(b)   MALRIGHT
       STATEMENT OF CHANGES IN EQUITY FOR THE YEAR ENDED 31 OCTOBER 20X7

	Ordinary shares $'000	Share premium $'000	Retained earnings $'000	Total $'000
Balance at 1 Nov 20X6	650	80	130	860
Total comprehensive income for the year			100	100
Dividends paid			(30)	(30)
Balance at 31 Oct 20X7	650	80	200	930

(c)   MALRIGHT
      STATEMENT OF FINANCIAL POSITION AS AT 31 OCTOBER 20X7

	$'000	$'000
Non-current assets		
Tangible assets (W3)		966
Current assets		
Inventory	75	
Trade receivables (320 – 16)	304	
		379
		1,345
Equity and liabilities		
Equity		
$1 ordinary shares		650
Share premium		80
Retained earnings (part (b))		200
		930
Non-current liabilities		
10 % loan notes		50
Current liabilities		
Trade payables	250	
Bank overdraft	50	
Tax payable	45	
Loan interest payable	5	
Energy expense accrual	15	
		365
Total equity and liabilities		1,345

Workings

1   *Cost of sales/distribution costs/administration expenses*

	Cost of sales $'000	Distribution cost $'000	Administrative expenses $'000
Purchases	1,105		
Discounts received			(90)
Wages (40:25:35)	72	45	63
Energy expenses ($105 + $15) (40:20:40)	48	24	48
Opening inventory	160		
Administrative expenses			80
Increase in allowance for receivables (W2)			6
Director's remuneration			70
Closing inventory	(75)		
Depreciation – buildings (30:30:40) (W3)	11	11	15
Depreciation – plant (W3)	22		
	1,343	80	192

2   *Allowance for receivables*

	$'000
Trade receivables at 31 October 20X7	320
∴ Allowance needed: $320 × 5%	16
Allowance at 1 November 20X6	10
∴ Increase	6

3 Tangible non-current assets

	Land $'000	Buildings $'000	Plant $'000	Total $'000
Cost	235	740	220	1,195
Accumulated dep'n at 1.11.X6	–	60	110	170
Charge for year				
Buildings:				
$740,000 × 5%		37		37
Plant:				
(220 – 110) × 20%			22	22
	–	97	132	229
Carrying value at 31.10.X7	235	643	88	966

4 Revenue

	$'000
Per trial balance	1,800
Less returns inward	(35)
	1,765

17.4 Sondaw

(a) SONDAW
STATEMENT OF PROFIT OR LOSS FOR THE YEAR ENDED 31 MAY 20X4

	$'000
Revenue	5,876
Cost of sales (W1)	(3,072)
Gross profit	2,804
Distribution costs (W2)	(492)
Administrative expenses (W3)	(763)
Finance cost	1,549
	(30)
Profit before tax	1,519
Income tax	(250)
Profit for the period	1,269

(b) SONDAW
STATEMENT OF FINANCIAL POSITION AS AT 31 MAY 20X4

	$'000	$'000
Assets		
Non-current assets		
Property, plant and equipment (W5)		3,193
Current assets		
Inventory	800	
Receivables (W6)	386	
Cash	50	
		1,236
Total assets		4,429
Equity and liabilities		
Equity		
$1 ordinary shares		1,500
Retained earnings (280 + 1,269)		1,549
		3,049
Non-current liabilities		
5% Loan notes		600
Current liabilities		
Payables (W7)	530	
Taxation	250	
		780
Total equity and liabilities		4,429

Workings

1   *Cost of sales*

	$'000
Opening inventory	1,200
Purchases	2,200
	3,400
Closing inventory	(800)
	2,600
Share of other expenses	
General expenses: 600 × 10/100	60
Heat and light: 90 × 50/100	45
Wages: (490 + 10) × 60/100	300
Depreciation (W5)	
Buildings: 250 × 50/100	125
Plant and equipment	92
Discounts received	(150)
	3,072

2   *Distribution costs*

	$'000
General expenses: 600 × 40/100	240
Heat and light: 90 × 30/100	27
Wages: 500 × 30/100	150
Depreciation (W5)	
Buildings: 250 × 20/100	50
Motor vehicles	25
	492

3   *Administrative expenses*

	$'000
General expenses: 600 × 50/100	300
Heat and light: 90 × 20/100	18
Marketing and advertising: 248 – 6	242
Wages: 500 × 10/100	50
Irrecoverable debts and allowance for receivables (W4)	58
Depreciation: buildings	75
Audit fee	20
	763

4   *Irrecoverable debts and allowance for receivables*

	$'000
Allowance required: 5% × (438 – 38)	20
Allowance b/fwd	nil
∴ Increase in allowance	20
Add irrecoverable debt written off	38
	58

5   *Non-current assets and depreciation*

	Buildings	Vehicles	Plant and equipment	Total
	$'000	$'000	$'000	$'000
Cost at 1.6.Y3	5,000	160	700	5,860
Accumulated depn. at 1.6.X3	2,000	60	240	2,300
Charge for year				
5% × 5,000	250			
25% × (160 – 60)		25		
20% × (700 – 240)			92	367
At 31.5.X4	2,250	85	332	2,667
Carrying value at 31.3.X4	2,750	75	368	3,193

6   *Receivables*

	$'000
Per list of balances	438
Less irrecoverable debt written off	(38)
	400
Less allowance	(20)
	380
Prepayment	6
	386

7   *Payables*

	$'000	$'000
Per list of balances		500
Accruals: wages	10	
audit fee	20	
		30
		530

17.5 Tonson

(a)   TONSON
STATEMENT OF PROFIT OR LOSS FOR THE YEAR ENDED 30 OCTOBER 20X6

	$'000	$'000
Sales revenue		5,780
Less returns inward		(95)
		5,685
Cost of sales (W1)		(3,670)
		2,015
Discounts received		50
Gross profit		2,065
Expenses		
Insurance	75	
General expenses	60	
Energy expenses	66	
Marketing expenses (50 – 5)	45	
Wages and salaries (675 + 40)	715	
Telephone expenses	80	
Property expenses	100	
Debenture interest	33	
Irrecoverable debt expense (W2)	155	
Depreciation (W3)	347	
		(1,676)
Net profit before taxation		389
Taxation		(150)
Profit for the year		239

(b) TONSON
STATEMENT OF FINANCIAL POSITION AS AT 31 OCTOBER 20X6

	$'000 Cost/ valuation	$'000 Accumulated depn.	$'000
Land	740	–	740
Buildings	1,800	–	1,800
Motor vehicles (W3)	240	112	128
Furniture and equipment (W3)	1,200	660	540
	3,980	772	3,208
Current assets			
Inventory (W1)		250	
Receivables	900		
Less allowance	(45)		
		855	
Prepayments (marketing expenses)		5	
Cash in hand		15	
			1,125
			4,333
Equity and liabilities			
Equity			
$1 Ordinary shares (W4)			1,980
Share premium account (W4)			20
Revaluation reserve (W3)			735
Retained earnings (315 + 239)			554
			3,289
Non-current liabilities			
7% loan note			470
Current liabilities			
Trade payables		290	
Accruals (wages)		40	
Tax		150	
Bank overdraft		94	
			574
			4,333

Workings

1   Cost of sales

	$'000	$'000
Opening inventory		350
Purchases		3,570
		3,920
Closing inventory		
Per question	275	
Less write-down to NRV (45 – 20)	(25)	
		(250)
		3,670

2   Irrecoverable debt expense

	$
Receivables per trial balance	900,000
Allowance required 900,000 × 5%	45,000
Allowance per trial balance	40,000
Increase	5,000
Irrecoverable debt written off	150,000
Total irrecoverable debt expense	155,000

3   Non-current assets and depreciation

	Land $'000	Buildings $'000	Motor vehicles $'000	Furniture and equipment $'000
Cost	740	1,500	240	1,200
Depreciation at 1.11.X5	–	360	80	420
Charge for the year				
1,500 × 5%		75		
(240 – 80) × 20%			32	
1,200 × 20%				240
	–	435	112	660
Carrying value at 31.10.X6	740	1,065	128	540

Total depreciation charge: 75 + 32 + 240 = $347,000

Revaluation of buildings:

	$
Carrying value at 31.10.X6	1,065
Revaluation surplus (bal)	735
Valuation at 31.10.X6	1,800

4   Equity

	$
Share capital	
Per trial balance	1,800
Bonus issue one for ten	180
	1,980
Share premium	
Per trial balance	200
Bonus issue	(180)
	20

17.6 Emma

EMMA
STATEMENT OF CASH FLOWS FOR THE YEAR ENDED 31 DECEMBER 20X2

	$'000	$'000
Cash flows from operating activities		
Net profit before taxation	300	
Adjustments for:		
Depreciation (W1)	90	
Loss on sale for non-current assets (45-32)	13	
Profit on sale of non-current asset investments	(5)	
Interest received	(25)	
Interest expense	75	
Operating profit before working capital changes	448	
Increase in inventories	(48)	
Increase in receivables	(75)	
Increase in payables	8	
Cash generated from operations	333	
Interest paid	(75)	
Income taxes paid (W2)	(190)	
Net cash from operating activities		68

	$'000	$'000
Cash flows from investing activities		
Purchase of intangible non-current assets	(50)	
Purchase of tangible non-current assets (W3)	(201)	
Receipts from sale of non-current assets (32+30)	62	
Interest received	25	
Net cash used in investing activities		(164)
Cash flows from financing activities		
Proceeds from issue of share capital	60	
Long-term loan	100	
		160
Net increase in cash and cash equivalents		64
Cash and cash equivalents at 1 January 20X2 (Note 1)		(97)
Cash and cash equivalents at 31 December 20X2 (Note 1)		(33)

Note 1 Cash and cash equivalents

	31 December	
	20X2	20X1
	$'000	$'000
Cash in hand	2	1
Bank overdraft	(85)	(98)
Short-term investments	50	
	(33)	(97)

Workings

1 *Depreciation charge*

	$'000	$'000
Depreciation at 31 December 20X2		340
Depreciation 31 December 20X1	290	
Depreciation on assets sold (85 – 45)	40	
		250
Charge for the year		90

2 *Tax paid*

INCOME TAX

	$'000		$'000
Tax paid	190	1.1.X2 balance b/d	240
31.12.X2 balance c/d	290	Statement of profit or loss	240
	480		480

3 *Purchase of tangible non-current assets*

TANGIBLE NON-CURRENT ASSETS

	$'000		$'000
1.1.X2 Balance b/d	595	Disposals	85
Revaluation (100 – 91)	9		
Purchases (bal fig)	201	31.12.X2 Balance c/d	720
	805		805

205

17.7 Sioux

SIOUX
STATEMENT OF CASH FLOWS FOR THE YEAR ENDED 31 DECEMBER 20X4

	$'000	$'000
Net profit before tax	2,350	
Add: depreciation (W)	1,250	
Less: profit on disposal (500 – 350)	(150)	
Add: Interest	300	
Operating profit before working capital changes	3,750	
Decrease in inventories	400	
Increase in receivables	(900)	
Increase in payables	500	
Cash generated from operations	3,750	
Interest paid (3,000 × 10%)	(300)	
Tax paid	(600)	
		2,850
Cash flows from investing activities		
Payments to acquire non-current assets (W)	(3,300)	
Proceeds from sale of non-current assets	500	
Net cash used in investing activities		(2,800)
Cash flows from financing activities		
Proceeds from issue of loan notes (3,000 – 2,000)	1,000	
Dividends paid	(750)	
Net cash from financing activities		250
Net increase in cash		300
Cash at 1 January 20X4		100
Cash at 31 December 20X4		400

Workings

Non-current assets

NON-CURRENT ASSETS AT COST

	$		$
Opening balance	8,000	Disposal	800
Revaluation	500	Closing balance	11,000
Additions (balance figure)	3,300		
	11,800		11,800

NON-CURRENT ASSETS – ACCUMULATED DEPRECIATION

	$		$
Disposal (800 – 350)	450	Opening balance	4,800
Closing balance	5,600	Charge for year (balance figure)	1,250
	6,050		6,050

17.8 Snowdrop

SNOWDROP LIMITED
STATEMENT OF CASH FLOWS FOR THE YEAR ENDED 31 MAY 20X5

	$'000	$'000
Cash flows from operating activities		
Net profit before tax	1,032	
Adjustments for		
Depreciation	700	
Loss on sale of tangible non-current assts	20	
Interest	10	
	1,762	
Operating profit before working capital changes		
Increase in inventory	(80)	
Increase in receivables	(130)	
Increase in payables	85	
Cash generated from operations	1,637	
Interest paid	(10)	
Tax paid (W1)	(145)	
Dividends paid	(270)	
Net cash from operating activities		1,212
Cash flow from investing activities		
Purchase of non-current assets (W2)		(2,800)
Receipts from sales of tangible non-current assets		180
Cash flows from financing activities		
Proceeds from issue of share capital	1,280	
Repayment of long term borrowing	(100)	
		1,180
Net increase/(decrease) in cash and cash equivalents		(228)
Cash and cash equivalents at the beginning of period		170
Cash and cash equivalents at end of period		(58)

Note. Dividends paid and interest paid may be shown in either operating activities or financing activities.

Workings

1   *Tax paid*

TAXATION

	$'000		$'000
Tax paid (bal fig)	145	Balance b/fwd	145
Balance c/fwd	180	Statement of profit or loss	180
	325		325

2   *Payments for tangible non-current assets*

TANGIBLE NON-CURRENT ASSETS

	$'000		$'000
Balance b/fwd	2,700	Depreciation	700
Additions (bal fig)	2,800	Disposals (carrying value)	200
		Balance c/fwd	4,600
	5,500		5,500

17.9 Geofost

GEOFOST
STATEMENT OF CASH FLOWS FOR THE YEAR ENDED 31 OCTOBER 20X7

	$	$
Cash flows from operating activities		
Net profit before tax	15,000	
Adjustments for		
Depreciation	4,658	
Finance cost	730	
Profit on disposal of non-current assets (W1)	(720)	
Operating profit before working capital changes	19,668	
Decrease in inventory	6,075	
Increase in receivables	(1,863)	
Increase in payables	3,178	
Cash generated from operations	27,058	
Interest paid (W2)	(710)	
Tax paid (W3)	(4,090)	
Net cash from operating activities		22,258
Cash flows from investing activities		
Payments to acquire property, plant and equipment	(24,340)	
Proceeds from sale of property, plant and equipment	2,694	
Net cash used in investing activities		(21,646)
Cash flows from financing activities		
Proceeds from issue of share capital	1,869	
Repayment of long term borrowing	(2,300)	
Dividend paid	(1,486)	
Net cash used in financing activities		(1,917)
Net decrease in cash and cash equivalents		(1,305)
Cash and cash equivalents at the beginning of period		634
Cash and cash equivalents at end of period		(671)

Workings

1   *Profit on sale of tangible non-current asset*

	$'000
Sale proceeds	2,694
Net book value	1,974
Profit	720

2   *Interest paid*

INTEREST PAYABLE

	$'000		$'000
Interest paid (bal fig)	710	Balance b/f	100
Balance c/f	120	Statement of profit or loss	730
	830		830

3   *Tax paid*

TAXATION

	$'000		$'000
Tax paid (bal fig)	4,090	Balance b/f	2,760
Balance c/f	3,020	Statement of profit or loss	4,350
	7,110		7,110

18 Incomplete records

18.1 B

	$
Opening inventory	386,200
Purchases	989,000
Closing inventory	(422,700)
Cost of sales	952,500

952,500 × 100/60 = 1,587,500

18.2 A Closing net assets plus drawings minus capital introduced minus opening net assets.

18.3 B Cost of sales = $114,000

Therefore sales should be = $114,000 × 100/60 = $190,000

Theft = $190,000 – 181 600 = $8,400

18.4 C

TOTAL RECEIVABLES ACCOUNT

	$		$
Opening balance	130,000	Cash received	686,400
Sales (balancing figure)	744,960	Discounts allowed	1,400
		Irrecoverable debts	4,160
		Contra	2,000
		Closing balance	181,000
	874,960		874,960

18.5 D

TOTAL PAYABLES ACCOUNT

	$		$
Cash paid	302,800	Opening balance	60,000
Discounts received	2,960	Purchases (balancing figure)	331,760
Contra	2,000		
Closing balance	84,000		
	391,760		391,760

18.6 C Cost of sales = $281,250 × 2/3 = $187,500
Loss of inventory = $228,200 – 187,500 = $40,700

18.7 D

	$
Opening inventory	318,000
Purchases	412,000
Closing inventory	(214,000)
	516,000
Notional cost of sales (612,000 × 75%)	(459,000)
Inventory lost	57,000

18.8 A

	$'000
Profit for the year	1,175
Add back depreciation	100
	1,275
Add: issue of shares	1,000
Less: repayment of loan notes	(750)
Less: purchase of non current assets	(200)
	1,325
Less: increase in working capital	(575)
Increase in bank balance	750

18.9 C

	$
Capital at 1 April 20X7	6,500
Add: profit (after drawings)	32,500
Less: sales tax element	(70)
Capital at 31 March 20X8	38,930

18.10 B $937,050

PURCHASES CONTROL ACCOUNT

	$		$
Payments to suppliers	888,400	Opening balance	130,400
Discounts received	11,200	Goods taken	1,000
Closing balance	171,250	Refunds received	2,400
		Purchases (bal fig)	937,050
	1,070,850		1,070,850

18.11 A $669,375

Cost of sales

	$
Opening inventory	243,000
Purchases	595,400
Less: purchases returns	(41,200)
	797,200
Less: closing inventory	(261,700)
	535,500

Sales = 535,500 × 100/80 = $669,375

18.12 A   RECEIVABLES LEDGER CONTROL ACCOUNT

	$		$
Opening balance	29,100	Cash from credit customers	381,600
Refunds	2,100	Cash sales	112,900
Sales (balancing figure)	525,300	Expenses paid out of cash	6,800
		Irrecoverable debts w/off	7,200
		Discounts allowed	9,400
		Closing balance	38,600
	556,500		556,500

18.13 D   Cost of sales: $17,000 + $91,000 − $24,000 = $84,000

Sales	100%
Cost of sales	60%
Gross profit	40%

Sales: $\dfrac{\$84,000}{60\%}$ = $140,000

18.14 B

	$
Sales (100%)	64,800
Cost of sales (70%)	45,360
Gross profit (30%)	19,440

	$
Opening inventory	28,400
Purchases	49,600
	78,000
Calculated closing inventory (bal fig)	(32,640)
Cost of sales	45,360
Calculated closing inventory	32,640
Actual closing inventory	-
Destroyed by fire	32,640

18.15 A

	$
Cost of sales	
Opening inventory	38,000
Purchases	637,000
Less: closing inventory	(45,000)
	630,000

Sales 630,000 × 100/70 = $900,000

18.16 C   Opening net assets + Profit + Capital introduced – Drawings = Closing net assets

210,000 + Profit + 100,000 – 48,000 = 400,000

Profit = $138,000

19 Company financial statements

19.1 D   Paid ordinary dividend only: 10m × 2c = $200,000. The dividend paid on the redeemable preference shares will be recognised in the financial statements as a finance cost.

The proposed ordinary dividend will not be recognised in the financial statements, but will be disclosed in the notes to the accounts.

Only the paid interim ordinary dividend will be recognised as a deduction from equity reserves in the statement of financial position.

19.2 A   A rights issue will increase cash and therefore assets. Retained earnings remain the same and the share premium account will be increased.

19.3 D   The revaluation surplus is part of equity. Dividends paid on redeemable preference shares are treated like interest paid on loans, and are therefore accrued for as finance costs in the financial statements.

19.4 B   Share capital will be credited with the nominal value of the shares – the balance goes to share premium.

19.5 B   Profit on disposal of properties will be included in profit in the statement of profit or loss and other comprehensive income. Equity dividends proposed after the reporting period are disclosed by note.

19.6 B

	$
Receivables and prepayments	
Insurance 9,000 × 8/12 prepayment	6,000
Loan (receivable)	12,000
Interest due 12,000 × 2% (receivable)	240
Rent due (receivable)	4,000
	22,240

19.7 B

	$
Ordinary shares at start of year	50,000
Add: bonus issue 50,000 × 50c	25,000
Add: new issue 60,000 × 50c	30,000
	105,000
Share premium at start of year	180,000
Less: bonus issue 50,000 × 50c	(25,000)
Add: new issue 60,000 × 30c	18,000
	173,000

19.8 B $9,000 is payable (SPL), but only $6,000 paid (April and July).

19.9 C   Dividends paid on ordinary shares are included in the statement of changes in equity, not the statement of profit or loss and other comprehensive income. Dividends paid on redeemable preference shares are treated like interest on loans and are shown in the statement of profit or loss and other comprehensive income as a finance charge. The gain on revaluation of non-current assets is shown in the statement of profit or loss and other comprehensive income, as other comprehensive income.

19.10 D   All of these items are disclosed, either on the face of the main financial statements or in the notes. Although dividends proposed are not included in the statement of changes in equity, they must still be disclosed in the notes.

19.11 B

		$
Ordinary shares		
Opening balance		125,000
Rights issue	250,000 × 25c	62,500
Bonus issue	150,000 × 25c	37,500
		225,000
Share premium		
Opening balance		100,000
Rights issue	250,000 × 75c	187,500
Bonus issue	150,000 × 25c	(37,500)
		250,000

19.12 D

		$
July – September	1,000,000 × 8% × 3/12	20,000
October – March	750,000 × 8% × 6/12	30,000
April – June	750,000 × 8% × 3/12	15,000
	500,000 × 7% × 3/12	8,750
		73,750

19.13 A   Adjusting events after the reporting period should be adjusted for, not just disclosed.

19.14 C   The loss on sale of investments will have been recognised in the statement of profit or loss and other comprehensive income. Dividends proposed after the year end are disclosed in the notes, they are not recognised in the accounts.

19.15 B   This is the transfer of the premium to the share premium account.

19.16 C   A bonus issue does not involve cash but can be financed from the share premium account.

19.17 D   A bonus issue does not raise any funds, instead other reserves are capitalised and reclassified as share capital. A rights issue is an issue of shares for cash, the right to buy the shares are initially offered to existing shareholders. If the existing shareholders do not take up their right to buy the shares, then their shareholding will be diluted.

19.18 D   Loan stock is a non-current liability.
  A   This is statutory reserve.
  B   Otherwise known as the revenue reserve.
  C   This is an unrealised reserve.

19.19 D   Correct, company will usually include this under distribution costs or administrative expenses.

  A   Incorrect, the contents of cost of sales are not defined by any IFRS.

  B   Depreciation will be included under the relevant expense heading (eg office equipment depreciation will go into administrative expenses).

  C   Incorrect, net profit is calculated after interest.

19.20 C

	$
Share capital @ 1.1.20X0	500,000
Issue on 1.4.20X0 (200,000 @ 50c)	100,000
Bonus issue (1.2m ÷ 4) @ 50c	150,000
Share capital as at 31.12.20X0	750,000
Share premium @ 1.1.20X0	300,000
1.4.20X0 200,000 shares @ (130c – 50c)	160,000
Bonus issue (as above)	(150,000)
	310,000

19.21 B   The statement of changes in equity.

19.22 C   A revaluation reserve arises when a non-current asset is **revalued**. Loan notes are not part of share capital.

20 Disclosure notes

20.1 A   Disclosure notes provide more detail about the information in the main financial statements.

20.2 B   A reconciliation of the opening and closing carrying amounts is required by IAS 16 for tangible non-current assets and by IAS 38 for intangible assets.

20.3 B   IAS 2 requires disclosure of the accounting policies adopted in measuring inventories, including the cost formula used, the total carrying amount of inventories and the carrying amount in classifications appropriate to the entity and the carrying amount of inventories carried at net realisable value.

20.4 C   The disclosure requirements in IAS 16 are comprehensive, particularly in relation to revalued assets.

20.5 A   IAS 38 does not require the net realisable value of deferred development costs to be disclosed.

20.6 C   Both statements are correct.

20.7 B   These are the disclosure requirements given in IAS 37 for contingent liabilities.

20.8 C   IAS 16 does not require disclosure of the market value of all tangible non-current assets.

20.9 B   Inventories must be valued at the lower of cost and net realisable value. The amount of any write-down in the period must be disclosed, and so too must the carrying value of inventories classified by type and the cost of inventories recognised as an expense in the period. There is no requirement to disclose the original cost of inventories that have been written down in value.

20.10 D   IAS10 requires disclosure of the nature of material non-adjusting events after the reporting period and either an estimate of the financial effect of the event or a statement that a reasonable estimate cannot be made.

21 Events after the reporting period

21.1 A   All of these events are indicative of conditions that existed at the reporting period.

21.2 A   2 and 3 do not affect the company's position at the end of the reporting period.

21.3 B   These affect valuation of receivables and inventory at the end of the reporting period.

21.4 B   These events are adjusting if discovered between the reporting date and the date the financial statements are authorised for issue as they provide evidence about conditions that existed at the reporting date: insolvency of an account receivable which was outstanding at the end of the reporting period, discovery of fraud or error which shows that the financial statements were incorrect, sale of inventory which gives evidence about its value at the end of the reporting period.

21.5 B   2 and 4 both affect the valuation of assets at the end of the reporting period.

21.6 C   IAS 10 requires the financial statements to be adjusted for events that reflect conditions that existed at the reporting date. Only event 3 is indicative of conditions at the reporting date – ie the recoverability of the receivable balance. Events 1 and 2 are non-adjusting events, however, they are material so they should be disclosed.

21.7 D   None of these events require adjustment in the financial statements.

21.8 A   An adjusting event after the reporting date is event that occurs between the reporting date and the date on which the financial statements are authorised for issue that provides further evidence of conditions that existed at the reporting date. The event must occur *after* the reporting period but *before* the date the financial statements are authorised for issue.

22 Statements of cash flows

22.1 C   Only the proceeds of a share issue and dividends received involve the movement of cash.

22.2 D   Loss on sale of non-current assets should be added back to net profit before tax.

22.3 D

	$
Add: depreciation charge	980,000
Less: profit on sale of assets	(40,000)
Less: increase in inventories	(130,000)
Add: decrease in receivables	100,000
Add: increase in payables	80,000
Addition to operating profit	990,000

22.4 B   Depreciation should be added back as it not a cash flow and proceeds of sale of non-current assets appears under 'investing' cash flows.

22.5 D   1   Proceeds from sale of premises appears under investing activities.
             2   Dividends received appears under operating or investing activities.
             3   A bonus issue of shares is not a cash flow.

22.6 C   1   The direct and indirect methods will give the correct figure.

             2   A rights issue of shares is a cash flow.

             4   The profit on sale of a non-current asset appears as an adjustment to profit in order to reach net cash flow from operations.

22.7 D   The depreciation charge and the increase in payables should both have been added.

22.8 B   Neither a proposed dividend nor a bonus issue of shares involve the movement of cash.

22.9 B   Proceeds from sale of equipment are included in investing activities.

22.10 B

		$'000
Cash flows from financing:		
Issue of share capital	(120 + 60) – (80 + 40)	60
Repayment of bank loan	(100 – 150)	(50)
		10

22.11 D   2 and 4. Decrease in inventories should be added, decrease in payables should be deducted.

22.12 B   The corrected extract is as follows:

	$'000
Net cash flow from operating activities	
Profit before tax	484
Depreciation charges	327
Profit on sale of property, plant and equipment	(35)
Increase in inventories	(74)
Decrease in trade and other receivables	41
Increase in trade payables	29
Cash generated from operations	772

22.13 D   Interest received and proceeds from the sale of property are cash flows from investing activities; taxation paid is a cash flow from operating activities.

22.14 A   The net cash flows from operating activities will be the same using the two methods.

22.15 D

	$'000
Carrying value of assets at beginning of the year	462
Increase in revaluation reserve during the year	50
Book value of assets disposed of (110 – 65)	(45)
Depreciation charge for the year	(38)
	429
Carrying value of assets at end of the year	633
Purchases of property, plant and equipment during the year	204

22.16 C   A loss on disposal of a non-current asset is added back as an adjustment in the calculation of cash flows from operating activities (using the indirect method), and the cash received from the disposal is included within cash flows from investing activities

23 15 mark questions: preparing simple consolidated financial statements

23.1 Swing and Cat

SWING GROUP
CONSOLIDATED STATEMENT OF PROFIT OR LOSS FOR THE YEAR ENDED 31 DECEMBER 20X8

	$'000
Revenue (5,000 + 1,000 – 100*)	5,900
Cost of sales (2,900 + 600 – 100* + 10(W2))	3,410
Gross profit	2,490
Other expenses (1,700 + 320)	2,020
Net profit	470
Tax (130 + 25)	155
Profit for the year	315

Profit attributable to:	
Owners of the parent (bal fig)	304
Non-controlling interest (20% × $55,000)	11
	315

* to remove the intra-group sale

CONSOLIDATED STATEMENT OF FINANCIAL POSITION AS AT 31 DECEMBER 20X8

	$'000	$'000
Non-current assets		
Goodwill (W1)	10	
Tangible non-current assets (1,880 + 200)	2,080	
		2,090
Current assets		
Inventory (500 + 120 - 10(W2))	610	
Trade receivables (650 + 40)	690	
Bank and cash (390 + 35)	425	
		1,725
		3,815
Equity and liabilities		
Equity attributable to owners of the parent		
Share capital (Swing only)		2,000
Retained earnings (W3)		510
		2,510
Non-controlling interest (W4)		70
Total equity		2,580
Current liabilities		
Trade payables (910 + 30)	940	
Tax (230 + 65)	295	
		1,235
Total equity and liabilities		3,815

Workings

1   *Goodwill*

	$	$'000
Fair value of consideration transferred		120
Plus fair value of non-controlling interest at acquisition		40
Less fair value of net assets acquired as represented by		
Ordinary share capital	100	
Retained earnings	50	
		(150)
Goodwill		10

2   *Provision for unrealised profit*

	$
Profit on intra-group sale (100,000 – 80,000)	20,000
Unrealised profit (50% × 20,000)*	10,000

* 50% of the inventories from the intra-group sales remain in inventories at the year end, therefore the unrealised profit is 50% of the overall profit made on the intra-group sales. The rest of the profit from the intra-group sales is now realised as the inventories have been sold outside the group.

3   *Retained earnings*

	Swing $'000	Cat $'000
Per question	400	200
Adjustments (unrealised profit (W2))	(10)	
Pre-acquisition retained earnings		(50)
		150
Group share of post-acq'n retained earnings:		
Cat (80% × 150)	120	
Group retained earnings	510	

4   *Non-controlling interest at reporting date*

	$'000
Fair value of NCI at acquisition	40
Plus NCI's share of post-acquisition retained earnings (20% × 150)	30
NCI at reporting date	60

23.2 Black and Bury

(a)   *Calculation of goodwill*

	$'000	$'000
Fair value of consideration transferred	21,000	
Plus fair value of NCI at acquisition	11,800	
		32,800
Less net acquisition-date fair value of identifiable assets acquired and liabilities assumed:		
Share capital	30,000	
Retained earnings at acquisition	2,000	
		(32,000)
Goodwill		800

(b)   (i)   BLACK GROUP
CONSOLIDATED STATEMENT OF PROFIT OR LOSS
FOR THE YEAR ENDED 31 OCTOBER 20X5

	$'000
Revenue (245 + 95 – 16.8 (W2))	323,200
Cost of sales (140 + 52 -16.8 +1.44)	(176,640)
Gross profit (W2)	146,560
Distribution costs (12 + 10)	(22,000)
Administrative expenses (55 + 13)	(68,000)
Profit before tax	56,560
Tax (13.25 + 5)	(18,250)
Profit for the year	38,310
Attributable to	
Owners of the parent (bal.fig.)	33,810
Non-controlling interest (30% × 15)	4,500
	38,310

(ii)   BLACK GROUP
CONSOLIDATED STATEMENT OF FINANCIAL POSITION AS AT 31 OCTOBER 20X5

	$'000	$'000
Non-current assets		
Goodwill	800	
Property, plant and equipment (110 + 40)	150,000	
		150,800
Current assets		
Inventory (W3)	15,810	
Trade receivables (W4)	12,420	
Bank (3.5 + 2.57)	6,070	
		34,300
Total assets		185,100

Equity and liabilities
Equity attributable to owners of the parent
    Share capital   100,000
    Retained earnings (W6)   37,856

                                           137,856
Non controlling interest (W7)   14,284

Current liabilities
    Trade payables (W5)   9,960
    Dividends (20+ (10× 30%))   23,000

                                           32,960
Total equity and liabilities   185,100

Workings

1   *Group structure*

        Black
        |
        | 70%
        |
        Bury

2   *Intragroup sale*

    Sale price to be eliminated from consolidated revenue:

                                            $'000
    Cost to Black   12,000
    40% mark up   4,800
    Cost to Bury   16,800

    Unrealised profit in inventory: $4,800,000 × 30% = $1,440,000

    Gross profit   = $105,000,000 + $43,000,000 – $1,440,000
                       = $146,560,000

3   *Inventory*

                                            $'000
    Black   13,360
    Bury   3,890
    Less unrealised profit (W2)   (1,440)
                                         15,810

4   *Trade receivables*

                                  $'000 $'000
    Black   14,640
    Less dividend receivable   (7,000)

                                         7,640
    Bury   6,280
    Less intragroup   (1,500)
                                         12,420

5   *Trade payables*

                                            $'000
    Black   9,000
    Bury   2,460
    Less intragroup   (1,500)
                                         9,960

6   Retained earnings

	Black	Bury
	$'000	$'000
Per question	33,500	10,280
Adjustment (unrealised profit (W2))	(1,440)	-
Pre-acquisition retained earnings		(2,000)
		8,280
Group share of post-acq'n ret'd earnings:		
Bury (70% × 8,280)	5,796	
Group retained earnings	37,856	

7   Non-controlling interest

	$'000
Fair value of NCI at acquisition	11,800
Plus NCI's share of post-acquisition retained earnings (30% × 8,280)	2,484
NCI at reporting date	14,284

23.3 Prestend

(a)   Calculation of goodwill on the acquisition of Northon

	$	$'000
Fair value of consideration transferred		3,345
Plus fair value of NCI at acquisition		1,415
Less net acquisition-date fair value of identifiable assets acquired and liabilities assumed:		
Ordinary share capital	4,000	
Retained earnings at acquisition	60	
		(4,060)
Goodwill		700

(b)   PRESTEND GROUP
CONSOLIDATED STATEMENT OF FINANCIAL POSITION AS AT 31 OCTOBER 20X7

	$'000	$'000
Non-current assets		
Goodwill	700	
Tangible non-current assets (4,200 + 3,300)	7,500	
		8,200
Current assets		
Inventory (1,500 + 800 – 20 (W2))	2,280	
Receivables (1,800 + 750 – 30)	2,520	
Bank (600 + 350)	950	
		5,750
		13,950
Equity and liabilities		
Equity		
$1 Ordinary shares		9,000
Retained earnings (W3)		603
Non-controlling interest (W4)		1,457
		11,060
Current liabilities		
Payables (1,220 + 200 – 30)	1,390	
Tax (700 + 800)	1,500	
		2,890
Total equity and liabilities		13,950

Workings

1   *Group structure*

Prestend

$$\frac{2,800,000}{4,000,000} = 70\%$$

Northon

2   *Unrealised profit on intra-group sale*

Profit on intra-group sale is $240,000 \times \dfrac{20}{120} = \$40,000$

∴ Unrealised profit is $40,000 × 50% = $20,000

3   *Retained earnings*

	Prestend $'000	Northon $'000
Per question	525	200
Adjustment (unrealised profit (W2))	(20)	
Pre-acquisition retained earnings		(60)
		140
Group share of post-acq'n ret'd earnings:		
Northon (70% × 140)	98	
Group retained earnings	603	

4   *Non-controlling interest*

	$'000
Fair value of NCI at acquisition	1,415
Plus NCI's share of post-acquisition retained earnings (30% × 140)	42
NCI at reporting date	1,457

23.4 Liverton and Everpool

(a)   *Calculation of goodwill on acquisition of Everpool*

	$'000	$'000
Fair value of consideration transferred		3,500
Plus fair value of NCI at acquisition		1,000
		4,500
Less net acquisition-date fair value of identifiable assets acquired and liabilities assumed:		
Share capital	4,000	
Retained earnings at acquisition	200	
		4,200
Goodwill		300

(b)   LIVERTON

CONSOLIDATED STATEMENT OF PROFIT OR LOSS FOR THE YEAR ENDED 31 MAY 20X6

	$'000
Sales revenue (6,400 + 2,600 – 200)	8,800
Cost of sales (W)	(5,004)
Gross profit (W)	3,796
Distribution costs (1,110 + 490)	(1,590)
Administration expenses (700 + 320)	(1,020)
Profit before tax	1,186
Tax (400 + 80)	(480)
Profit for the year	706
Profit attributable to	
Owners of the parent	641
Non-controlling interest (25% × 260)	65
	706

Working: group structure

Liverton

$$\frac{3,000}{4,000} = 75\%$$

Everpool

Working: Consolidated gross profit

Profit on sale by Liverton to Everpool: $200,000 – $110,000 = $90,000

Unrealised profit: $90,000 × 60% = $54,500

Consolidated gross profit: $2,700,000 + $1,150,000 – $54,000 = $3,796,000

Cost of sales is the balancing figure.

24 Consolidated financial statements

24.1	C		$	$
		Fair value of consideration		270,000
		Plus fair value of NCI at acquisition		42,000
		Less net acquisition-date fair value of identifiable assets acquired and liabilities assumed:		
		Share capital	100,000	
		Retained earnings at acquisition	90,000	
				190,000
		Goodwill in statement of financial position		122,000

24.2	A		$
		Non-controlling interest	
		Fair value of NCI at acquisition	42,000
		Plus NCI's share of post-acq'n retained earnings (10% × (160 – 90))	7,000
		NCI at reporting date	49,000

24.3	D		$
		Alpha retained earnings	210,000
		Group share post-acq'n ret'd earnings:	
		Beta ((160,000 – 90,000) × 90%)	63,000
			273,000

24.4   C   Iota is a subsidiary as Gamma has power to cast a majority of votes at meetings of the board of directors. Kappa is a subsidiary as Gamma owns >50% of the ordinary shares of Kappa, it doesn't make any difference that Kappa is based overseas or pays tax in that country. Zeta is not a subsidiary of Gamma because Gamma's investment in the non-voting preference shares will not give it the ability to control Zeta.

24.5 C

		$	$
Fair value of consideration			280,000
Plus fair value of NCI at acquisition			65,000
Less net acquisition-date fair value of identifiable assets acquired and liabilities assumed:			
Share capital		140,000	
Share premium		50,000	
Retained earnings at acquisition		60,000	
			250,000
Goodwill			95,000

24.6 C

Non-controlling interest

	$
Fair value of NCI at acquisition	65,000
Plus NCI's share of post-acq'n retained earnings (20% × (100 − 60))	8,000
NCI at reporting date	73,000

24.7 D

	$'000
Fair value of net assets acquired:	
Ordinary shares	400
Retained earnings at 1 January 20X7	100
Retained earnings for 9 months to acquisition date (80 × 9/12)	60
	560
Add goodwill	30
	590

24.8 B   Deciduous is an associate of Evergreen. Under equity accounting, the Evergreen group's share of the profit after tax of Deciduous is added to the group profit before tax.

24.9 A

	$
Mercedes Co retained earnings	450,000
Benz Co retained earnings	
Unrealised profit in closing inventory (50,000 × 25/125)	(10,000)
Consolidated retained earnings at 31 March 20X9	560,000

24.10 B

	$	$
Fair value of consideration		300,000
Plus fair value of NCI at acquisition		75,000
Less net acquisition-date fair value of identifiable assets acquired and liabilities assumed:		
Share capital	100,000	
Retained earnings at acquisition	156,000	
Fair value adjustment at acquisition	20,000	
		276,000
Goodwill		99,000

24.11 D

	$'000
Unrealised profit (30,000 × 25% × 40%)	3
Gross profit (330 + 300 − 3)	627

24.12 C   3 and 4 are incorrect.

An investor must have significant influence over the investee in order for the investee to be classified as an associate. If the investor owns between 20% and <50% of the ordinary shares of the investee, significant influence can be assumed, therefore 1 is true. For an investee to be classified as a subsidiary, the investor must have control over the investee. Control can be demonstrated if the investor has the power to appoint the majority of board members of the investee, so 2 is true. 3 is incorrect because the power to govern the financial and operating policies of F make F a subsidiary of E. Likewise, 4 is incorrect as the power to govern the financial and operating policies of H makes H a subsidiary of G.

24.13 C   Tangerine is an associate of Clementine, however because Clementine has no other investments in other companies, it will not produce consolidated accounts. Therefore the investment will appear in the single company accounts of Clementine as a simple investment. The statement of financial position will show an investment at cost and the statement of profit or loss will show dividends received from Tangerine. If Clementine instead did produce consolidated accounts, Tangerine would be accounted for using the equity method and B would instead be correct.

24.14 B   A parent may hold less than 50% of the share capital but more than 50% of the voting rights. Goodwill only appears in the **consolidated** statement of financial position. Consolidated financial statements present the substance of the relationship between parent and subsidiaries, rather than the legal form.

24.15 D   S is not a subsidiary as P's shareholdings in S do not give it the power to control S. R is a subsidiary as P has the right to appoint or remove the directors of R, and so control it.

24.16 C   Investments in associates are accounted for using equity accounting. An investment is an associate if the investor has significant influence over the investee. Significant influence is presumed if the investor owns at least 20% of the voting equity of the investee. Therefore 2 is not an associate. 1 and 4 are subsidiaries as Company A investor has control over them.

24.17 C

	$'000	$'000
Fair value of consideration (bal fig)		620
Plus fair value of NCI at acquisition		150
Less net acquisition-date fair value of identifiable assets acquired and liabilities assumed:		
Share capital	500	
Retained earnings at acquisition	150	
Revaluation surplus at acquisition	50	
		(700)
Goodwill		70

24.18 A $950 + $1,250 + $50 = $2,250,000

24.19 A   The $30,000 owed by Seven Co to Six Co is included within the receivables of Six Co and the payables of Seven Co. These inter-company balances should be eliminated for the purpose of consolidation.

Trade receivables = $(64,000 + 39,000 – 30,000) = $73,000

Trade payables = $(37,000 + 48,000 – 30,000) = $55,000

The unrealised profit on closing inventory will be an adjustment to inventory on consolidation, and does not affect consolidated receivables and payables.

24.20 D

	$'000
Fair value of consideration given (60,000 × $3.50)	210
Fair value of net assets acquired	50
Goodwill	160

24.21 B

	$
Fair value of NCI at date of acquisition	25,000
NCI share of retained post-acquisition earnings: 20% × $(60,000 – 40,000)	4,000
	29,000
NCI share in unrealised profit: 20% × 50% × $12,000	(1,200)
Non-controlling interest at 31 December 20X4	27,800

24.22 A Retained post-acquisition earnings of Lava Co = 4/12 × $(336,000 – 264,000) = $24,000.

	$000
Volcano retained earnings	650
Parent company share of post-acquisition earnings: 75% × $24,000	18
Parent company's share of consolidated retained earnings at 31 Dec 20X3	668

24.23 B Post-acquisition earnings of Drum Co = 9/12 × $60,000 = $45,000.

	$
Tin Co profit for the year	70,000
Parent company share of post-acquisition profit of Drum Co: 90% × $45,000	40,500
Parent company's share of consolidated retained earnings at 31 Dec 20X3	110,500

24.24 C The unrealised profit in the closing inventory of Sand Co = 25% × 40% × $40,000 = $4,000.
The NCI share of this is 20% × $4,000 = $800.

	$	$
NCI share of profit of Sun Co: 20% × $35,000		7,000
Less: NCI share of unrealised profit		(800)
		6,200
Combined profits of Sand Co and Sun Co: (120,000 + 35,000)	155,000	
Less: Unrealised profit in closing inventory	(4,000)	
Total consolidated profit for the year		151,000
Attributable to the parent company		144,800

25 15 mark question: interpretation of financial statements

25.1 Binky and Smokey

(a)

		Binky		Smokey
Gross profit percentage	$\frac{\text{Gross profit}}{\text{Sales}} \times 100$	$\frac{129}{284} \times 100$	= 45.4%	$\frac{154}{305} \times 100 = 50.5\%$
Net profit percentage	$\frac{\text{Net profit}}{\text{Sales}} \times 100$	$\frac{61}{284} \times 100$	= 21.5%	$\frac{47}{305} \times 100 = 15.4\%$
Asset turnover ratio	$\frac{\text{Sales}}{\text{Capital employed}} \times 100$	$\frac{284}{258} \times 100$	= 110.1%	$\frac{305}{477} \times 100 = 63.9\%$
Current ratio	$\frac{\text{Current assets}}{\text{Current liabilities}}$	$\frac{201}{188}$	= 1.1:1	$\frac{383}{325} = 1.2:1$
Quick ratio	$\frac{\text{Current assets} - \text{inventory}}{\text{Current liabilities}}$	$\frac{110}{188}$	= 0.6:1	$\frac{90}{325} = 0.3:1$
Receivables collection period	$\frac{\text{Receivables}}{\text{Sales}} \times 365$	$\frac{46}{284} \times 365$	= 59.1 days	$\frac{75}{305} \times 365 = 89.8 \text{ days}$

(b) The **gross profit percentage** is high for both companies. **Smokey**, which has a higher sales figure in absolute terms, also has a **higher** gross profit percentage. It is possible that its marginally greater sales volume enables it to take advantage of **discounts**. As the two companies operate in the same market, it is possibly geographical location that makes the difference in the profit margin Smokey can make.

The picture is different when it comes to **net profit percentage**. At 21.5%, that of Binky is significantly higher than that of Smokey (15.4%). The main reason for this is that **expenses in all categories are higher for Smokey**. In addition, Smokey is paying loan interest, while Binky does not have any loans.

The **asset turnover** ratios show that **Binky is making more efficient use of assets** than Smokey, as it is generating proportionally more sales from the assets. As discussed below, the inefficiency of Smokey may be partly because **working capital is tied up in inventory**.

The **current ratios** of both companies are **greater than one**, with Smokey having the edge slightly. These ratios indicate that the companies have sufficient current assets to meet their current liabilities. However, the quick ratios are more worrying.

Both companies have **quick ratios of less than one**, indicating potential liquidity problems. In the case of **Smokey, the quick ratio is very low** at 0.3:1. Much of Smokey Ltd's working capital is tied up in inventory, and the high inventory level suggests that inventory is not selling. Smokey, with its low cash balance and **lack of liquidity**, may have problems paying debts as they fall due.

The **receivables collection period is high** for both companies, but for Smokey, at 89.8 days it is considerably higher than that of Binky, which has 59.1 days. **Smokey Ltd needs to pay attention to credit control**. The longer a debt remains unpaid, the less likely it is to be paid.

In conclusion, although Smokey has a higher profit margin, it has liquidity problems, is less efficient and has ineffective credit control. **Binky is therefore a better investment prospect**.

26 Interpretation of financial statements

26.1 A Issuing further loan notes and paying dividends will *increase* gearing. A bonus issue simply capitalises reserves, so has no effect.

26.2 C Undervaluing closing inventory will increase cost of sales and therefore reduce the gross profit percentage.

26.3 D Understatement of the December 20X1 closing inventory will lead to understatement of December 20X2 opening inventory and therefore understatement of cost of sales.

26.4 A Profit will be an addition to owner's capital.

26.5 D Purchases $= \$(32,500 - 6,000 + 3,800)$
$= \$30,300$

$\therefore$ Accounts payable payment period $= \dfrac{4,750}{30,300} \times 365 = 57$ days

26.6 A Gearing $= \dfrac{\text{Total long term debt}}{\text{Total long term debt + share holders equity}} = \dfrac{75}{75 + 500} = 13\%$

26.7 C This ratio is used to assess how much the company owes in relation to its size.

26.8 C A - Increased prices may result in reduced sales so asset turnover may fall. B - Selling price increases should increase margins. D - The effect of a price increase will be increased margins but reduced asset turnover, therefore effects on return on capital may be nil.

26.9 B

	%	$
Sales	100	2,400
Cost of sales	$66\,^2/_3$	1,600
Gross profit	$33\,^1/_3$	800
Expenses	$28\,^1/_3$	680
Net profit	5	120

26.10 A Long-term loans raise gearing, shareholders funds reduce it.

26.11 C Current ratio is 2,900 : 1,100 = 2.6: 1 ie high

Acid test ratio is 1,000 : 1,100 = 0.9 ie acceptable

26.12 A   Current ratio = 1,390:420 = 3.3:1 (ie high)

           Acid test   = 420:420 = 1:1 (ie ideal)

26.13 B   Analysis of financial statements is carried out so that the significance of the financial statements can be better understood. Comparisons through time and with other companies help to show how well the company is doing.

27   Mixed bank 1

27.1 A

	$
Increase in net assets	88,000
Capital introduced	(50,000)
Drawings (68,000 + 20,000)	88,000
Profit for the year	126,000

27.2 A

	$
Debit cash	1,100,000
Credit share capital	250,000
Credit share premium	850,000

27.3 C   Closing inventory should be valued at the lower of cost and NRV as per IAS 2.

27.4 D

	Share capital	Share premium
	$	$
1 July 20X4	500,000	400,000
1 January 20X5 – bonus issue (250,000 × 50c)	125,000	(125,000)
1 April 20X5 – rights issue	62,500	125,000
	687,500	400,000

27.5 D   2 and 4. Journal entry 1 has debits and credits transposed and journal entry 3 uses the wrong amount.

27.6 B

RECEIVABLES LEDGER CONTROL ACCOUNT

	$		$
Opening balance	138,400	Cash received	78,420
Credit sales	80,660	Payables contra	1,000
Dishonoured cheques	850	Discounts allowed	1,950
		Irrecoverable debts written off	3,000
		Closing balance	135,540
	219,910		219,910

27.7 A

SUSPENSE ACCOUNT

	$		$
Opening balance	14,550	To cash account	10,000
		To rent account	4,550

27.8 D   A revaluation of a non-current asset and a bonus issue of shares are both non-cash transactions.

27.9 D

	$
Opening inventory	138,600
Purchases	716,100
Closing inventory	(149,100)
Cost of sales	705,600

Sales = 705,600 × 100/70 = 1,008,000

27.10 C

	SPLOCI	SOFP
	$	$
Prepaid insurance	8,200	
Payment January 20X5	38,000	
Prepayment July-Sept 20X5	(9,500)	9,500
	36,700	9,500

27.11 B   (i) is the definition of a provision from IAS 37, (ii) is correct – a provision is a liability of uncertain timing or amount, (iii) is not correct, a contingent liability is not recognised in the financial statements, it is simply disclosed in the notes.

27.12 D   Beta has issued a credit note for $500 to Alpha which Alpha has not yet received.

27.13 A   Research expenditure is never capitalised.

27.14 D   (i) and (iv) provide information about conditions which existed at the reporting date and are therefore adjusting.

27.15 A

RENT RECEIVED

	$		$
Arrears b/f	3,800	In advance b/f	2,400
Rent in advance	3,000	Cash received	83,700
Balance c/f	84,000	In arrears	4,700
	90,800		90,800

27.16 B

	$
Allowance for receivables ((517,000 – 37,000) × 5%)	24,000
Previous allowance	(39,000)
Reduction	(15,000)
Debts written off	37,000
Charge to statement of profit or loss	22,000

27.17 D   2 and 3 only. Attributable overheads should be included in finished goods inventories.

27.18 B   The proceeds will appear under *investing activities* and any profit will be deducted under *operating activities*.

27.19 C   All four items will appear in the statement of changes in equity.

27.20 A

	$
Balance per bank statement	(38,600)
Bank charges	200
Lodgements	14,700
Cheque payments	(27,800)
Cheque payment misposted	8,400
Balance per cash book	(43,100)

28 Mixed bank 2

28.1 C

	$
Balance b/f ((280,000 − 14,000) × 20%)	53,200
Addition 1 April (48,000 × 20% × $\frac{9}{12}$)	7,200
Addition 1 Sept (36,000 × 20% × $\frac{4}{12}$)	2,400
	62,800
Sale (14,000 × 20% × $\frac{1}{2}$)	1,400
	64,200

28.2 D Item 1 is wrong, as inventory should be valued at the **lower** of cost and net realisable value. Items 2, 3 and 4 are all correct.

28.3 D

RENT RECEIVABLE

	$			$
31.1.X6 Statement of profit or loss	27,500	1.2.X5 Balance b/f ($\frac{2}{3}$ × $6,000)		4,000
		1.4.X5 Received		6,000
		1.7.X5 Received		7,500
		1.10.X5 Received		7,500
31.1. X6 Balance c/f ($\frac{2}{3}$ × $7,500)	5,000	1.1.X6 Received		7,500
	32,500			32,500

28.4 D 20%. ROCE is defined as the profit on ordinary activities before interest and tax divided by capital employed = $300,000/$1.5m = 20%

28.5 D Items 1 and 4 are adjusting events. Item 2 is a non-adjusting event but might be disclosed by way of note if material. Item 3 is a non-adjusting event that is disclosed by way of note.

28.6 D

	$
Balance per Alta	3,980
Cheque not yet received	(270)
Goods returned	(180)
Contra entry	(3,200)
Revised balance per Alta	330
Balance per Ordan	(230)
Remaining difference	100

28.7 C For discounts, we need to debit the discounts received account $13,000 to reverse the entry and debit the discounts allowed account $13,000 to record the entry correctly. The credit of $26,000 will be to suspense. So journal 2 is correct.

For machinery, we need to debit plant and machinery $18,000 and credit suspense $18,000. So journal 4 is correct.

28.8 B Item (1), as the plant register is not part of the double entry system, the adjustment does not go through the suspense account.

Item (2), the transaction has been completely omitted from the records.

Therefore only items (3) and (4) affect the suspense account.

28.9 D

	$
Initial profit	630,000
Item (1) – increase in depreciation (4,800 – 480)	(4,320)
Item (2) – bank charges	(440)
Item (3) – no effect on P/L	–
Item (4) – no effect on P/L	–
Revised profit	625,240

28.10 A   Statements 1 and 2 are correct.

28.11 B   Only statements 2 and 4 are correct.

28.12 B

	$
Closing receivables	458,000
Irrecoverable debts w/off	(28,000)
	430,000
Allowance required (5% × 430,000)	21,500
Existing allowance	(18,000)
Increase required	3,500
Charge to statement of profit or loss (28,000 + 3,500)	31,500

28.13 A

PLCA

	$		$
Cash paid to suppliers	988,400	Opening balance	384,600
Discounts received	12,600	Purchases	963,200
Purchases returns	17,400		
Contras	4,200		
Closing balance	325,200		
	1,347,800		1,347,800

28.14 A   We need to increase drawings (debit) and reduce purchases (credit). Therefore journal A is the correct answer. Remember that we only adjust inventory at the year end.

28.15 D

	$	$
Sales (balancing figure)		1,080,000
Opening inventory	77,000	
Purchases	763,000	
	840,000	
Closing inventory	84,000	
Cost of sales (70%)		756,000
Gross profit ($\frac{30}{70}$ × 756,000)		324,000

28.16 C   Statements (3) and (4) are correct. Statement (1) is incorrect because land is not usually depreciated. Statement (2) is incorrect as the gain on revaluation for property accounted for in accordance with IAS 16 is shown in the statement of profit or loss and other comprehensive income, under 'other comprehensive income' or in the separate statement of other comprehensive income. (NB gains on property classified as investment property per IAS 40 are recognised in profit or loss, but this is beyond the scope of this syllabus).

28.17 B

	$
Balance per bank (overdrawn)	(38,640)
Add: outstanding lodgements	19,270
	(19,370)
Less: unpresented cheques	(14,260)
Balance per cash book (overdrawn)	(33,630)

28.18 C   48,000 + 400 + 2,200 = 50,600

28.19 B   Opening inventory: debit statement of profit or loss, credit inventory account

Closing inventory: debit inventory account, credit statement of profit or loss

Remember that inventory is part of cost of sales, which is included in the statement of profit or loss.

28.20 D

	$'000
Fair value of consideration	4,000
Plus fair value of NCI at acquisition	2,200
Less net acquisition-date fair value of identifiable assets acquired and liabilities assumed	(4,750)
Goodwill	1,450

29   Mixed bank 3

29.1 A

	$
Sales (100%)	650,000
Cost of sales (70%)	455,000
Gross profit (30%)	195,000
Opening inventory	380,000
Purchases	480,000
	860,000
Closing inventory (bal. fig.)	(405,000)
Cost of sales	455,000
Calculated inventory	405,000
Actual inventory	220,000
Lost in fire	185,000

29.2 A

Transaction	Effect
1	+ 500
2	+ 500
3	No effect
	+ 1,000

29.3 B   Income from investments and dividends paid on redeemable preference shares are recognised in the statement of profit or loss.

29.4 D   Dividends paid go through the SOCIE, not the statement of profit or loss and other comprehensive income. Also dividends declared after the end of the reporting period, are disclosed by way of note to the accounts.

29.5 D   Goose Co has control over all three of these investments, and hence they are all subsidiaries.

29.6 B   Trade receivables   = 838,000 – 72,000

= 766,000

Allowance for receivables   = 60,000

Net balance   = 766,000 – 60,000

= 706,000

29.7 C   1 and 4 are correct. Overheads must be included in the value of finished goods. Inventories should be valued at the lower of cost and net realisable value, not replacement cost.

29.8 C   Inventory is correctly recorded, so 2 and 4 are incorrect. Purchases are understated, so cost of sales are understated and so profit for 20X6 is overstated. Therefore 1 only is the correct answer.

29.9 D   1.26:1. (Receivables 176,000)/(trade payables 61,000 + overdraft 79,000).

29.10 A   All four items are correct.

29.11 A

INSURANCE

	$		$
Prepayment b/f	8,100	SPL	11,100
(3/4 × 10,800)		Prepayments c/f	9,000
Paid	12,000	(3/4 × 12,000)	
	20,100		20,100

29.12 C Statements 2 and 3 are incorrect. A bounced cheque is credited to the cash book and bank errors do not go through the cash book at all.

29.13 B

SHARE CAPITAL

	$m		$m
		Bal b/f	100
		Bonus (1/2 × 100m)	50
Bal c/f	210	Rights (2/5 × 150m)	60
	210		210

SHARE PREMIUM

	$m		$m
Bonus	50	Bal b/f	80
Bal c/f	60	Rights	30
	110		110

29.14 A All three statements are correct

29.15 A Items 2, 3 and 4 preserve double entry and so would not show up in a trial balance.

29.16 D

	$'000
Fair value of consideration transferred	8,000
Plus fair value of NCI at acquisition ($1.20 × 3,000,000)	3,600
Less net acquisition-date fair value of identifiable assets acquired and liabilities assumed	(8,750)
Goodwill	2,850

29.17 B

	$
Opening inventory	40,000
Purchases	60,000
	100,000
Closing inventory	(50,000)
Cost of sales	50,000
This implies sales	100,000 (50,000 × 2)

So either 1 is correct or 3 is correct.

29.18 D

RENT RECEIVED

	$		$
Arrears b/f	4,800	Prepayments b/f	134,600
		Cash received	834,600
SPL	828,700		
Prepayments c/f	144,400	Arrears c/f	8,700
	977,900		977,900

29.19 A

PLCA

	$		$
Purchases returns	41,200	Bal b/f	318,600
Cash paid	1,364,300	Purchases	1,268,600
Discounts received	8,200	Refunds	2,700
Contras	48,000		
Bal c/f	128,200		
	1,589,900		1,589,900

29.20 A $150,000

	$
Carrying value at 1st August 20X0	200,000
Less depreciation	(20,000)
	180,000
Proceeds	25,000
Loss	5,000
Carrying value of asset sold	(30,000)
Therefore carrying value	150,000

30 Mixed bank 4

30.1   A   Share capital (1m × $1)   =   1,000,000

Share premium (1m × 50c)   =   500,000

30.2   C   The correct answer is decrease current ratio and decrease quick ratio. Proposed dividends are not accrued for, so the only impact on the financial statements is to decrease cash.

30.3   C   Prudence and consistency

30.4   D

RENTAL INCOME

	$		$
Arrears b/f	42,300	Prepayments b/f	102,600
SPL	858,600	Received	838,600
Prepayments c/f	88,700	Arrears c/f	48,400
	989,600		989,600

30.5   C   Journals A and B have their entries reversed and Journal D should not include the suspense account at all.

30.6   A   Per IAS 37 *provide* for probable losses of known amount and for which there is a constructive obligation, disclose possible losses, ignore remote ones.

30.7   A

RENT PAID

	$		$
Prepayment b/f	10,000		
(1/12 × 120,000)			
Paid – 1/1	30,000	SPL	136,000
– 1/4	36,000		
– 1/7	36,000		
– 1/10	36,000	Prepayments c/f	12,000
		(1/3 × 36,000)	
	148,000		148,000

30.8 A

	$	$
Trade receivables	863,000	
Irrecoverable debts w/off	(23,000)	
	840,000	
Closing allowance for receivables (5% × 840,000)		42,000
Opening allowance		49,000
Reduction		(7,000)

Charge = 23,000 – 7,000
= 16,000

30.9 C

SHARE CAPITAL

	$m		$m
		Bal b/f	1.0
		Share issue (note 1)	0.5
Bal c/f	2.0	Bonus (note 2)	0.5
	2.0		2.0

SHARE PREMIUM

	$m		$m
Bonus (note 2)	0.5	Bal b/f	1.4
Bal c/f	1.8	Share issue (note 1)	0.9
	2.3		2.3

Notes

1   Share issues of 1,000, 000 shares raises $1,400,000. Shares are 50c each, so share capital is $500,000 and share premium $900,000

2   Share capital is $1.5m or 3m shares. Therefore the bonus issue is 1m shares.

30.10 C   Inventory should be valued at the lower of cost and net realisable value, so statement 1 is incorrect.

30.11 B

	$
Held all year ((960,000 – 84,000) × 20%)	175,200
Addition (48,000 × 20% × 1/2)	4,800
Disposal (84,000 × 20% × 3/4)	12,600
	192,600

30.12 B   Items 1 and 4 involve completed double entry and so do not go through the suspense account.

30.13 D   Debit drawings and credit the cost to purchases.

30.14 A   This is a contingent liability, rather than a provision. Provisions should only be provided where the outcome is probable, which is not the case here.

30.15 D   Cost   +   Profit   =   Selling price

100   25   125

PUP = (25/125 × 15,000) × 2/3   = $2,000

Inventories = $40,000 + $20,000 - $2,000   = $58,000

30.16 D   Tax is separately disclosed in the statement of profit or loss and other comprehensive income only, while profit for the period is shown in the statement of profit or loss and other comprehensive income and in the statement of changes in equity.

30.17 D   The reducing balance method charges more depreciation in earlier years.

30.18 D   A decrease in receivables should be added and so should an increase in payables. Therefore 3 and 4 are correct.

30.19 C $47,429

	$	$
Balance per P Johnson		46,747
Add: Whitchurch Co invoice, previously omitted from ledger	267	
Rectofon Co balance, previously omitted from list	2,435	
		3,102
		49,449
Less: Error on posting of Bury Inc's credit note to ledger	20	
P Fox & Son (Swindon) Co's balance included twice	2,000	
		2,020
Revised balance per receivables ledger		47,429

30.20 B   Only B fully accounts for the difference of $12,780 credit.

31 Mixed bank 5

31.1 B   Closing inventory $1,700

Purchases units	Sales units	Balance units	Inventory value $	Unit cost $
10		10	3,000	300
12			3,000	250
		22	6,000	
	8		(2,400)	
		14	3,600	
6			1,200	200
		20	4,800	
	12		(3,100)*	
		8	1,700	

* 2 @ $300 + 10 @ $250 = $3,100

31.2 A   The IFRS Advisory Council

31.3 D

SUSPENSE ACCOUNT

	$		$
Cash	1,512	Bal b/f	759
		Receivables	131
		Bal c/f	622
	1,512		1,512

31.4 D   The sales daybook has been totalled incorrectly so the incorrect total has been posted to the control account. Each individual transaction has been posted to the individual accounts so when the two are compared there will be a difference of $200.

31.5 C

	$
Receivables allowance at 30/11/X8 (598,600 × 2%)	11,972
Opening provision at 1/12/X7	(12,460)
Reduction in provision (credit to statement of profit or loss)	(488)

Total credit to statement of profit or loss = 488 + 635 = $1,123

31.6 C

	$
Rent accrual (4/12 × $12,000)	(4,000)
Insurance prepayment (10/12 × $6,000)	5,000
Net increase in profit	1,000

31.7 D

	$
Non-current assets at 1 December 20X7	2,500,000
Depreciation charge for the year	(75,000)
Non-current asset disposed of (carrying value)	(120,000)
Revaluation of non-current assets	500,000
	2,805,000
Non-current assets at 30 November 20X8	4,200,000
Therefore non-current assets acquired during the year	(1,395,000)
Sales proceeds from disposal of non-current asset	150,000
To be included in 'net cash flows from investing activities'	(1,245,000)

NON-CURRENT ASSETS

	$'000		$'000
Bal b/f	2,500	Depreciation	75
Revaluation	500	Disposal	120
Additions (bal fig)	1,395	Bal c/f	4,200
	4,395		4,395

31.8 A A transposition error in the sales day book will not cause a difference between the SLCA and the receivables ledger as the total of the SDB is posted to the SLCA and the individual balances in the SDB to the receivables ledger, therefore the same error will be posted to both the SLCA and the receivables ledger.

31.9 A Make sure you read the **dates carefully** as some of the goods are returned after 31 May and we are only concerned with sales returns at that date, which is the goods with a list price of $3,000. The value of the original sale is after the trade discount of 10%, so the actual amount invoiced for those goods is $2,700 ($3,000 × 90%).

31.10 C Only statement 2 is correct. Development expenditure should be capitalised in accordance with IAS 38, however, research expenditure should be written off to the statement of profit or loss as incurred. Goodwill arising in a business combination should be capitalised as a non-current asset in the statement of financial position.

31.11 D All of the suggestions are flawed. FIFO is not permitted under IAS 2. Provisions cannot be created unless a constructive obligation exists, the amount can be reliably estimated and the likelihood of having to pay out cash is probable – none of these conditions are met, therefore a provision cannot be made. Development expenditure must be amortised over its useful life.

31.12 C Journal entries 1 and 2 should both be reversed.

31.13 C Carriage outwards is a distribution expense.

31.14 C

	Frog	Toad
	$'000	$'000
Per question	650	160
Pre-acquisition retained earnings		(145)*
		15
Post-acquisition retained earnings of Toad	15	
Group retained earnings	665	

* 100 + (60/12 × 9)

31.15 D

	$
Profit before tax	36,000
Dividend	(21,000)
Added to retained earnings	15,000

31.16 D It reduces receivables.

31.17 A $2,185. Prepayment b/f $60 (2/3 × 90) + $2,145 – prepayment c/f $60 – accrual b/f $80 + accrual c/f $120 = $2,185.

31.18 B   In option 2, receivables and drawings are debits but discount received is a credit. In option 4, capital and trade payables are credits but operating expenses are debits.

31.19 B $205

Profit = Drawings + Increase in net assets – Capital introduced
        = $77 + $173 – $45
        = $205

31.20 B $130 loss

Capital = Assets – Liabilities

$50 + $100 + profit for the year = $90 – $70

$150 + profit for the year = $20

Therefore, the profit for the year is in fact a *loss* of $130.

32   Mixed bank 6

32.1   A   X is a receivable of Y.

32.2   A $47,429

RECEIVABLES LEDGER CONTROL

	$		$
Balance b/d	50,241	Returns inwards	41,226
Sales	472,185	Irrecoverable debts written off	1,914
Cheques dishonoured	626	Discounts allowed	2,672
		Cheques received	429,811
		Balance c/d	47,429
	523,052		523,052

32.3   C $1,681

CASH BOOK

	$		$
20X8		*20X8*	
31 Dec Balance b/d	1,793	31 Dec Bank charges	18
31 Dec Dividend	26	Standing order	32
		Direct debit	88
		Balance c/d	1,681
	1,819		1,819

32.4   A $2,098

CASH BOOK

	$		$
20X3		*20X3*	
31 May Balance b/d	873	31 May Bank charges	630
Error $(936 – 693)	243	Trade journals	52
Balance c/d	2,098	Insurance	360
		Business rates	2,172
	3,214		3,214
		1 May Balance b/d	2,098

32.5   B $87 loss

	$
Carrying value: 9,000 × 0.7 × 0.7 × 0.7	3,087
Proceeds of sale	(3,000)
Loss on disposal	87

32.6 A Depreciation is an application of the accruals principle.

32.7 C Original annual depreciation = $(160,000 – 40,000)/8 years = $15,000 per year.

The change in the estimated life of the asset is made on 31 December 20X3, and this means that the change should be applied for the year ending 31 December 20X3.

		$
Cost		160,000
Accumulated depreciation to 31 December 20X2	(2 years × $15,000)	30,000
Carrying amount at 1 January 2008		130,000
Residual value		40,000
Remaining depreciable amount as at 1 January 20X3		90,000

Remaining life from 1 January 20X3 = 4 years

Annual depreciation = $90,000/4 years = $22,500.

Net book value (carrying amount at 31 December 20X3 = $130,000 – $22,500 = $107,500.

32.8 B $200 debit which should have been credited – correction will bring trial balance into agreement

32.9 C IAS 1 requires revenue to be disclosed on the face of the statement of profit or loss and other comprehensive income. It does not specify that a company must disclose profit before tax or gross profit on the face of the statement of profit or loss and other comprehensive income, however, most companies choose to do this. Dividends are disclosed in the statement of changes in equity if they are paid or are declared before the period end.

32.10 D ($73,680) + 102,480 – 87,240 = (58,440) $58,440 overdrawn

32.11 C 1, 2 and 3 are all incorrect.

32.12 C

TRADE RECEIVABLES				ALLOWANCE FOR RECEIVABLES		
	$		$			$
B/d	31,450	Irrecoverable debt	1,000		b/d	450
		c/d	30,450			
				c/d 3,445 (W1)		
	31,450		31,450			

	$
Net trade receivables	30,450
Less: Horrids	(800)
	29,650
Allowance @ 10%	2,965

	$
General allowance	2,965
Specific allowance = 800 × 60%	480
	3,445

32.13 A

32.14 B $952,500 × 100/60 = $1,587,500

32.15 C

	$
Theoretical gross profit ($130,000 × 30%)	39,000
Actual gross profit ($130,000 – $49,800 – $88,600 + $32,000)	23,600
Shortfall – missing inventory	15,400

32.16 A

	$	$
Sales		240,000
Purchases	134,025	
∴ Drawings	(2,640)	
Inventory adjustment	(11,385)	
Cost of sales (50% × 240,000)		120,000
		120,000

32.17 D   Incorrect answers: Goods purchased for cash – current assets remain the same, Payables paid out of an overdraft – current liabilities remain the same

32.18 D

PUP = 50,000 × 25/125 × 40% = $4,000

	Lexus group
	$'000
Revenue (350 + 150 – 50*)	450
Cost of sales (200 + 60 – 50* + 4)	214

* to remove intragroup sales

32.19 D

Share capital 75,000 + 15,000 + 30,000 =	120,000
Share premium 200,000 + 57,000 – 30,000 =	227,000
(Remember shares are 25c)	

32.20 D

33   Mixed bank 7

33.1 A

PLANT AND EQUIPMENT (CARRYING VALUE)

	$'000		$'000
b/d	155	Depreciation charge in year	25
Purchases of P+E	10	∴ Carrying value of sale	15
		c/d	125
	165		165

		$'000
So,	Carrying value	15
	Proceeds	(7)
	Loss	8

33.2 D   (2c + 3c) × 10,000,000. The final ordinary dividend is declared before the year end and so is accrued for. The preference dividend is classified as a finance cost.

33.3 A   Working capital is increased as the company will receive cash for the share issue. Share premium is not reduced as it is not a bonus issue of shares, it will probably increase as the shares will probably be issued at a premium.

33.4 D   A revaluation surplus will be presented as part of equity, not current liabilities.

33.5 C   In statement (i) both sides of the double entry posting from the cash book would be incorrect but equal in value, so this would not cause a trial balance imbalance. In statement (ii), both expenses and non-current assets are debit balances in the trial balance, so posting to the wrong account in this case would not cause a trial balance imbalance.

33.6 D   The dividends actually paid will go through the statement of changes in equity. The final proposed dividend of $120,000 is disclosed in the notes to the statement of financial position.

33.7 D   Deferred development expenditure should be amortised over its useful life. If the conditions in IAS 38 are met, development expenditure *must* be capitalised. Trade investments are not intangible assets, they should be reported under non-current assets: investments in the SOFP.

33.8 D

RENT

	$		$
Bal b/f (rent in arrears)	4,800	Bal b/f (rent in advance)	134,600
SPL (bal. fig.)	828,700	Bank	834,600
Bal c/f (rent in advance)	144,400	Bal c/f (rent in arrears)	8,700
	977,900		977,900

33.9 D   A, B and C are all income items reflected in the statement of profit or loss and other comprehensive income. In contrast D is reflected in the statement of financial position.

33.10 B   Items A, C and D are all capital items, reflected in the statement of financial position.

33.11 A

33.12 A

PAYABLES LEDGER CONTROL ACCOUNT

	$		$
Cash paid to suppliers	1,364,300	Opening balance	318,600
Discounts received	8,200	Purchases	1,268,600
Purchases returns	41,200	Refunds received from suppliers	2,700
Contras	48,000		
Closing balance	128,200		
	1,589,900		1,589,900

33.13 C   We need to increase the rent expenses (debit) and set up a liability to pay this amount (credit accruals).

33.14 D   For the purpose of consolidation, 100% of the goodwill in the subsidiary is included in the consolidated statement of financial position, because the parent company controls all of it.

33.15 C   Wastage of inventory means that cost of sales is high relative to revenue.

33.16 A   Sales: current assets = 5:1

Therefore current assets ($30m/5) = $6m

Current ratio = 2:1

Therefore current liabilities ($6m/2) = $3m

Acid test ratio = 1.5:1

Therefore current assets – inventory ($3m × 1.5) = $4.5m

Hence, Inventory ($6m – $4.5m) = $1.5m

33.17 C   All three statements are correct.

33.18 A   485,000 + 48,600 + 18,100 – 368,400

33.19 B   = 60,000 + ((1,232,000 – 60,000) × 5%) – 90,000

33.20 A   Although we may use a trial balance as a step in preparing management or financial accounts, the main reason is A.

Mock Exams

ACCA
Paper FFA/F3
Financial Accounting

Mock Examination 1
(Specimen exam)

Question Paper	
Time allowed	2 hours
This paper is divided into two sections:	
Section A – ALL 35 questions are compulsory and MUST be attempted	
Section B – BOTH questions are compulsory and MUST be attempted	

DO NOT OPEN THIS PAPER UNTIL YOU ARE READY TO START UNDER EXAMINATION CONDITIONS

SECTION A – ALL 35 questions are compulsory and MUST be attempted

1   Which of the following calculates a sole trader's net profit for a period?

   A   Closing net assets + drawings – capital introduced – opening net assets
   B   Closing net assets – drawings + capital introduced – opening net assets
   C   Closing net assets – drawings – capital introduced – opening net assets
   D   Closing net assets + drawings + capital introduced – opening net assets   **(2 marks)**

2   Which of the following explains the imprest system of operating petty cash?

   A   Weekly expenditure cannot exceed a set amount.
   B   The exact amount of expenditure is reimbursed at intervals to maintain a fixed float.
   C   All expenditure out of the petty cash must be properly authorised.
   D   Regular equal amounts of cash are transferred into petty cash at intervals.   **(2 marks)**

3   Which of the following statements are TRUE of limited liability companies?

   1   The company's exposure to debts and liability is limited
   2   Financial statements must be produced
   3   A company continues to exist regardless of the identity of its owners

   A   1 and 2 only
   B   1 and 3 only
   C   2 and 3 only
   D   1, 2 and 3   **(2 marks)**

4   Annie is a sole trader who does not keep full accounting records. The following details relate to her transactions with credit customers and suppliers for the year ended 30 June 20X6:

	$
Trade receivables, 1 July 20X5	130,000
Trade payables, 1 July 20X5	60,000
Cash received from customers	686,400
Cash paid to suppliers	302,800
Discounts allowed	1,400
Discounts received	2,960
Contra between payables and receivables ledgers	2,000
Trade receivables, 30 June 20X6	181,000
Trade payables, 30 June 20X6	84,000

   What figure should appear for purchases in Annie's statement of profit or loss for the year ended 30 June 20X6?

   A $325,840
   B $330,200
   C $331,760
   D $327,760   **(2 marks)**

5   Which TWO of the following errors would cause the total of the debit column and the total of the credit column of a trial balance not to agree?

   1   A transposition error was made when entering a sales invoice into the sales day book
   2   A cheque received from a customer was credited to cash and correctly recognised in receivables
   3   A purchase of non-current assets was omitted from the accounting records
   4   Rent received was included in the trial balance as a debit balance

   A   1 and 2
   B   1 and 3
   C   2 and 3
   D   2 and 4   **(2 marks)**

6   At 31 December 20X5 the following require inclusion in a company's financial statements:

1   On 1 January 20X5 the company made a loan of $12,000 to an employee, repayable on 1 January 20X6, charging interest at 2% per year. On the due date she repaid the loan and paid the whole of the interest due on the loan to that date.

2   The company paid an annual insurance premium of $9,000 in 20X5, covering the year ending 31 August 20X6.

3   In January 20X6 the company received rent from a tenant of $4,000 covering the six months to 31 December 20X5.

For these items, what total figures should be included in the company's statement of financial position as at 31 December 20X5?

A   Current assets $10,000   Current liabilities $12,240
B   Current assets $22,240   Current liabilities $nil
C   Current assets $10,240   Current liabilities $nil
D   Current assets $16,240   Current liabilities $6,000   **(2 marks)**

7   A company's statement of profit or loss for the year ended 31 December 20X5 showed a net profit of $83,600. It was later found that $18,000 paid for the purchase of a motor van had been debited to the motor expenses account. It is the company's policy to depreciate motor vans at 25% per year on the straight line basis, with a full year's charge in the year of acquisition.

What would the net profit be after adjusting for this error?

A $106,100
B $70,100
C $97,100
D $101,600   **(2 marks)**

8   Xena has the following working capital ratios:

	20X9	20X8
Current ratio	1.2:1	1.5:1
Receivables days	75 days	50 days
Payables days	30 days	45 days
Inventory turnover	42 days	35 days

Which of the following statements is correct?

A   Xena's liquidity and working capital has improved in 20X9
B   Xena is receiving cash from customers more quickly in 20X9 than in 20X8
C   Xena is suffering from a worsening liquidity position in 20X9
D   Xena is taking longer to pay suppliers in 20X9 than in 20X8   **(2 marks)**

9   Which of the following statements is/are correct?

1   A statement of cash flows prepared using the direct method produces a different figure to net cash from operating activities from that produced if the indirect method is used.

2   Rights issues of shares do not feature in a statement of cash flows.

3   A surplus on revaluation of a non-current asset will not appear as an item in a statement of cash flows.

4   A profit on the sale of a non-current asset will appear as an item under cash flows from investing activities in the statement of cash flows.

A   1 and 3 only
B   3 and 4 only
C   2 and 4 only
D   3 only   **(2 marks)**

10   A company receives rent from a large number of properties. The total received in the year ended 30 April 20X6 was $481,200.

The following were the amounts of rent in advance and in arrears at 30 April 20X5 and 20X6:

	30 April 20X5	30 April 20X6
	$	$
Rent received in advance	28,700	31,200
Rent in arrears (all subsequently received)	21,200	18,400

What amount of rental income should appear in the company's statement of profit or loss for the year ended 30 April 20X6?

A $486,500
B $460,900
C $501,500
D $475,900   (2 marks)

11   Which of the following are differences between sole traders and limited liability companies?

1   A sole trader's financial statements are private and never made available to third parties; a company's financial statements are sent to shareholders and may be publicly filed.

2   Only companies have share capital.

3   A sole trader is fully and personally liable for any losses that the business might make.

4   Drawings would only appear in a sole trader's financial statements.

A   1 and 4 only
B   2, 3 and 4
C   2 and 3 only
D   1, 3 and 4   (2 marks)

12   Which of the following statements is true?

A   The interpretation of an entity's financial statements using ratios is only useful for potential investors.

B   Ratios based on historical data can predict the future performance of an entity.

C   The analysis of financial statements using ratios provides useful information when compared with previous performance or industry averages.

D   An entity's management will not assess an entity's performance using financial ratios. (2 marks)

13   A company's motor vehicles cost account at 30 June 20X6 is as follows:

MOTOR VEHICLES - COST

	$		$
Balance b/f	35,800	Disposal	12,000
Additions	12,950	Balance c/f	36,750
	48,750		48,750

What opening balance should be included in the following period's trial balance for Motor vehicles – cost at 1 July 20X6?

A $36,750 Dr
B $48,750 Dr
C $36,750 Cr
D $48,750 Cr   (2 marks)

14 Which TWO of the following items must be disclosed in the note to the financial statements for intangible assets?

1 The useful lives of intangible assets capitalised in the financial statements
2 A description of the development projects that have been undertaken during the period
3 A list of all intangible assets purchased or developed in the period
4 Impairment losses written off intangible assets during the period

A 1 and 4
B 2 and 3
C 3 and 4
D 1 and 2 **(2 marks)**

15 Which of the following statements are correct ?

1 Capitalised development expenditure must be amortised over a period not exceeding five years.

2 Capitalised development costs are shown in the statement of financial position under the heading of non-current assets.

3 If certain criteria are met, research expenditure must be recognised as an intangible asset.

A 2 only
B 2 and 3
C 1 only
D 1 and 3 **(2 marks)**

16 The following transactions relate to Rashid's electricity expense ledger account for the year ended 30 June 20X9:

	$
Prepayment brought forward	550
Cash paid	5,400
Accrual carried forward	650

What amount should be charged to the statement of profit or loss in the year ended 30 June 20X9 for electricity?

A $6,600
B $5,400
C $5,500
D $5,300 **(2 marks)**

17 At 30 June 20X5 a company's allowance for receivables was $39,000. At 30 June 20X6 trade receivables totalled $517,000. It was decided to write off debts totalling $37,000 and to adjust the allowance for receivables to the equivalent of 5% of the trade receivables based on past events.

What figure should appear in the statement of profit or loss for the year ended 30 June 20X6 for receivables expense?

A $61,000
B $52,000
C $22,000
D $37,000 **(2 marks)**

18 The total of the list of balances in Valley's payables ledger was $438,900 at 30 June 20X6. This balance did not agree with Valley's payables ledger control account balance. The following errors were discovered:

1   A contra entry of $980 was recorded in the payables ledger control account, but not in the payables ledger.

2   The total of the purchase returns daybook was undercast by $1,000.

3   An invoice for $4,344 was posted to the supplier's account as $4,434.

What amount should Valley report in its statement of financial position for accounts payable at 30 June 20X6?

A $436,830
B $438,010
C $439,790
D $437,830   (2 marks)

19 According to IAS 2 *Inventories*, which TWO of the following costs should be included in valuing the inventories of a manufacturing company?

1   Carriage inwards
2   Carriage outwards
3   Depreciation of factory plant
4   General administrative overheads

A   1 and 4
B   1 and 3
C   3 and 4
D   2 and 3   (2 marks)

20 Prisha has not kept accurate accounting records during the financial year. She had opening inventory of $6,700 and purchased goods costing $84,000 during the year. At the year end she had $5,400 left in inventory. All sales are made at a mark up on cost of 20%.

What is Prisha's gross profit for the year?

A $13,750
B $17,060
C $16,540
D $20,675   (2 marks)

21 At 31 December 20X4 a company's capital structure was as follows:

	$
Ordinary share capital (500,000 shares of 25c each)	125,000
Share premium account	100,000

In the year ended 31 Decemebr 20X5 the company made a rights issue of 1 share for every 2 held at $1 per share and this was taken up in full. Later in the year the company made a bonus issue of 1 shrae for every 5 held, using the share premium account for the purpose.

What was the company's capital structure at 31 December 20X5?

	Ordinary share capital	Share premium account	
A	$450,000	$25,000	
B	$225,000	$250,000	
C	$225,000	$325,000	
D	$212,500	$262,500	(2 marks)

22   Which of the following should appear in a company's statement of changes in equity?

      1   Total comprehensive income for the year
      2   Amortisation of capitalised development costs
      3   Surplus on revaluation of non-current assets

      A   1, 2 and 3
      B   2 and 3 only
      C   1 and 3 only
      D   1 and 2 only   **(2 marks)**

23   The plant and machinery account (at cost) of a business for the year ended 31 December 20X5 was as
      follows:

                              PLANT AND MACHINERY - COST

20X5	$	20X5	$
1 Jan Balance b/f	240,000	31 Mar Transfer to disposal account	60,000
30 Jun Cash purchase of plant	160,000	31 Dec Balance c/f	340,000
	400,000		400,000

      The company's policy is to charge depreciation at 20% per year on the straight line basis, with
      proportionate depreciation in the years of purchase and disposal.

      What should be the depreciation charge for the year ended 31 December 20X5?

      A $68,000
      B $64,000
      C $61,000
      D $55,000   **(2 marks)**

24   The following extracts are from Hassan's financial statements:

	$
Profit before interest and tax	10,200
Interest	(1,600)
Tax	(3,300)
Profit after tax	5,300
Share capital	20,000
Reserves	15,600
	35,600
Loan liability	6,900
	42,500

      What is Hassan's return on capital employed?

      A   15%
      B   29%
      C   24%
      D   12%   **(2 marks)**

25   Which of the following statements about sales tax is/are true?

      1   Sales tax is an expense to the ultimate consumer of the goods purchased
      2   Sales tax is recorded as income in the accounts of the entity selling the goods

      A   1 only
      B   2 only
      C   Both 1 and 2
      D   Neither 1 nor 2   **(2 marks)**

26 Q's trial balance failed to agree and a suspense account was opened for the difference. Q does not keep receivables and payables control accounts. The following errors were found in Q's accounting records:

1 In recording an issue of shares at par, cash received of $333,000 was credited to the ordinary share capital account as $330,000

2 Cash of $2,800 paid for plant repairs was correctly accounted for in the cash book but was credited to the plant asset account

3 The petty cash book balance of $500 had been omitted from the trial balance

4 A cheque for $78,400 paid for the purchase of a motor car was debited to the motor vehicles account as $87,400.

Which of the errors will require an entry to the suspense account to correct them?

A   1, 2 and 4 only
B   1, 2, 3 and 4
C   1 and 4 only
D   2 and 3 only   **(2 marks)**

27 Prior to the financial year end of 31 July 20X9, Cannon Co has received a claim of $100,000 from a customer for providing poor quality goods which have damaged the customer's plant and equipment. Cannon Co's lawyers have stated that there is a 20% chance that Cannon will successfully defend the claim.

Which of the following is the correct accounting treatment for the claim in the financial statements for the year ended 31 July 20X9?

A   Cannon should neither provide for nor disclose the claim.
B   Cannon should disclose a contingent liability of $100,000.
C   Cannon should provide for the expected cost of the claim of $100,000.
D   Cannon should provide for an expected cost of $20,000.   **(2 marks)**

28 Gareth, a sales tax registered trader purchased a computer for use in his business. The invoice for the computer showed the following costs related to the purchase:

	$
Computer	890
Additional memory	95
Delivery	10
Installation	20
Maintenance (1 year)	25
	1,040
Sales tax (17.5%)	182
Total	1,222

How much should Gareth capitalise as a non-current asset in relation to the purchase?

A $1,193
B $1,040
C $1,222
D $1,015   **(2 marks)**

29   The following bank reconciliation statement has been prepared by a trainee accountant:

	$
Overdraft per bank statement	3,860
Less: Unpresented cheques	9,160
	5,300
Add: Outstanding lodgements	16,690
Cash at bank	21,990

What should be the correct balance per the cash book?

A $21,990 balance at bank as stated
B $3,670 balance at bank
C $11,390 balance at bank
D $3,670 overdrawn   **(2 marks)**

30   The IASB's *Conceptual Framework for Financial Reporting* identifies characteristics which make financial information faithfully represent what it purports to represent.

Which of the following are examples of those characteristics?

1   Accruals
2   Completeness
3   Going concern
4   Neutrality

A   1 and 2
B   2 and 4
C   2 and 3
D   1 and 4   **(2 marks)**

31   The following control account has been prepared by a trainee accountant:

RECEIVABLES LEDGER CONTROL ACCOUNT

	$		$
Opening balance	308,600	Cash	147,200
Credit sales	154,200	Discounts allowed	1,400
Cash sales	88,100	Interest charged on overdue accounts	2,400
Contras	4,600	Irrecoverable debts	4,900
		Allowance for receivables	2,800
		Closing balance	396,800
	555,500		555,500

What should the closing balance be when all the errors made in preparing the receivables ledger control account have been corrected?

A $395,200
B $304,300
C $309,500
D $307,100   **(2 marks)**

32   Which of the following material events after the reporting date and before the financial statements are approved are adjusting events?

1   A valuation of property providing evidence of impairment in value at the reporting date.
2   Sale of inventory held at the reporting date for less than cost.
3   Discovery of fraud or error affecting the financial statements.
4   The insolvency of a customer with a debt owing at the reporting date which is still outstanding.

A   1, 2 and 4 only
B   1, 2, 3 and 4
C   1 and 4 only
D   2 and 3 only   **(2 marks)**

33 A company values its inventory using the FIFO method. At 1 May 20X5 the company had 700 engines in inventory, valued at $190 each. During the year ended 30 April 20X6 the following transactions took place:

20X5
1 July   Purchased 500 engines at $220 each
1 November   Sold 400 engines for $160,000

20X6
1 February   Purchased 300 engines at $230 each
15 April   Sold 250 engines for $125,000

What is the value of the company's closing inventory of engines at 30 April 20X6?

A $188,500
B $195,500
C $166,000
D $106,000   **(2 marks)**

34 Amy is a sole trader and had assets of $569,400 and liabilities of $412,840 on 1 January 20X8. During the year ended 31 December 20X8 she paid $65,000 capital into the business and she paid herself wages of $800 per month.

At 31 December 20X8, Amy had assets of $614,130 and liabilities of $369,770.

What is Amy's profit for the year ended 31 December 20X8?

A $32,400
B $23,600
C $22,800
D $87,800   **(2 marks)**

35 Bumbly Co extracted the trial balance for the year ended 31 December 20X7. The total of the debits exceeded the credits by $300.

Which of the following could explain the imbalance?

A   Sales of $300 were omitted from the sales day book.
B   Returns inward of $150 were extracted to the debit column of the trial balance.
C   Discounts received of $150 were extracted to the debit column of the trial balance.
D   The bank ledger account did not agree with the bank statement by a debit of $300.

                                                                 (2 marks)

SECTION B – BOTH questions are compulsory and MUST be attempted

Please write your answer within the answer booklet in accordance with the detailed instructions provided within each of the questions in this section of the exam paper.

1 Keswick Co acquired 80% of the share capital of Derwent Co on 1 June 20X5. The summarised draft statements of profit or loss for Keswick Co and Derwent Co for the year ended 31 May 20X6 are shown below:

	Keswick Co	Derwent Co
	$'000	$'000
Revenue	8,400	3,200
Cost of sales	(4,600)	(1,700)
Gross profit	3,800	1,500
Operating expenses	(2,200)	(960)
Profit before tax	1,600	540
Tax	(600)	(140)
Profit of the year	1,000	400

During the year Keswick Co sold goods costing $1,000,000 to Derwent Co for $1,500,000. At 31 May 20X6, 30% of these goods remained in Derwent Co's inventory.

Required

(a) Prepare the Keswick group consolidated statement of profit or loss for the year ended 31 May 20X6.

Note: The statement should stop once the consolidated profit for the year has been determined. The amounts attributable to the non-controlling interest and equity owners of Keswick are not required. Show all workings as credit will be awarded to these as appropriate.   (7 marks)

(b) Which of the following formulas describes the amount to be entered in the consolidated statement of profit or loss as '*Profit attributable to: Equity owners of Keswick Co*'?

A Group profit after tax – non-controlling interest
B Group profit after tax + non-controlling interest
C Keswick Co's profit after tax
D Group profit after tax   (2 marks)

(c) What amount should be shown in the consolidated statement of profit or loss for the non-controlling interest?   (2 marks)

(d) The following table shows factors to be considered when determining whether a parent–subsidiary relationship exists.

Factor Description

A Significant influence
B Control
C Non-controlling interest
D Greater than 50% of the equity shares being held by an investor
E 100% of the equity shares being held by an investor
F Greater than 50% of the preference shares being held by an investor
G 50% of all shares and all debt being held by an investor
H Greater than 50% of preference shares and debt being held by an investor

Required

Which of the above factors A to H illustrate the existence of a parent–subsidiary relationship?
                                        (4 marks)

(15 marks)

2   Malright, a limited liability company, has an accounting year end of 31 October. The accountant is preparing the financial statements as at 31 October 20X7 and requires your assistance. The following trial balance has been extracted from the general ledger.

Account	Dr $'000	Cr $'000
Buildings at cost	740	
Buildings accumulated depreciation, 1 November 20X6		60
Plant at cost	220	
Plant accumulated depreciation, 1 November 20X6		110
Bank balance		70
Revenue		1,800
Net purchases	1,140	
Inventory at 1 November 20X6	160	
Cash	20	
Trade payables		250
Trade receivables	320	
Administrative expenses	325	
Allowance for receivables at 1 November 20X6		10
Retained earnings at 1 November 20X6		130
Equity shares, $1		415
Share premium account		80
	2,925	2,925

The following additional information is also available:

–   The allowance for receivables is to be increased to 5% of trade receivables. The allowance for receivables is treated as an administrative expense.

–   Plant is depreciated at 20% per annum using the reducing balance method and buildings are depreciated at 5% per annum on their original cost. Depreciation is treated as a cost of sales expense.

–   Closing inventory has been counted and is valued at $75,000.

–   An invoice of $15,000 for energy costs relating to the quarter ended 30 November 20X7 was received on 2 December 20X7. Energy costs are included in administrative expenses.

Required

Prepare the statement of profit or loss and the statement of financial position of Malright Co as at 31 October 20X7.   **(15 marks)**

Answers to
Mock Exam 1
(Specimen exam)

Note: The ACCA examiner's answers follow these BPP Learning Media answers.

SECTION A

1   A   Remember that: closing net assets = opening net assets + capital introduced + profit − drawings.

2   B   Under the imprest system, a reimbursement which equals the total of expense vouchers paid out, is made at intervals to maintain the petty cash balance at a certain amount.

3   C   The shareholder's exposure to debts is limited, not the company's.

4   C

PAYABLES CONTROL ACCOUNT

	$		$
Cash paid to suppliers	302,800	Balance b/f	60,000
Discounts received	2,960	Purchases (bal fig)	331,760
Contra	2,000		
Balance c/f	84,000		
	391,760		391,760

5   D   Errors (1) and (3) will not cause a trial balance imbalance. In error 1, the incorrect amount will be posted to both sales and receivables (Dr receivables, Cr sales). In error 3, the complete omission of the transaction will have no effect on the trial balance.

6   B

Current assets	$
Loan asset	12,000
Interest (12,000 × 12%)	240
Prepayment (8/12 × 9,000)	6,000
Accrued rent	4,000
	22,240

7   C

	$
Profit	83,600
Purchase of van	18,000
Depreciation 18,000 × 25%	(4,500)
	97,100

8   C   The ratios given relate to working capital and liquidity. The ratios have all worsened from 20X8 to 20X9, suggesting a worsening liquidity position. Receivables days have gone up, meaning that customers are taking longer to pay. Payables days have gone down, meaning that Xena is paying suppliers more quickly. Inventory turnover days have gone up, meaning inventories are being held for longer.

9   D   Only item (3) is correct. The direct and indirect method both produce the same figure for cash from operating activities. A rights issue of shares does feature in a statement of cash flows as cash is received for the issue, a bonus issue, however, would not feature as no cash is received. A profit on the sale of a non-current asset would not appear as an investing cash flow, rather the cash received from the sale would appear as an investing cash flow and the profit on the sale would be added back to profit before tax under the indirect method of calculating cash from operating activities.

10   D

	$
Balance b/f (advance)	28,700
Balance b/f (arrears)	(21,200)
Cash received	481,200
Balance c/f (advance)	(31,200)
Balance c/f (arrears)	18,400
	475,900

11   B   A sole trader's financial statements are not publicly available, but they might be made available to some third parties, for example, the tax authorities.

12   C   Ratio analysis is useful for different users of financial statements, including management, potential investors, the government, employees and so on. Historical performance can give an indication of what might occur in the future, especially if a trend is shown, but it cannot be used to accurately predict the future.

13   A   Motor vehicles – cost account is an asset and so the balance brought forward must be a debit. It is $36,750 as this is the figure that balances the account.

14   A   An entity is **not** required to disclose a description of the development projects undertaken in the period, or a list of all intangible assets purchased or developed in the period. It is however, required to: disclose a description, the carrying amount and remaining amortisation period of any individual intangible asset that is **material** to the entity's financial statements, and distinguish between internally generated intangible assets capitalised in the period and those acquired in the period.

15   A   Statement 2 is the only correct statement. Statement 1 is incorrect because capitalised development expenditure is amortised over its useful life. Statement 3 is incorrect because research expenditure is never capitalised.

16   A

	$
Balance b/f	550
Expense incurred (cash)	5,400
Accrual c/f	650
	6,600

17   C

	$	$
Debts written off		37,000
Movement in allowance:		
(517 – 37) × 5%	24,000	
Less opening allowance	39,000	
		(15,000)
Receivables expense		22,000

18   D

	$
Balance per ledger	438,900
Less contra	(980)
Posting error	(90)
Corrected balance	437,830

The individual returns from the purchase returns day book are posted to the individual accounts in the memorandum payables ledger, so the list of balances does not need to be adjusted for error (2).

19   B   Carriage outwards is a distribution expense. General administrative overheads should not be included per IAS 2.

20   B   (6,700 + 84,000 – 5,400) × 20% = $17,060

21   B   Share capital = 125,000 + 62,500 rights issue of 250,000 25c shares (500,000/2) + 37,500 bonus issue of 150,000 25c shares (750,000/5) = 225,000

Share premium = 100,000 + 187,500 rights issue (250,000 × 75c) – 37,500 bonus issue (150,000 x 25c) = 250,000

22   C   Amortisation of development costs will appear in the statement of profit or loss, not the statement of changes in equity.

23   D

	$
Depreciation:	
Jan–Mar 240,000 × 20% × 3/12	12,000
Apr–Jun (240,000 – 60,000) × 20% × 3/12	9,000
Jul–Dec (180,000 + 160,000) × 20% × 6/12	34,000
	55,000

24   C   10,200/42,500

25   A   Sales tax is merely collected by the business, the ultimate consumer bears the expense.

26   B   All of the errors would require an entry to the suspense account to correct them.

27   C   It is probable that Canon will have to pay $100,000 for the claim, therefore a provision is required.

28   D   1,040 – 25 = $1,015. The maintenance costs should not be capitalised. The sales tax is recoverable as Gareth is registered for sales tax, therefore is should not be capitalised.

29   B

	$
Overdraft per bank statement	(3,860)
Less: Unpresented cheques	(9,160)
Add: Outstanding lodgements	16,690
Cash at bank	3,670

30   B   Completeness and neutrality are two characteristics given in the *Conceptual framework*. Going concern is the underlying assumption and accruals is not a stated characteristic.

31   D

RECEIVABLES LEDGER CONTROL ACCOUNT

	$		$
Opening balance	308,600	Cash	147,200
Credit sales	154,200	Discounts allowed	1,400
Interest charged on overdue accounts	2,400	Contras	4,600
		Irrecoverable debts	4,900
		Closing balance	307,100
	465,200		465,200

32   B   All of the events are adjusting events.

33   A   Closing inventory:

	$
50 × $190	9,500
500 × $220	110,000
300 × $230	69,000
	188,500

34   A   Closing net assets = opening net assets + capital introduced + profit – drawings

	$
Opening assets	569,400
Opening liabilities	(412,840)
Capital introduced	65,000
Drawings (800 × 12)	(9,600)
	211,960
Profit (bal fig)	32,400
Closing net assets (614,130 – 369,770)	244,360

35   C   Discounts received are recorded as a credit balance and appear as other income in the statement of profit or loss: Dr payables, Cr discounts received.

SECTION B

1   (a)   KESWICK GROUP

CONSOLIDATED STATEMENT OF PROFIT OR LOSS FOR THE YEAR ENDED 31 MAY 20X6

	$'000
Revenue (8,400 + 3,200 − 1,500)	10,100
Cost of sales (4,600 + 1,700 − 1,500 + 150)	(4,950)
Gross profit	5,150
Operating expenses (2,200 + 960))	(3,160)
Profit before tax	1,990
Tax (600 + 140)	(740)
Profit of the year	1,250

(b)   A

(c)   Non-controlling interest = $80,000 ($400,000 × 20%)

(d)   The following factors illustrate the existence of a parent–subsidiary relationship: B, C, D, E.

2   MALRIGHT CO

STATEMENT OF PROFIT OR LOSS FOR THE YEAR ENDED 31 OCTOBER 20X7

	$'000
Revenue	1,800
Cost of sales (W1)	(1,284)
Gross profit	514
Administrative expenses (325 + 10 (W4) + (16 (W3) −10))	(314)
Profit for the year	175

STATEMENT OF FINANCIAL POSITION AS AT 31 OCTOBER 20X7

	$'000	$'000
Assets		
Non-current assets (W2)		731
Current assets		
Inventories	75	
Trade receivables (W3)	304	
Cash	20	
		399
Total assets		1,130
Equity and liabilities		
Equity		
Share capital	415	
Retained earnings (130 + 175)	305	
Share premium	80	
		800
Current liabilities		
Trade and other payables (250 + 10 (W4))	260	
Bank overdraft	70	
		330
Total equity and liabilities		1,130

Workings

1 *Cost of sales*

	$'000
Opening inventory	160
Purchases	1,140
Closing inventory	(75)
	1,225
Depreciation (W2)	59
	1,284

2 *Non-current assets*

	Property $'000	*Plant* $'000	*Total* $'000
Cost	740	220	960
Depreciation b/f	(60)	(110)	(170)
Depreciation for year			
740 × 5%	(37)		
(220 – 110) × 20%)		(22)	(59)
Net book value 31 October 20X7	643	88	731

3 *Trade receivables*
Allowance = 320,000 × 5% = $16,000
320,000 – 16,000 = $304,000

4 *Trade and other payables*

Energy cost accrual
15,000 × 2/3 = $10,000

ACCA examiner's answers to
Specimen exam

ACCA examiner's answers to

Specimen exam

SECTION A

1   A

2   B

3   C

4   C

Payables:	$
Balance b/f	60,000
Cash paid to suppliers	(302,800)
Discounts received	(2,960)
Contra	(2,000)
Balance c/f	(84,000)
Purchases	331,760

5   D

6   B

Current assets	$
Loan asset	12,000
Interest (12,000 × 12%)	240
Prepayment (8/12 × 9,000)	6,000
Accrued rent	4,000
	22,240

7   C

	$
Profit	83,600
Purchase of van	18,000
Depreciation 18,000 × 25%	(4,500)
	97,100

8   C

9   D

10   D

	$
Balance b/f (advance)	28,700
Balance b/f (arrears)	(21,200)
Cash received	481,200
Balance c/f (advance)	(31,200)
Balance c/f (arrears)	18,400
	475,900

11   B

12   C

13   A

14   A

15   A

16   A

	$
Balance b/f	550
Expense incurred (cash)	5,400
Accrual c/f	650
	6,600

17   C

	$	$
Debts written off		37,000
Movement in allowance:		
(517 – 37) × 5%	24,000	
Less opening allowance	39,000	
		(15,000)
Receivables expense		22,000

18   D

	$
Balance per ledger	438,900
Less contra	(980)
Posting error	(90)
Corrected balance	437,830

19   B

20   B   (6,700 + 84,000 – 5,400) × 20% = $17,060

21   B

	Share capital	Share premium
	$	$
Balance b/f	125,000	100,000
Rights issue	62,500	187,500
Bonus issue	37,500	(37,500)
Balance c/f	225,000	250,000

22   C

23   D

	$
Depreciation:	
Jan–Mar 240,000 × 20% × 3/12	12,000
Apr–Jun (240,000 – 60,000) × 20% × 3/12	9,000
Jul–Dec (180,000 + 160,000) × 20% × 6/12	34,000
	55,000

24   C   10,200/42,500

25   A

26   B

27   C

28   D   1,040 – 25 = $1,015

29   B

	$
Overdraft per bank statement	(3,860)
Less: Unpresented cheques	(9,160)
Add: Outstanding lodgements	16,690
Cash at bank	3,670

30   B

31   D

Receivables ledger control account

	$		$
Opening balance	308,600	Cash	147,200
Credit sales	154,200	Discounts allowed	1,400
Interest charged on overdue accounts	2,400	Contras	4,600
		Irrecoverable debts	4,900
		Closing balance	307,100
	465,200		465,200

32   B

33   A

Closing inventory:

	$
50 × $190	9,500
500 × $220	110,000
300 × $230	69,000
	188,500

34   A

	$
Opening assets	569,400
Opening liabilities	(412,840)
Capital introduced	65,000
Drawings (800 × 12)	(9,600)
	211,960
Profit (bal fig)	32,400
Closing net assets (614,130 – 369,770)	244,360

35   C

SECTION B

1   (a)   Consolidated statement of profit or loss for the year ended 31 May 20X6

	$'000
Revenue (W1)	10,100
Cost of sales (W1)	(4,950)
Gross profit	5,150
Operating expenses (W1)	(3,160)
Profit before tax	1,990
Tax	(740)
Profit of the year	1,250

(b)   A

(c)   Non-controlling interest = $80,000 ($400,000 (W1) × 20%)

(d)   The following factors illustrate the existence of a parent–subsidiary relationship: B, C, D, E.

Workings

Working 1

	Keswick Co $'000	Derwent Co $'000	Adjustments $'000	Consolidated $'000
Revenue	8,400	3,200	(1,500)	10,100
Cost of sales	(4,600)	(1,700)	1,500	(4,950)
Unrealised profit	(150)			
Operating expenses	(2,200)	(960)		(3,160)
Tax	(600)	(140)		(740)
	850	400		

2   Statement of profit or loss for the year ended 31 October 20X7

	$'000
Revenue	1,800
Cost of sales (W1)	(1,284)
Gross profit	514
Administrative expenses (325 + 10 (W4) + (16 (W3) –10))	(314)
Profit for the year	175

Statement of financial position as at 31 October 20X7

	$'000	$'000
Assets		
Non-current assets (W2)		731
Current assets		
Inventories	75	
Trade receivables (W3)	304	
Cash	20	
		399
Total assets		1,130
Equity and liabilities		
Equity		
Share capital	415	
Retained earnings (130 + 175)	305	
Share premium	80	
		800
Current liabilities		
Trade and other payables (250 + 10 (W4))	260	
Bank overdraft	70	
		330
Total equity and liabilities		1,130

Workings

Working 1

	$'000
Cost of sales	
Opening inventory	160
Purchases	1,140
Closing inventory	(75)
	1,225
Depreciation (W2)	59
	1,284

Working 2

	Property $'000	Plant $'000	Total $'000
Cost	740	220	960
Depreciation b/f	(60)	(110)	(170)
Depreciation for year			
740 × 5%	(37)		
(220 – 110) × 20%)		(22)	(59)
Net book value 31 October 20X7	643	88	731

Working 3

Trade receivables
Allowance = 320,000 × 5% = $16,000
320,000 – 16,000 = $304,000

Working 4

Energy cost accrual
15,000 × 2/3 = $10,000

Mock Exam 2

ACCA
Paper FFA/F3
Financial Accounting

Mock Examination 2

Question Paper	
Time allowed	2 hours
This paper is divided into two sections:	
Section A – ALL 35 questions are compulsory and MUST be attempted	
Section B – BOTH questions are compulsory and MUST be attempted	

DO NOT OPEN THIS PAPER UNTIL YOU ARE READY TO START UNDER EXAMINATION CONDITIONS

ACCA

Paper FFA/F3

Financial Accounting

Mock Examination 2

Question Paper	
Time allowed	2 hours

Both sections are divided into two sections:

Section A – ALL 35 questions are compulsory and MUST be attempted

Section B – BOTH questions are compulsory and MUST be attempted

DO NOT OPEN THIS PAPER UNTIL YOU ARE READY TO START UNDER
EXAMINATION CONDITIONS

SECTION A

1   In accordance with IAS37 *Provisions, Contingent Liabilities and Contingent Assets*, which of the following criteria must be present in order for a company to recognise a provision?

    1   There is a present obligation as a result of past events.
    2   It is probable that a transfer of economic benefits will be required to settle the obligation.
    3   A reliable estimate of the obligation can be made.

    A   All three criteria must be present.
    B   1 and 2 only
    C   1 and 3 only
    D   2 and 3 only   **(2 marks)**

2   Which one of the following types of book-keeping error is never indicated when a trial balance of nominal ledger account balances is extracted?

    A   Errors of commission
    B   Errors of omission
    C   Errors of principle
    D   Transposition errors   **(2 marks)**

3   Nooma Co owns 55% of the ordinary shares of Matic Co. What is the correct accounting treatment of the revenues and costs of Matic Co in the consolidated statement of profit or loss of the Nooma Group?

    A   The revenues and costs of Matic Co are added to the revenues and costs of Nooma Co on a line by line basis.

    B   55% of the profit after tax of Matic Co should be added to Nooma Co's consolidated profit after tax.

    C   55% of the revenues and costs of Matic Co are added to the revenues and costs of Nooma Co on a line by line basis.

    D   Only dividends received from Matic Co are shown in the consolidated statement of profit or loss of Nooma Co.   **(2 marks)**

4   The following information relates to a bank reconciliation.

    (i)   The bank balance in the cashbook before taking the items below into account was $8,970 overdrawn.

    (ii)   Bank charges of $550 on the bank statement have not been entered in the cashbook.

    (iii)   The bank has credited the account in error with $425 which belongs to another customer.

    (iv)   Cheque payments totalling $3,275 have been entered in the cashbook but have not been presented for payment.

    (v)   Cheques totalling $5,380 have been correctly entered on the debit side of the cashbook but have not been paid in at the bank.

What was the balance as shown by the bank statement *before* taking the above items into account?

    A $9,520 overdrawn
    B $11,200 overdrawn
    C $9,520 in credit
    D $11,200 in credit   **(2 marks)**

5   W Co, a sales tax registered trader, bought a new printing machine. The cost of the machine was $80,000, excluding sales tax at 17.5%. The delivery costs were $2,000 and installation costs were $5,000. Before using the machine to print customers' orders, a test was undertaken and the paper and ink cost $1,000.

What should be the cost of the machine in the company's statement of financial position?

A $80,000
B $82,000
C $87,000
D $88,000   **(2 marks)**

6   The electricity account for Jingles Co for the year ended 30 June 20X1 was as follows.

	$
Opening balance for electricity accrued at 1 July 20X0	300
Payments made during the year	
1 August 20X0 for three months to 31 July 20X0	600
1 November 20X0 for three months to 31 October 20X0	720
1 February 20X1 for three months to 31 January 20X1	900
30 June 20X1 for three months to 30 April 20X1	840

Jingles Co expects the next bill due in September to be for the same amount as the bill received in June.

What are the appropriate amounts for electricity to be included in the financial statements of Jingles Co for the year ended 30 June 20X1?

	Statement of financial position	Statement of profit or loss
A	$560	$3,320
B	$560	$3,060
C	$860	$3,320
D	$860	$3,060

(2 marks)

7   Which of the following is a fundamental qualitative characteristic of useful financial information included in the IASB's *Conceptual framework for financial reporting*?

A   Relevance
B   Reliability
C   Prudence
D   Accruals   **(2 marks)**

8   S & Co sell three products – A, B and C. The following information was available at the year end.

	Basic $ per unit	Super $ per unit	Luxury $ per unit
Original cost	10	9	20
Estimated selling price	9	12	26
Selling and distribution costs	1	4	5
	units	units	units
Units of inventory	500	1,250	850

In accordance with IAS2 *Inventories*, what is the value of inventory at the year end?

A $23,500
B $31,000
C $31,850
D $32,750   **(2 marks)**

9   A car was purchased by a business in May 20X1 for:

	$
Cost	10,000
Road fund licence	150
Total	10,150

The business adopts a date of 31 December as its year end.

The car was traded in for a replacement vehicle in August 20X4 at an agreed value of $5,000.

It has been depreciated at 25% per annum on the reducing-balance method, charging a full year's depreciation in the year of purchase and none in the year of sale.

What was the profit or loss on disposal of the vehicle during the year ended December 20X4?

A   Loss of $2,890
B   Profit of $781
C   Profit of $2,500
D   Profit of $3,750   **(2 marks)**

10   At 1 January 20X3, Attila Co had an allowance for receivables of $35,000. At 31 December 20X3, the trade receivables of the company were $620,000. It was decided to:

1   Write off (as uncollectable) receivables totalling $30,000, and
2   Adjust the allowance for receivables to 5% of receivables, based on past experience.

What is the combined expense that should appear in the company's statement of profit or loss for the year, for irrecoverable debts and the allowance for receivables?

A $24,500
B $26,000
C $34,000
D $35,500   **(2 marks)**

11   The annual sales of a company are $235,000 including sales tax at 17.5%. Half of the sales are on credit terms, half are cash sales. The receivables in the statement of financial position are $23,500.

What is the output tax?

A $17,500
B $20,562.5
C $35,000
D $41,125   **(2 marks)**

12   Beta purchased some plant and equipment on 1 July 20X1 for $40,000. The scrap value of the plant in ten years' time is estimated to be $4,000. Beta's policy is to charge depreciation on the straight line basis, with a proportionate charge in the period of acquisition.

What is the depreciation charge on the plant in Beta's financial statements for the year ended 30 September 20X1?

A $900
B $1,000
C $3,600
D $4,000   **(2 marks)**

13 The following figures are taken from the statement of financial position of GEN Co.

	$m
Inventory	2
Receivables	3
Cash	1
Payables	3
Bank loan repayable in 5 years time	3

What is the current ratio?

A   1.33
B   2.00
C   1.00
D   0.33

(2 marks)

14 A particular source of finance has the following characteristics: fixed payments, a fixed repayment date, it is secured on the assets of the company and the payments are classified as an expense.

Which of the following best describes this source of finance?

A   A redeemable preference share
B   An irredeemable preference share
C   A loan note
D   An overdraft

(2 marks)

15 Tong Co acquired 100% of the $100,000 ordinary share capital of Cheek Co for $1,200,000 on 1 January 20X5 when the retained earnings of Cheek Co were $550,000 and the balance on the revaluation surplus was $150,000. At the date of acquisition the fair value of plant held by Cheek Co was $80,000 higher than its carrying value.

What is the goodwill arising on the acquisition of Cheek Co?

A $320,000
B $400,000
C $470,000
D $550,000

(2 marks)

16 During the year ended 31 December 20X1, Alpha Rescue had the following transactions on the receivables ledger.

	$
Receivables at 1 January 20X1	100,000
Receivables at 31 December 20X1	107,250
Goods returned	12,750
Amounts paid into the bank from receivables	225,000
Discount received	75,000
Discounts allowed	5,000

What were the sales for the year?

A $107,250
B $240,000
C $250,000
D $320,000

(2 marks)

17 Financial analysts calculate ratios from the published financial statements of large companies. Which one of the following reasons is UNLIKELY to be a reason why they calculate and analyse financial ratios?

A   Ratios can reduce lengthy or complex financial statements into a fairly small number of more easily-understood indicators.

B   Ratios can indicate whether a business is at serious risk of insolvency.

C   Ratios can help with comparisons between businesses in the same industry.

D   Ratios can indicate changes in the financial performance and financial position of a business over time.

(2 marks)

18   Cat Co has held 85% of the share capital of Dog Co for many years. During the current year Cat Co sold goods to Dog Co for $15,000, including a mark up of 25% on cost. 60% of these goods were still in inventory at the year end.

The following extract was taken from the accounting records of Cat Co and Dog Co at 31 March 20X8.

	Cat Co $'000	Dog Co $'000
Opening inventory	650	275
Closing Inventory	750	400

What is the figure for inventory to be included in the statement of financial position of the Cat Group at 31 March 20X8?

A $1,151,800
B $1,152,250
C $1,197,750
D $1,148,200   **(2 marks)**

19   A company's quick ratio has increased from 0.9:1 at 31 December 20X1 to 1.5:1 at 31 December 20X2. Which of the following statements relating to this increase is correct?

A   The increase was due to an improvement in inventory management procedures so that more inventory is sold before it becomes obsolete.

B   The increase was caused by the repayment of a long-term loan during the period.

C   The increase was caused by an increase in selling price in the period of the company's main product.

D   The increase was caused by an increase in the price during the period of the main raw material necessary for production.   **(2 marks)**

20   Which of the following represents an error of original entry?

A   The purchase of goods for resale using cash was debited to the purchases account and credited to the cash book using the incorrect amount in both cases.

B   The purchase of goods for resale using cash was debited to the motor vehicles account and credited to the cash book using the correct amount in both cases.

C   The purchase of goods for resale using cash was debited to the purchases account and credited to the sales day book using the correct amount in both cases.

D   The purchase of goods for resale using cash was debited to the purchases account but no credit entry was made.   **(2 marks)**

21   A machine was purchased for $100,000 on 1 January 20X1 and was expected to have a useful life of 10 years. After 3 years, management revised their expectation of the remaining useful life to 20 years. The business depreciates machines using the straight line method.

What is the carrying value of the machine at 31 December 20X5?

A $50,000
B $63,000
C $72,000
D $75,000   **(2 marks)**

22 Your organisation has received a statement of account from one of its suppliers, showing an outstanding balance due to them of $1,350. On comparison with your ledger account, the following is determined:

- Your ledger account shows a credit balance of $260
- The supplier has disallowed a cash discount of $80 due to late payment of an invoice
- The supplier has not yet allowed for goods returned at the end of the period of $270
- Cash in transit of $830 has not been received by the supplier

Following consideration of these items, what is the unreconciled difference between the two records?

A $nil
B $10
C $90
D $(180)   **(2 marks)**

---

23 A company is preparing its statement of cash flows for the year ended 31 December 20X2. Relevant extracts from the accounts are as follows.

Statement of profit or loss	$	
Depreciation	15,000	
Profit on sale of non-current assets	40,000	

Statement of financial position	*20X2*	*20X1*
	$	$
Plant and machinery - cost	185,000	250,000
Plant and machinery - depreciation	45,000	50,000

Plant and machinery additions during the year were $35,000. What is the cash flow arising from the sale of non-current assets?

A $40,000
B $100,000
C $120,000
D $135,000   **(2 marks)**

---

24 Which body is responsible for issuing IFRSs?

A IFRSIC
B IFRSAC
C IASB
D National governments   **(2 marks)**

---

25 Teo Co acquired 95% of the ordinary share capital of Mat Co 31 December 20X0. The following information relates to Mat Co:

	20X0	*20X1*
	$'000	$'000
Retained earnings	700	800
Revaluation surplus	-	100
	700	900

The fair value of the non-controlling interest in Mat Co at the date of acquisition was $45,000.

What is the amount reported for non-controlling interest in the statement of financial position of the Teo Group as at 31 December 20X1?

A $45,000
B $55,000
C $85,000
D $90,000   **(2 marks)**

26 Which of the following statements is/are correct?

   1   AZ owns 25% of the preferred (non-voting) share capital of BX, which means that BX is an associate of AZ.

   2   CW has a 10% shareholding in DY and can appoint 4 out of 6 directors to the board of DY, so DY is classified as a subsidiary of CW.

   3   ES has significant influence over FT, which means that FT is an associate of ES.

   4   GR owns 55% of the share capital of HU, but by agreement with the minority shareholder, does not have control or significant influence over the financial and operating policies of HU, so HU is a simple investment of GR.

   A   1 and 2 only
   B   2 and 3 only
   C   2, 3 and 4 only
   D   4 only   (2 marks)

27 Which, if any, of the following journal entries is correct according to their narratives?

		Debit $	Credit $
1	B receivables ledger account	450	
	Irrecoverable debts account		450
	Irrecoverable balance written off		
2	Investments: Q ordinary shares	100,000	
	Share capital		100,000
	80,000 shares of 50c each issued at $1·25 in exchange for shares in Q.		
3	Suspense account	1,000	
	Motor vehicles account		1,000
	Correction of error – debit side of Motor vehicles account undercast by $1,000		

   A   None of them
   B   1 only
   C   2 only
   D   3 only   (2 marks)

28 Jay Co values inventories on the first in first out (FIFO) basis. Jay Co has 120 items of product A valued at $8 each in inventory at 1 October 20X9. During October 20X9, the following transactions in product A took place.

3 October	Purchases	180 items at $9 each
4 October	Sales	150 items at $12 each
8 October	Sales	80 items at $15 each
18 October	Purchases	300 items at $10 each
22 October	Sales	100 items at $15 each

   What is the closing balance on the inventory account at 31 October 20X9?

   A $1,500
   B $2,560
   C $2,628
   D $2,700   (2 marks)

29 Fred's trial balance did not balance so he opened a suspense account with a debit balance of $346. Control accounts are maintained for receivables and payables.

Fred discovered the following:

1   The sales day book was undercast by $400.

2   Purchases of $520 from the purchases day book have only been recorded in the payables ledger control account.

3   Profit on sale of non-current assets of $670 had been recorded in the sundry income account as $760.

What is the remaining balance on Fred's suspense account after these errors have been corrected?

A $264 credit
B $136 debit
C $956 debit
D $1,266 debit   **(2 marks)**

---

30 Charles Co entered into the following transactions:

1   He sold goods on credit to Cody with a list price of $3,200. He allows a 10% trade discount and a further 2% discount for payment within seven days. Cody paid within two days.

2   He made a credit sale to Mary allowing a 5% trade discount on the list price of $640.

3   He purchased goods for $600 and paid $590, receiving a discount for immediate cash payment.

How much discount should be recorded in the Discount Allowed account as a result of the above transactions?

A $57.60
B $10.00
C $352.00
D $409.60   **(2 marks)**

---

31 Where, in a company's financial statements complying with International Financial Reporting Standards, should you find the proceeds of non-current assets sold during the period?

A   Statement of cash flows and statement of financial position
B   Statement of changes in equity and statement of financial position
C   Statement of profit or loss and other comprehensive income and statement of cash flows
D   Statement of cash flows only   **(2 marks)**

---

32 If the current ratio for a company is equal to its quick ratio, which of the following statements is true?

A   The current ratio must be greater than one.
B   The company does not carry any inventory.
C   Receivables plus cash is greater than payables minus inventories.
D   Working capital is positive.   **(2 marks)**

---

33 The closing inventory of Epsilon amounted to $284,000 at 30 September 20X1, the reporting date. This total includes two inventory lines about which the inventory taker is uncertain.

1   500 items which had cost $15 each and which were included at $7,500. These items were found to have been defective at the end of the reporting period. Remedial work after the reporting period cost $1,800 and they were then sold for $20 each. Selling expenses were $400.

2   100 items which had cost $10 each. After the reporting period they were sold for $8 each, with selling expenses of $150.

What figure should appear in Epsilon's statement of financial position for inventory?

A $283,650
B $283,800
C $284,000
D $284,450   **(2 marks)**

34   Which of these statements about research and development expenditure are correct?

1   If certain conditions are satisfied, research and development expenditure must be capitalised.

2   One of the conditions to be satisfied if development expenditure is to be capitalised is that the technical feasibility of the project is reasonably assured.

3   The amount of capitalised development expenditure for each project should be reviewed each year. If circumstances no longer justify the capitalisation, the balance should be written off over a period not exceeding five years.

4   Development expenditure may only be capitalised if it can be shown that adequate resources will be available to finance the completion of the project.

A   1 and 2 only
B   1 and 4 only
C   2 and 3 only
D   2 and 4 only   **(2 marks)**

35   A company measures the average time to collect receivables as:

[Receivables at end of financial year/Annual credit sales] × 365 days

Accounting ratios have just been calculated from the financial statements for the financial year that has just ended. These show an abnormally high average time to collect receivables, compared with ratios calculated for the previous financial year.

Which of the following may help to explain this unusually high turnover period for trade receivables?

1   There was an unusually large sale on credit close to the end of the financial year.

2   The company has seasonal trade, and sales in the final quarter of the year are always higher than in the other quarters.

3   However, sales in the final quarter of the year that has just ended were lower than in the previous year.

A   Reason 1 only
B   Reason 2 only
C   Reason 3 only
D   Reasons 1, 2 and 3   **(2 marks)**

SECTION B

1   You have been given the following information relating to a limited liability company called Nobrie. This company is preparing financial statements for the year ended 31 May 20X4.

NOBRIE
STATEMENT OF PROFIT OR LOSS
FOR THE YEAR ENDED 31 MAY 20X4

	$'000
Revenue	66,600
Cost of sales	(13,785)
Gross profit	52,815
Distribution costs	(7,530)
Administrative expenses	(2,516)
Investment income	146
Finance cost	(1,177)
Profit before tax	41,738
Tax	(9,857)
Profit for the year	31,881
Retained earnings brought forward at 1 June 20X3	28,063
Retained earnings carried forward at 31 May 20X4	59,944

NOBRIE
STATEMENTS OF FINANCIAL POSITION AS AT 31 MAY

	20X4 $'000	20X4 $'000	20X3 $'000	20X3 $'000
Assets				
Non-current assets				
Cost		144,844		114,785
Accumulated depreciation		(27,433)		(26,319)
		117,411		88,466
Current assets				
Inventory	24,931		24,065	
Trade receivables	18,922		13,238	
Cash	3,689		2,224	
		47,542		39,527
Total assets		164,953		127,993
Equity and liabilities				
Equity				
Ordinary share capital	27,000		23,331	
Share premium	14,569		10,788	
Revaluation surplus	15,395		7,123	
Retained earnings	59,944		28,063	
		116,908		69,305
Non current liabilities				
6% loan note		17,824		24,068
Current liabilities				
Bank overdraft	5,533		6,973	
Trade payables	16,699		20,324	
Taxation	7,989		7,323	
		30,221		34,620
Total equity and liabilities		164,953		127,993

Additional information

(a) During the year ended 31 May 20X4, the company sold a piece of equipment for $3,053,000, realising a profit of $1,540,000. There were no other disposals of non-current assets during the year.

(b) Depreciation of $5,862,000 has been charged.

(c) There were no amounts outstanding in respect of interest payable or receivable as at 31 May 20X3 or 20X4.

(d) There were no dividends paid or declared during the year.

Required

Prepare a statement of cash flows for Nobrie for the year ended 31 May 20X4 in accordance with IAS 7 Statement of cash flows.
(15 marks)

---

2   The draft statements of financial position of Spyder and its subsidiary company Phly at 31 October 20X5 are as follows.

	Spyder		Phly	
	$'000	$'000	$'000	$'000
Assets				
Non-current assets				
Tangible assets				
Land and buildings		315,000		278,000
Plant		285,000		220,000
		600,000		498,000
Investment				
Shares in Phly at cost		660,000		-
Current assets				
Inventory	357,000		252,000	
Receivables	525,000		126,000	
Bank	158,000		30,000	
		1,040,000		408,000
		2,300,000		906,000
Equity and liabilities				
Equity				
$1 ordinary shares		1,500,000		600,000
Reserves		580,000		212,000
		2,080,000		812,000
Current liabilities				
Payables		220,000		94,000
Total equity and liabilities		2,300,000		906,000

The following information is also available.

(a) Spyder purchased 480 million shares in Phly some years ago, when Phly had a credit balance of $95 million in reserves. The fair value of the non-controlling interest at the date of acquisition was $165 million.

(b) At the date of acquisition the freehold land of Phly was valued at $70 million in excess of its book value. The revaluation was not recorded in the accounts of Phly.

(c) Phly's inventory includes goods purchased from Spyder at a price that includes a profit to Spyder of $12 million.

(d) At 31 October 20X5 Phly owes Spyder $25 million for goods purchased during the year.

Required

(a) Calculate the total goodwill on acquisition.
(b) Prepare the consolidated statement of financial position for Spyder as at 31 October 20X5.
(15 marks)

Answers to Mock Exam 2

SECTION A

1   A   All three criteria must be present.

2   C   The existence of a transposition error should always be revealed by a trial balance. Errors of omission and commission may or may not be revealed, depending on the nature of the error and whether the error has resulted in a mismatch between debt and credit entries in the nominal ledger accounts. An error of omission is never revealed, because there have been no entries in the nominal ledger for the omitted item.

3   A   Matic Co is a subsidiary of Nooma Co, so the results of Matic Co should be consolidated on a line by line basis with the results of Nooma Co.

4   B $11,200 overdrawn

Cash book	$	Bank statement	$
Balance	(8,970)	Balance b/f (bal fig)	(11,200)
Bank charges	(550)	Credit in error	(425)
		Unpresented cheques	(3,275)
		Outstanding deposits	5,380
	(9,520)		(9,520)

5   D $88,000

	$
Cost of machine	80,000
Installation	5,000
Delivery	2,000
Testing	1,000
	88,000

6   A   Statement of financial position $560, Statement of profit or loss $3,320.

ELECTRICITY ACCOUNT

		$		$
			Balance b/fwd	300
20X9:				
1 August	Paid bank	600		
1 November	Paid bank	720		
20Y0:				
1 February	Paid bank	900		
30 June	Paid bank	840		
30 June	Accrual c/d $840 × $^2/_3$	560	SPL	3,320
		3,620		3,620

7   A   Relevance is a fundamental qualitative characteristic.

8   B $31,000

	Cost	Net realisable value	Lower of cost & NRV	Units	Value
	$	$	$		$
A	10	8	8	500	4,000
B	9	8	8	1,250	10,000
C	20	21	20	850	17,000
					31,000

9　B　$781 profit

	$
Cost	10,000
20X1 Depreciation	2,500
	7,500
20X2 Depreciation	1,875
	5,625
20X3 Depreciation	1,406
	4,219
20X4 Part exchange	5,000
Profit	781

10　A

	$	$
Amount written off		30,000
Allowance for receivables at 31 December 20X3	29,500	
5% × $(620,000 − 30,000)		
Allowance for receivables at 1 January 20X3	35,000	
Reduction in allowance for receivables		(5,500)
Combined expense		24,500

11　C　$35,000

$$\text{Output tax} = \frac{235,000}{117.5} \times 17.5$$

12　A　$900. ($36,000/10) × $^3/_{12}$

13　B　This is the ratio of current assets to current liabilities. C is wrong as the five year bank loan would not normally be included with current liabilities. A is the quick ratio (excludes inventory).

14　C　It is a loan note. It is not a preference share because it is secured. An overdraft does not have a fixed return or a fixed repayment date and is not secured.

15　A

	$	$
Fair value of consideration		1,200,000
Net assets at acquisition as represented by		
Share capital	100,000	
Retained earnings	550,000	
Revaluation surplus	150,000	
Fair value adjustment	80,000	
		(880,000)
Goodwill		320,000

16　C　$250,000

RECEIVABLES LEDGER CONTROL ACCOUNT

	$		$
Bal b/f	100,000	Bank	225,000
Sales (balancing figure)	250,000	Discounts allowed	5,000
		Returns	12,750
		Bal c/f	107,250
	350,000		350,000

Discounts received refer to purchases and go in the payables ledger control account.

17　B　Ratios can be used to analyse financial performance, and to make comparisons of performance over time and between different businesses in the same industry, but they cannot usually provide a reliable indicator of insolvency, especially if they are prepared only once a year.

18   D $1,148,200

	$'000
Unrealised profit (15,000 × 25/125 × 60%)	1.8
Inventory (750 + 400 − 1.8)	1,148.2

19   C   Quick ratio = (current assets − inventories)/current liabilities.

The quick ratio does not include inventories or long term loans, so A and B will have no effect. An increase in suppliers prices will lead to an increase in payables, which will reduce the quick ratio.

20   A   B and C are errors of principle, D is an error of omission.

21       $63,000.

Carrying value at the end of year 3:   100,000 − (100,000 × 3/10) = $70,000

Carrying value at the end of year 5:   70,000 − (70,000 × 2/20)   = $63,000

22   C $90

	$
Ledger balance	260
Add back: disallowed discount	80
returns goods	270
cash in transit	830
Total balance	1,440
As stated by the supplier	1,350
Unreconciled difference	90

23   C $120,000

	$
Sale proceeds (balancing figure)	120,000
Carrying amount (see below)	80,000
Profit on sale	40,000
Carrying amount at 31 December 20X1 (250,000 − 50,000)	200,000
Additions	35,000
	235,000
Carrying amount of disposals (balancing figure)	(80,000)
Depreciation	(15,000)
Carrying amount at 31 December 20X2 (185,000 − 45,000)	140,000

24   C   The IASB is responsible for issuing IFRSs.

25   B

	$
Fair value of NCI at acquisition	45,000
Plus NCI's share of post-acquisition retained earnings (and other reserves)	
((800 − 100) × 5% + 100 × 5%)	10,000
NCI at reporting date (31 December 20X1)	55,000

26   C   An investor must have significant influence over the investee in order for the investee to be classified as an associate, therefore 3 is correct. If the investor owns between 20% and <50% of the **ordinary shares (voting)** of the investee, significant influence can be assumed, 1 is not true as the shares held do not have voting rights. For an investee to be classified as a subsidiary, the investor must have control over the investee. Control can be demonstrated if the investor can appoint the majority of board members of the investee, so 2 is correct. 4 is also correct as despite its 55% shareholding, GR does not have control or significant influence over HU and as such is not classified as a subsidiary or as an associate, but as a simple trade investment.

27   A   All three are incorrect. In 1 and 3 the debit and credit entries should be reversed and 2 should show a credit of $60,000 to the share premium account.

28 **D** $2,700

Date		No. of items	Unit price $	Value $
1.10.X9	Balance	120	8	960
3.10.X9	Purchases	180	9	1,620
	Balance	300		2,580
4.10.X9	Sales	(120)	8	(960)
	Sales	(30)	9	(270)
	Balance	150		1,350
8.10.X9	Sales	(80)	9	(720)
	Balance	70		630
18.10.X9	Purchases	300	10	3,000
	Balance	370		3,630
22.10.X9	Sales	(70)	9	(630)
	Sales	(30)	10	(300)
	Balance	270		2,700

29 **A**

SUSPENSE ACCOUNT

	$		$
Bal b/f	346	Purchases (2)	520
Bal c/f	264	Sundry income (3)	90
	610		610

30 **A** Selling price = $3,200 × 90% = $2,880. Early settlement discount = 2% × $2,880 = $57.60.

31 **D** Proceeds of a sale of non-current assets will only be shown in the statement of cash flows.

32 **B** The company does not carry any inventory.

33 **A** $283,650

	$	
	284,000	
Item 1	–	No change as NRV exceeds cost
Item 2	(350)	Reduce to NRV (1,000 – 650)
	283,650	

34 **D** 2 and 4 only are correct. Statements 1 and 3 are incorrect.

35 **A** If there has been a large credit sale near the end of the financial year, the amount owed will be included within receivables at the year end and trade receivables may be unusually high. If so, the average time for receivables to pay may be distorted, because year-end receivables are used to calculate the turnover ratio.

A large volume of sales in the final quarter of every year may explain why the measurement of the average collection period is long every year, but not why the collection period should be unusually long compared with the previous year.

Comparatively low sales in the final quarter would be more likely to result in a shorter-than-normal measurement of the average collection period.

SECTION B

1

NOBRIE
STATEMENT OF CASH FLOWS FOR THE YEAR ENDED 30 MAY 20X4

	$'000	$'000
Cash flow from operating activities		
Net profit before tax	41,738	
Adjustments for		
Depreciation	5,862	
Profit on equipment disposal	(1,540)	
Investment income	(146)	
Interest paid	1,177	
Operating profit before working capital changes	47,091	
Increase in inventory	(866)	
Increase in receivables	(5,684)	
Decrease in payables	(3,625)	
Cash generated from operations	36,916	
Interest received*	146	
Interest paid*	(1,177)	
Tax paid (W1)	(9,191)	
Net cash flows from operating activities		26,694
Cash flows from investing activities		
Purchase at property plant and equipment (W2)	(28,048)	
Proceeds from sale of equipment	3,053	
Net cash used in investing activities		(24,995)
Cash flows from financing activities		
Proceeds from issue of share capital		
(27,000 + 14,569) – (23,331 + 10,788)	7,450	
Repayment of long term borrowings (24,068 – 17,824)	(6,244)	
Net cash flows from financing activities		1,206
Increase in cash and cash equivalents		2,905
Cash and cash equivalents at beginning of period (2,224 – 6,973)		(4,749)
Cash and cash equivalents at end of period (3,689 – 5,533)		(1,844)

* *Note*. Interest paid can be either an operating cash flow or a financing cash flows. Interest received can be either an operating cash flow or an investing cash flow.

Workings

1   *Tax paid*

TAXATION

	$'000		$'000
Tax paid (bal fig)	9,191	Balance b/fwd	7,323
Balance c/fwd	7,989	Statement of profit or loss	9,857
	17,180		17,180

2   *Purchases of property, plant and equipment*

PROPERTY, PLANT AND EQUIPMENT

	$'000		$'000
Balance b/fwd (carrying value)	88,466	Disposals (carrying value) (W3)	1,513
Revaluation (15,395 – 7,123)	8,272	Depreciation	5,862
Purchases (bal fig)	28,048	Balance c/fwd (carrying value)	117,411
	124,786		124,786

3   *Disposals*

	$'000
Proceeds	3,053
Profit	1,540
∴Carrying value of disposals	1,513

2

(a) *Calculation of goodwill*

	$'000	$'000
Fair value of consideration transferred		660,000
Plus fair value of NCI at acquisition		165,000
Less net acquisition-date fair value of identifiable assets acquired and liabilities assumed:		
Share capital	600,000	
Retained earnings at acquisition	95,000	
Fair value adjustment at acquisition	70,000	
		(765,000)
Goodwill		60,000

(b) SPYDER GROUP

CONSOLIDATED STATEMENT OF FINANCIAL POSITION AS AT 31 OCTOBER 20X5

	$'000	$'000
Assets		
Non-current assets		
Goodwill		60,000
Land and buildings (315 + 278 + 70)		663,000
Plant (285 + 220)		505,000
		1,228,000
Current assets		
Inventory (357 + 252 - 12)	597,000	
Receivables (525 + 126 – 25)	626,000	
Bank (158 + 30)	188,000	
		1,411,000
		2,639,000
Equity and liabilities		
Equity attributable to owners of the parent		
$1 ordinary shares		1,500,000
Reserves (W2)		661,600
Non-controlling interest (W3)		188,400
		2,350,000
Current liabilities		
Payables (220 + 94 – 25)		289,000
Total equity and liabilities		2,639,000

Workings

1   *Group structure*

$$\frac{480m}{600m} = 80\%$$

2   *Retained earnings*

	Spyder	Phly
	$m	$m
Per question	580.0	212
Adjustment (unrealised profit)	(12.0)	
Pre-acquisition retained earnings		(95)
		117
Group share of post-acq'n ret'd earnings:		
Phly (80% × 117)	93.6	
Group retained earnings	661.6	

3   *Non-controlling interest*

	$m
Fair value of NCI at acquisition	165.0
Plus NCI's share of post-acquisition retained earnings (20% × 117)	23.4
NCI at reporting date	188.4

REVIEW FORM

Name: _____ Address: _____

_____

Date:_____

How have you used this Practice & Revision Kit?
(Tick one box only)

☐ Distance learning (book only)

☐ On a course: college _____

☐ As a tutor

☐ With 'correspondence' package

☐ Other _____

Why did you decide to purchase this Practice & Revision Kit? *(Tick one box only)*

☐ Have used complementary Interactive Text

☐ Have used BPP Texts in the past

☐ Recommendation by friend/colleague

☐ Recommendation by a lecturer at college

☐ Saw advertising

☐ Other _____

☐ Our advertisement in *ACCA Student Accountant*

☐ Our advertisement in *Teach Accounting*

☐ Other advertisement _____

☐ Our brochure with a letter through the post

☐ ACCA E-Gain email

☐ BPP email

☐ Our website www.bpp.com

Which (if any) aspects of our advertising do you find useful?
(Tick as many boxes as are relevant)

☐ Prices and publication dates of new editions

☐ Information on Practice & Revision Kit content

☐ Facility to order books off-the-page

☐ None of the above

During the past six months do you recall seeing/receiving any of the following?
(Tick as many boxes as are relevant)

Have you used the companion Interactive Text for this subject?   ☐ Yes   ☐ No

Your ratings, comments and suggestions would be appreciated on the following areas

	Very useful	Useful	Not useful
Introductory section (How to use this Practice & Revision Kit)	☐	☐	☐
'Do You Know' checklists	☐	☐	☐
'Did You Know' checklists	☐	☐	☐
Possible pitfalls	☐	☐	☐
Questions	☐	☐	☐
Answers	☐	☐	☐
Mock exams	☐	☐	☐
Structure & presentation	☐	☐	☐
Icons	☐	☐	☐

	Excellent	Good	Adequate	Poor
Overall opinion of this Kit	☐	☐	☐	☐

Do you intend to continue using BPP Interactive Texts/Kits?   ☐ Yes   ☐ No

Please note any further comments and suggestions/errors on the reverse of this page.

Please return to: Barry Walsh, BPP Learning Media Ltd, FREEPOST, London, W12 8BR

REVIEW FORM (continued)

Please note any further comments and suggestions/errors below